Technical Lands

editors

Jeffrey S Nesbit
Charles Waldheim

A Critical Primer

Contents

Acknowledgments

This book and the research project it stems from would not have been possible without countless conversations, contributions, and collaborations with an extraordinary group of colleagues, co-conspirators, and friends. It would equally have been inconceivable absent the intellectual and material contributions of many individuals and institutions.

We begin by acknowledging our essential debt to Peter L. Galison, Joseph Pellegrino University Professor in History of Science and Physics at Harvard University, for his collaboration and ongoing leadership. Galison's foundational work on the topic proposes to bridge the chasm between science and design by offering contingent histories and necessary arguments for why technical landscapes are a vital framework for contemporary inquiry. This project builds directly upon Galison's formulation of "technical landscapes" and his fall 2016 eponymous seminar at Harvard. Additionally, we owe our gratitude and many thanks to Tiffany Nichols, a doctoral candidate in the history of science at Harvard University. Early on, Nichols understood that "technical lands" implied and necessitated innovative and interdisciplinary approaches to the topic. The inception of this project derives from her groundbreaking work on place-based science. We thank Tiffany for her collegial collaboration and friendship.

We also acknowledge three recent convenings on the topic of "technical lands" and specifically recognize the organizers, contributors, and respondents for those discussions. This project builds upon the conversations brought forth from these events. First, we were compelled by the graduate student conference, "Technical Landscapes: Aesthetics and the Environment in the History of Science and Art," organized at Harvard in spring 2017 by Leah Aronowsky, Brad Bolman, and Walker Downey. The keynotes by Peter L. Galison, Caroline A. Jones, and Rebecca K. Uchill were particularly illustrative and inspirational. Second, we are thankful, once again, to Tiffany Nichols for her invitation to join the conference session, "Uneasy Alliances: Analyzing the Role of Nation States in the Administration of Place-Based Science Sites," at the History of Science Society conference in Seattle, WA, in 2018. Organized by Nichols, she brought together a diverse group of critical thinkers and academic scholars to reflect on the politics of land with presentations by Mary Mitchell, Jeffrey S. Nesbit, and Megan Raby. We are also thankful for the keen insights and reflections from moderator David Kaiser during the session. Third, this project grew directly out of the "Technical Lands Master Class" at Harvard in spring 2020. This interdisciplinary master class series co-organized by Tiffany Nichols and Jeffrey S. Nesbit, in collaboration with Harvard's Department of the History of Science and Graduate School of Design, was funded by the Research Workshops Committee in the Harvard Graduate School of Arts and Sciences. The master class was informed by keynotes from Peter Galison and Charles Waldheim, followed by presentations from scholars across diverse disciplines. We thank Wythe Marschall, Gretchen Heefner, Lisa Messeri, Robert Pietrusko, Matthew Spellberg, and S. Margaret Spivey-Faulkner for their essential contributions and engaging discussions.

We must thank several scholars from various fields who gave genuine attention and offered valuable reflections on the foundation and intellectual arguments made during the development of this book. We are grateful to Rosalind Williams, Bern Dibner Professor of the History of Science and Technology, Emerita, at MIT, for providing enthusiastic and encouraging feedback on earlier versions of the book abstract and for many discussions and support for this line of scholarship. We thank Benjamin Wilson for many thought-provoking discussions from his history seminar, "Science in the Cold War," in the Department of the History of Science at Harvard; Matthew Hersch for his willingness to engage the master class series and for several exchanges and informal discussions along the way; and special thanks to Mariano Gomez-Luque, for his time critically reflecting on an earlier draft of the literature review and for his continued feedback around the themes of this project. We also thank William Conroy and Christina Shivers for their work as research assistants helping us to uncover the origins, etymologies, and implications of the formulation "technical lands," and Magdalena Kerkmans for her work on gathering initial archival photographs on the topic.

We acknowledge the explicit material and implicit moral support of Dean Sarah Whiting at the Harvard Graduate School of Design and Dean Robert Gonzalez at the University of New Mexico School of Architecture + Planning, both of whom supported the project through faculty research funds from their respective institutions. Thanks to graphic designer Siena Scarff and Siena Scarff Design for their visual imagination of the topic and their careful crafting of the volume. Thanks to photographer Vincent Fournier for generously contributing the visual imaginary in which the topic is set and for agreeing to have his work reproduced here. We are equally indebted to the photographers who generously contributed their cultural production to illustrate the volume. Thanks to Jake Starmer for copyediting the volume to allow it to be (hopefully) readable by civilians. We also thank our wonderful partners at JOVIS Verlag, including Doris Kleilein, Charlotte Blumenthal, and Theresa Hartherz, who swiftly committed to the topic and its realization as a book.

Finally, we are indebted to the twenty authors who contributed their invaluable time and intellectual energies to illuminate the various themes of "technical lands." We remain thankful for their commitment and contribution to the collective intellectual project and themes that it illuminates.

What *A*re
Tec*hn*ical Land*s*?

Peter Galison

At the heart of physics for hundreds of years lay the foundation of Newtonian physics; space and time formed a stage on which the events of the physical world took place. Mechanical and gravitational forces shoved objects through space over the course of time; space and time in and of themselves were unchangeable. In Newton's words, behind mere appearances, space and time were "absolute, true, and mathematical."[1] When Albert Einstein introduced his General Theory of Relativity, he broke the frame of that sensorium of God. "Forgive me," he once said to the specter of Newton, as he demonstrated how matter and energy forged space-time, bending it.[2] Without mass-energy in Einstein's theory, there is no empty stage; there is no space-time at all. The curvature of space-time, then, dictates the paths along which matter travels. Or, as physicist John Wheeler once explained, "Space-time tells matter how to move; matter tells space-time how to curve."[3]

In this transformation, space-time offers a felicitous starting point for thinking about "technical lands." We might, as latter-day Newtonians, picture land itself as a fixed framework in which the action of culture, technology, habitation take place. True, one might say, we arrange and re-arrange the surface of the planet with roads and habitation, production and cultivation. True too, below the surface, here and there, we mine and tunnel. But we see the land, in some irreducible way, as a substrate, as external to us as space and time were to Newton and his followers. History, in this account, is about the *use* of land—it is borrowed, temporary, and reversible, the way a cast of actors might take over a theater for a Shakespearian drama one week, and a political party might rent it for a rally the next.

We no longer live in such a world: we need, land-theoretically, to be latter-day Einsteinans. For, in fact, land is not permanent, and it is simply not viable to consider it as a framework outside us. Our modification of the air has already altered the balance of land and sea, rivers and cities. Our restructuring of lakes and swamps as aquifers and farmland drives deserti-fication in some regions and deglaciation in others. In a fundamental sense, land is historical—not just in its use but also in its constitution.

I began thinking about technical lands—the term and the idea—around 2000. I had just finished writing and filming about the building of the hydro-gen bomb. There seemed no avoiding the idea after spending time at Los Alamos and elsewhere. I saw firsthand the trillion-dollar sprawl of nuclear weapons production and deployment. It comprised an interconnected complex ranging from West Coast sites such as the Hanford Reservation in Washington State to the East Coast's Savannah River Site in South Carolina; from test areas in the depths of Amchitka Island, Alaska, down through the South Pacific Atolls; and strewn across hundreds of factories, some active and others defunct.[4]

One particular site grabbed my attention: the Waste Isolation Pilot Plant (WIPP), about thirty miles northeast of Carlsbad, New Mexico. There, starting 850 feet below the surface, lies a 2,000-feet-thick salt bed deposited in the Permian about 250 million years ago. Amid this thick ancient seafloor, some 2,150 feet below ground, is the heart of the WIPP facility. The facility was

[1] From Sir Isaac Newton's Scholium to the Definitions in *Philosophiae Naturalis Principia Mathematica*, Bk. 1 (1689); trans., Andrew Motte (1729), rev., Florian Cajori (Berkeley, CA: University of California Press, 1934), 6.

[2] Albert Einstein, "Autobi-ographical Notes," in Paul Arthur Schilpp, ed., *Albert Einstein, Philosopher-Scientist* (New York, NY: Tudor Pub-lishing Company, 1951), 31.

[3] John Wheeler in his book with Kenneth William Ford, *Geons, Black Holes, and Quantum Foam: A Life in Physics* (New York, NY: Norton, 2000), 235.

[4] See the film *Containment* (2015) by Peter Galison and Robb Moss; see also Brinda Sarathy, Vivian Hamilton, and Janet Farrell Brodie, "Discussing Nuclear Waste with Peter Galison: Interview by Vivien Hamilton and Brinda Sarathy," *Inevitably Toxic: Historical Perspectives on Contamination, Exposure, and Expertise* (Pittsburgh, PA: Pittsburgh University Press, 2019); Peter Galison and Jamie Kruse, "Waste-Wilderness: A Conversation with Peter L. Galison," *Friends of the Pleistocene*, May 20, 2015, https://fopnews.wordpress.com/2011/03/31/galison/; and Mohsen Mostafavi, Gareth Doherty, and Peter Gal-ison, "Underground Future," *Ecological Urbanism* (Zürich, Switzerland: Lars Müller Publishers, 2010). I would like to thank members of my fall 2016 Technical Lands grad-uate seminar and associated 2016 research fieldwork; along with Leah Arnowsky, Brad Bolman, Walker Downey and the graduate conference on technical landscapes, April 6–8, 2017, https://dis-cardstudies.com/2016/12/08/cfp-technical-landscapes-aes-thetics-and-the-environment-in-the-history-of-science-and-art/. Tiffany Nichols and Jeffrey S. Nesbit ran an excellent faculty-student working group on technical lands starting in 2019. The idea of the struggle over the legibility, visibility, and obscuration of technical lands is explored in Peter Galison and Caroline Jones, *Invisibil-ities: Seeing and Unseeing the Anthropocene* (New York, NY: Zone, forthcoming).

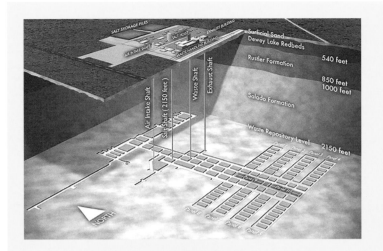

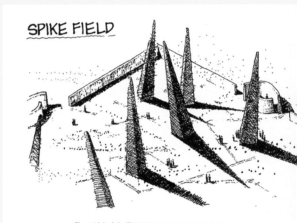

Figure 4.3-3. Spike Field, view 1 (concept and art by Michael Brill).

fig 1　　A diagram of the Waste Isolation Pilot Plant repository. "Quick Facts about EM's Waste Isolation Pilot Plant," U.S. Department of Energy

fig 2　　Spike Field, proposed warning to signal to the 10,000-year future that da[...] lurked in the earth below. K. M. Trauth et al., ' Judgment on Markers to Deter Inadvertent Hum[...] into the Waste Isolation Pilot Plant (Technical rep[...] Sandida National Labs and U.S. Department of E[...]

designed to be the final resting place for rags, gloveboxes, soil, machinery, sludge, and other materials that the nuclear weapons industry had contaminated by plutonium and other transuranic elements like americium; the mundane discard that makes up this nuclear waste. One day, when my collaborator Robb Moss and I were filming *Containment* in the WIPP underground, the then-chief-scientist Roger Nelson gestured to the wall of yellow containers stamped with radiation warnings and said: "*That* is the legacy of the Cold War."

Congress approved the construction of a waste site that would permanently encyst drums of radioactive detritus from the weapons production, up to 6.2 million cubic feet. After a decade of demonstrations and challenges, the first trucks bearing waste arrived at the Carlsbad "Pilot" site in 1999. By 2021, some 13,000 shipments had made their way to the site. Lowered in specially designed elevators, emplacement began in eight panels cut into the salt, each with seven rooms that were 33 feet wide, 13 feet tall, and 300 feet long.[5]

Salt remains stable; indeed, the idea was that this area, already having shown its longevity by the very fact of its continued existence, would isolate the radioactive materials for a time long enough that the material would lose most of its radioactivity. For millennia, the buried casks would be held in this salt. When the facility had received its legal limit of 6.2 million cubic feet of weapons waste, the operators would let the excavated volume collapse. Under the intense pressure of the salt this far underground, the floors, walls, and ceilings would creep and ultimately crush the drums along with their waste, securing them for the very long term. That was the intent, in any case.

Understanding the site and all technical lands is also always a question of laws and regulations. Technicity is judicial as well as a matter of pipes and drills. Indeed, when you look at the WIPP plant, you see regulations that have set the pace and structure of every aspect of its existence. There are rules governing the containers that arrive from the weapons complex and the details of their contents. Regulations become guides. If the regulations specify the total radioactivity allowed in a drum, then bottom-line thinking pushes the contractors to dilute the material precisely to that limit. If the regulations restrict to a certain level of surface radioactivity of the drum, then that too will become a blueprint for action. Throughout the process, the Department of Energy (DOE) controls all things radiological, with the waste under the legal specification of the 1976 Resource Conservation and Recovery Act (RCRA). Schedule C of that act gave the Environmental Protection Agency (EPA) control over hazardous and non-hazardous solid materials from "cradle to grave," as the expression goes.[6] But the WIPP site is also an extensive mine—and as such, it is regulated, inspected, and directed by the Mine Safety and Health Administration, which sits within the US Department of Labor. As they say on the ground, when a shovel is involved, the mining management and regulations dominate; absent the shovels, the DOE is in charge.[7]

When the 103rd Congress (1993–95) approved the construction of WIPP, they specified that the EPA oversaw the environmental safety of the site.

[5] On statutory limits, The WIPP Land Withdrawal Act, Public Law 102-579 as amended by Public Law 104-201 (1980).

[6] The Resource Conservation and Recovery Act (RCRA) legally controls the handling of hazardous and non-hazardous solid waste. The law, passed by Congress, assigns to the Environmental Protection Agency (EPA) the authority to develop the RCRA program more specifically. Somewhat confusingly, the term "RCRA" can be used interchangeably to "refer to the law, regulations and EPA policy and guidance." Environmental Protection Agency, "Resource Conservation and Recovery Act (RCRA) Laws and Regulations," EPA, accessed February 28, 2022, https://www.epa.gov/rcra.

[7] See Department of Energy and Mine Safety and Health Administration, "Memorandum of Understanding (MOU) Between the US Department of Energy (DOE) and the Mine Safety and Health Administration, US Department of Labor," n.d., https://www.msha.gov/sites/default/files/wipp-doe.pdf.

The EPA sought to do what it often did; it determined the length of time for the regulated materials to be isolated. For a chemical by-product that may leach into the ground, the needed containment time is often years, even decades. By contrast, plutonium-239—the manufactured element that lay at the core of the Nagasaki bomb and most all fission weapons since—has a half-life of 24,100 years. If you wanted to legislate an isolation period of ten half-lives, a standard measure chosen to reduce radioactivity by a factor of about 1,000, it would require 241,000 years. Facing that staggering interval, the EPA compromised, demanding "only" that the site of burial carry warnings to future generations not to dig for a period not less than 10,000 years. Not long enough, perhaps, to cover the decay of plutonium-239, but twice the time the world has had written language: the first traces of Sumerian cuneiform script date from 5,000 years ago.

Alas, even after the plutonium decays, it breaks into uranium-235, which has a half-life of 700 million years. Combining the various buried waste types and their decay products led to even longer cautionary periods for other nuclear sites. The once-but-never Yucca Mountain burial site was held by the courts to adhere to standards requiring a warning period of a *million* years. Modern homo sapiens might be 200,000 or 300,000 years old. That sets this legally mandated million-year period on an *evolutionary* time scale. Long before a megayear has ticked by, "we" may not be us.

With the more reasonable term (if one can say that) of 10,000 years, the regulations required that the DOE commission a team to construct scenarios by which our descendants, 400 generations removed, might inadvertently penetrate the site. (The scenarists saw no possibility of preventing intentional intrusion thousands of years from now.) To work they went, designing scenarios the way wargamers at RAND constructed plausible eruptions of armed conflict or industrial scenario planners at Shell Oil worked their way through worldlines that could affect oil, including imagined embargoes. In that same spirit, the WIPP planners wondered what would happen if the markers were taken away, just as people in the distant past carted off and repurposed some of the bluestone pillars at Stonehenge. What if underground mining robots bored into the site, out of sight of the warning markers? What if people saw the markers but believed their messages were deceptions put there to prevent the excavation of treasure?[8]

Using this form of state-sanctioned science fiction, another team—this one composed, inter alia, of architects, semioticians, linguists, and material scientists—began designing markers that were to be proof against the various imagined, blundering futures. Undoubtedly influenced by then-contemporary land-art and minimalist movements, the marker team contemplated massive spikes emerging from the ground, strewn fields of concrete blocks that impeded settled land use, and other monumental structures. However overly optimistic the WIPP futurists might have been, their mandated effort is unusual. Certainly, it contrasts with the utter *absence* of intergenerational equity in the myriad sites of other production waste: decaying barrels of toxic chemicals; contaminated run-off from chrome plating, copper smelting, and

[8] The complete list of scenarios dreamed up by Sandia scientists can be found in Appendix A of *Preliminary Identification of Scenarios That May Affect the Escape and Transport of Radionuclides from the Waste Isolation Pilot Plant, Southeastern New Mexico*, Robert V. Guzowski and Sandia National Laboratories, prepared for the United States Department of Energy, 1991. More on the development and influence of these scenarios can be found in my "Quand L'État Écrit De La Science-Fiction," *Angle Mort*, November 16, 2016, https://www.angle-mort.fr/fiction/quand-letat-ecrit-de-la-science-fiction/. See also Peter Galison, "The Half-Life of Story," *Hall of Half-Life*, ed., Tessa Giblin (Graz, Austria: Steirischer Herbst, 2015).

porcelain factories; and buried waste around missile factories, airports, and petrochemical plants.

WIPP is unique, of course. But technical lands across the world reshape their surroundings chemically, radioactively, and mechanically in ways that often cannot be seen from the surface alone. On the EPA's Superfund National Priority List stand more than 1,300 entries, each a memorial to the shifting focus of industrial production. Take the fifty-year-old, over-4,000-acre US Magnesium plant adjacent to the Great Salt Lake in Utah. When high water overflowed its evaporation ponds, the plant spewed metals (arsenic, chromium, mercury, copper, and zinc) into the soil, lake waters, groundwater, and air, along with acidic wastewater, polychlorinated biphenyls (PCBs), dioxins/furans, hexachlorobenzene (HCB), polycyclic aromatic hydrocarbons, and chlorine gas. Those highly carcinogenic PCBs and HCBs are in the biosphere *now*, not ten millennia in the future. These chemicals can be found in the eggshells of migratory birds that alight around the Great Salt Lake—and in the bodies of present-day workers.[9]

Technical lands bend time—their outflows, smokestacks, and leached and buried materials transform soil, groundwater, and wetlands. Radioactive territories, such as the WIPP plant and the many other Cold War plants, alter their surroundings in ways that force consideration of staggering chronologies from the past and into the future. WIPP's clock is set to the rhythm of isotopes. Here is a two-mile-by-two-mile outpost that qualified for opening, in part, by right of a salt formation laid down before dinosaurs and in part by predictions to a future longer than recorded human civilization.

Space, too, is altered by technical lands: processing, storage, distribution, and accidents. Perhaps the most dramatic reassignment of vast territories due to technical alteration came through nuclear "loss of containment" events. The catastrophic reactor fire at Chernobyl in April 1986 and its transnational exclusion zone certainly comes to mind; so too does the forbidden zone of Fukushima following the nuclear plant explosion of March 2011. In both cases, radioactive lands drove the mass relocation of residents. Some 300,000 people were pushed out of the 1,600 square miles surrounding the Chernobyl plant; the Fukushima zone peaked at 311 square miles forcing the evacuation of 165,000 people.[10] Paradoxically, human exclusion zones became havens for the more-than-human, creating a new category of land, which one can characterize as *waste-wilderness*.[11]

In the case of the WIPP Site, the non-local impact of the project issues from the national evacuation of nuclear materials. Trucks with transuranic waste roll down specified highways. The routes are highly regulated; drivers must have hundreds of thousands of miles under their belts merely to apply. After selection and training, they cart waste from Rocky Flats, Oak Ridge, Savannah River Site, Idaho National Laboratory, Hanford Site, and Los Alamos National Laboratory—in total, twenty-two nuclear waste "generator" facilities.[12] These plants were immense operations, some now relics almost exclusively devoted to cleaning up the spills, dumps, and storage of hot materials they generated over most of a century. They, in turn, depended

[9] On US Magnesium and the National Priority List: https://semspub.epa.gov/work/08/1570669.pdf. PCBs persist in the biosphere more than forty years after they were banned: Aaron Sidder, "A Look at How Long-Banned PCBs Persist in the Ocean," *Eos*, May 7, 2019, https://eos.org/research-spotlights/a-look-at-how-long-banned-pcbs-persist-in-the-ocean. On toxic sites, see Brinda Sarathy, Vivien Hamilton, Janet Farrell Brodie, eds., *Inevitably Toxic: Historical Perspectives on Contamination, Exposure, and Expertise* (Pittsburgh, PA: University of Pittsburgh Press, 2018).

[10] Adriana Petryna, *Life Exposed: Biological Citizens after Chernobyl* (Princeton, NJ: Princeton University Press, 2013). On Chernobyl, an excellent entry point into the literature can be found with Serhii Plokhy, *Chernobyl: The History of a Nuclear Catastrophe* (New York, NY: Basic Books, 2018). An excellent compact review with many further references on the Fukushima disaster can be found in Kai Vetter, "The Nuclear Legacy Today of Fukushima," *Annual Review of Nuclear and Particle Science* 70 (2020), 257–92; for forthcoming work, see Ryo Morimoto's book, *The Nuclear Ghost: Atomic Livelihoods in Fukushima's Gray Zone*.

[11] On waste-wilderness, Peter Galison and Jamie Kruse, "Waste-Wilderness: A Conversation with Peter L. Galison," Friends of the Pleistocene, May 20, 2015, https://fopnews.wordpress.com/2011/03/31/galison/, cited above.

[12] "22 Sites," US Department of Energy's Waste Isolation Pilot Plant home page, accessed March 8, 2022, https://www.wipp.energy.gov/.

fig 3   WIPP Plant. During the operating decades of WIPP, the tower contains a facility for handling radioactively hot materials. When the plant is eventually closed, the cell will become an "archaeological remnant," serving as an additional permanent marker. *Containment* (2015), Peter Galison and Robb Moss; See also John Hart Associates' report, "Permanent Markers Implementation Plan (DOE/WIPP 04-3302)," U.S. Department of Energy

fig 4   Waste shipping routes to WIPP, routes of radio-monitored, tracked deliveri[es] see an attempt, however difficult and impe[rative] to run the fabrication process in reverse. " Transuranic Waste Transportation Routes," U.S. De[pt.] of Energy

on a nationwide set of smaller sites that mined, enriched, and processed uranium; and from uranium, plutonium. WIPP became the continental drain into which the weapons-generated transuranic waste flowed, gathering materials from a catchment basin the size of the continental United States.

It is certainly a good thing that such great efforts kept the WIPP site isolated. It is vastly cheaper to keep toxics of any kind out of the environment rather than hunting escaped chemicals and isotopes once they have escaped. Alas, there are more ways to have a system break down than there are anticipatory safety measures. To absorb stray liquids, the "generator plants" pack kitty litter in with the waste. So at Los Alamos, planners ordered *inorganic*, clay-based kitty litter for their WIPP-destined containers. A staffer, untrained in chemistry, wrote down "an organic," putting in an order for sWheat Scoop™ made with "renewable wheat," as advertisements proudly proclaimed. Nitric acid is used to recover plutonium, leaving nitrate salts in the waste. When those nitrate salts mixed with the organic materials of the kitty litter, it acted like a miniature version of the fertilizer bomb domestic terrorists used to blow up the Alfred P. Murrah Federal Building in Oklahoma City. Communicative walls between agencies, training failures, poor ventilation design, fire in a salt truck engine, lack of a safety culture—a host of enabling conditions made the accident possible.

At 11:34 pm on February 14, 2014, a WIPP-site radiation alarm went off. A waste container exploded underground, propelling transuranic isotopes through the WIPP ventilation system and out of the plant. Radioactive isotopes, in small quantities, were detected all the way out to points twenty miles from the plant. It took a billion dollars and three years to get it operating again. Distressingly, the accident barely avoided being many times worse.[13] Containment is always aspirational, never complete, inevitably partial, and occasionally catastrophic. Localized plants are not local. This is why technical lands remain so for the very long term.

Building nuclear bombs—some 80,000 over the course of the Cold War— meant erecting a vast set of interconnected lands, from uranium ore mining, processing, and fabricating the cores of uranium-235 and plutonium-239, to assembling, testing, storing, and deploying the weapons. Then, in dismantling obsolete weapons and disposing waste, the whole process had to be run in reverse, all the way back to emplacement in the earth. Here, as in his work on quantum theory, Niels Bohr augured well. In 1939, he already judged that the atomic bomb could only be produced by turning the whole of America into a production facility. A few years later, with the wartime Manhattan Project going full throttle, after being briefed on the bomb by Edward Teller, Bohr remarked, "I told you it couldn't be done without turning the whole country into a factory."[14] Now, we might add with the perspective of almost a century, it could not be done without leaving radioactive lands across much of the country.

Bohr was right about the country becoming a factory—and not just in the case of nuclear weapons. Over the last decades, the petrochemical complex has also radically altered the land, air, and water. The 150 winding miles

[13] For an astute reading of the accident, see David M. Klaus, "What Really Went Wrong at WIPP: An Insider's View of Two Accidents at the Only US Underground Nuclear Waste Repository," *Bulletin of the Atomic Scientists* 75, no. 4 (2019): 197–204, https://doi.org/10.1080/009 63402.2019.1628516. Klaus's article contains references to the original accident reports, and is critical of them for not adequately attending to the institutional failures that surrounded the events.

[14] Richard Rhodes, *The Making of the Atomic Bomb* (London: Simon & Schuster, 2012), 500.

15 On the 140-plus chemical companies, see Tegan Wendland, "Louisiana's Chemical Corridor Is Expanding. So Are Efforts to Stop It," *NPR*, March 20, 2020, https://www.npr.org/2020/03/20/814882296/louisianas-chemical-corridor-is-expanding-so-are-efforts-to-stop-it. On chemical toxicity in the Great Lakes, see Michelle Murphy, "Alterlife and Decolonial Chemical Exposures," *Cultural Anthropology* 32, no. 4 (November 2017): 494–503.

16 Richard Misrach and Kate Orff, *Petrochemical America* (New York, NY: Aperture, 2014), 128–29; underground diagram, 134–35, export corridors, 140–41.

17 On the chemical corridor with significant digital and mapping see, for example, Lylla Younes et al., "Poison in the Air," ProPublica, November 2, 2021, https://www.propublica.org/article/toxmap-poison-in-the-air. For the view of the UN, see its report "USA: Environmental Racism in 'Cancer Alley' Must End—Experts," OHCHR, March 2, 2021, https://www.ohchr.org/EN/NewsEvents/Pages/DisplayNews.aspx?NewsID=26824&LangID=E. For the quotation "get sick, move, or die," see James Pasley, "Inside Louisiana's Horrifying 'Cancer Alley,' an 85-Mile Stretch of Pollution and Environmental Racism That's Now Dealing with Some of the Highest Coronavirus Death Rates in the Country," *Business Insider*, April 9, 2020, https://www.businessinsider.com/louisiana-cancer-alley-photos-oil-refineries-chemicals-pollution-2019-11.

along the Mississippi River between Baton Rouge and New Orleans host one of the most toxic environments in the United States. There are already some 140 chemical companies in the corridor, some expanding while more move in. For example, ExxonMobil has a major plant here, making gasoline and jet fuel along with other petrochemical products, including polyethylene, used in wrapping films, liquid containers, injection molding, caps, piping, and wire insulation. BASF Corporation has a chemical plant at Geismar, Louisiana, that in 2018 emitted a total of 7.6 tons of ethylene oxide.[15] Indeed, as landscape architect Kate Orff has done in collaboration with photographs by Richard Misrach, one can map the riverbanks with human-made products—here dioxolane, there isopropylamine, or elsewhere polyisobutylene. Or one can map by company name. Or, as Orff and her team also do, cut vertically and display the storage of ethylene, gasoline, and other products deep underground in hollowed-out salt domes.[16]

This vast petrochemical empire has fully altered the land; this territory is a technical object through and through. It is also land where environmental racism is manifest. The river parishes (St. James, St. John the Baptist, and St. Charles) bear the brunt of this massive set of plants, a burden that has fallen disproportionally on the Black populace of these counties. Study after study shows that people of color and low-income populations live, in far greater numbers, near petrochemical and other technical pollution sources and are systematically subjected to 40 percent more airborne toxins than wealthier communities. In Cancer Alley, as it is known to locals in St. James Parish close to the plants, the choice is stark: because of the emissions, you can get sick, move, or die.[17] So, too, is it in the nuclear domain. There is a long and terrible tradition of putting unsafe, poorly regulated uranium mines on Native American lands to negotiate with communities outside US regulations. More than 500 of these mines are now abandoned; many, which were drilled into aquifers, are leaching arsenic and other contaminants into groundwater; the mines remain a source of radon and other contaminated dust.[18] On the surface, in the underground, and through the air, the land is now entirely technical.

So, the question remains: What are technical lands? They are intensely local lands, meaning this soil, that evaporation pond, this underground storage tank exists right now. We need to understand better the implications for abutting residents who drink their well water and breathe the chemicals spewing from the smokestacks. It can matter whether one is a mile or five miles from a multibillion-dollar chemical plant, with their storage tanks and distillation columns. But technical lands also link us to a past and future through planetary and evolutionary time, leading to spaces that range far more extensively than we reckoned when we built our systems of airports, weapons factories, refineries, plastic production facilities, and toxic legacy sites.

The editors and authors of this present volume on technical lands face this challenge by addressing technical lands across economic, cultural, legal, aesthetic, architectural, and ideological approaches. We need this intersectional form of discourse—we need it because these lands are not peripheral. On the contrary, they are, in many ways, the core industrial and military structures of the United States and comparable economies. If we are going to understand these lands in the full spectrum of their local/non-local existences, it will require analysis from the fields of science, economics, art history, cultural studies, tax policy, administrative law, and foreign policy. It demands a grasp of an expanded remit for critical landscape architecture joined with ethnography, scientific history, and social justice. In the crossing of these various approaches, one thing is sure: however contained technical lands may seem at first glance, they cannot be grasped within the confines of county or parish or any single discipline.

Ask "why are these lands where they are?" and some part of the answer may be given by geography—you do not want a nuclear waste facility on a mountain or near a body of water; you avoid locating a refinery far from the entry point of the oil shipments. But that is not enough. The WIPP site and many other nuclear facilities are in New Mexico partly because other states had the political power to block them. The hundreds of chemical factories that sit in the river parishes along the Mississippi are partly because Louisiana has tax and regulatory breaks offered to them. The residents there, often minorities, often poor, had little ability to shift those subsidies and permits. All these forces, driven by some of the largest corporations in the world—profits, jobs, tax breaks, regulatory loopholes—have their origins far beyond a parish like St. James. Pressure comes from the state of Louisiana, the US federal government, and the international trade that brings in South American, Russian, and Middle Eastern oil and ships plastics, fertilizers, gasoline, jet fuel, and other petrochemical products out across the world.

Such considerations lead us to a functional definition: the more infrastructure expands to ever-wider circles—from local to state, national to international—the more they are technical lands. The scope of this shaping radius extends far out to the planet itself. From this perspective, the Anthropocene is precisely a recognition that we are converting the sea, atmosphere, and land to technical objects, with consequences that become more apparent with each passing year.

We shape our technical lands, airports, petrochemical plants, and nuclear facilities. They then determine whether we can drink the water, where we can live, how well we can live. Albeit less ethereal than Wheeler's beautiful formulation of Einstein's equations, a rephrasing comes to mind: *We build technical lands; technical lands shape how we will live.*

[18] There is by now a vast literature across many disciplines about the Cold War mining on Navajo lands. A good introduction with oral histories of miners and more can be found in Stewart L. Udall's foreword in *Navajo People and Uranium Mining*, eds. Doug Brugge, Timothy Benally, and Esther Yazzie-Lewis (Albuquerque, NM: University of New Mexico Press, 2006).

Reading Technical Lands

Jeffrey S Nesbit *&* **Charles Waldheim**

The past several years witnessed the emergence of academic discourse on "technical lands." This nascent dialogue has grown slowly, obliquely, and unevenly across the social sciences, humanities, and design disciplines. Harvard historian of science Peter Galison has been at the forefront of this discussion. His direct invocation of "technical landscapes" theorizes "sites where global knowledge practices and aesthetic categories have converged to literally transform the physical geography of the land."[1] This burgeoning discourse provides an initial inquiry of shared characteristics defining "technical lands" as a particular type and has yielded a catalog of unique sites, each spatially delimited and secured, with tightly regulated boundaries and perimeters. They are often geographically remote and highly invisible—subject to both heightened surveillance and painstaking forms of obfuscation. They maintain special legal status and, more specifically, exceptional protocols in relation to the nonhuman world. Established from distinct forms of technical subjectivity, these sites continuously rely on the rearticulation of performative parameters. "Technical lands" demonstrate varied sites of exclusion, administration, and regulation, including demilitarized zones, conservation easements, spaceports, prisons, sites of extractive industries, and military bases, to name but a few examples.

The empirical and theoretical contours of technical lands remain opaque. The discussion has been largely confined to seminar rooms, conference halls, and forthcoming publications. Crucial questions remain: how precisely do technical lands articulate, and perhaps confound, our conventional nomenclature of "'nature,' 'culture,' 'value,' 'capital,' 'territory,' and 'site?'"[2] How to do they relate to traditional understandings of landscape, either in its German (*landschaft*), Dutch (*landscap*), or English (*landskip*) etymologies? How do technical lands themselves function in the visual cultures or "scopic regimes" of modernity?

Technical Lands and Land Use

Writing on technical lands stretches across the twentieth century in ways that depart quite dramatically from the critical, reflexive usage suggested here. Technical lands appear in colonial and neocolonial documentation, city and urban planning land-use practices, and broadly construed developmentalist literature of the second half of the twentieth century. The phrase "technical lands" itself seems to have first appeared in 1814 in a document created by the Linnaean Society of London, a society concerned with the development and dissemination of knowledge regarding natural history. However, it was not until the late nineteenth century—as technical land came to designate a specific category of colonial land claimed by the British Empire—that the phrase truly entered the English language. For instance, the Khoti Settlement Amendment Act of 1880 addressed the existence and management of technical land, alongside a broader discussion of land ownership, tenure, taxation, and reform in British India. This usage of technical land continued into the late moments of the British colonial project and into the early postcolonial period. For example, technical land

[1] Peter Galison et al., "Technical Landscapes: Aesthetics and the Environment in the History of Science and Art," Harvard University, April 6–8, 2017.

[2] Galison et al., "Technical Landcapes."

offices and officers are mentioned throughout the colonial documents of the Anglophone Caribbean during the 1950s; and, among other places, in documentation regarding the formation of a Technical Land Use Committee in Ceylon in 1967.

During this period, the literature in urban and regional planning came to designate land—and kinds of landscape survey and analysis—as technical. In this context, the language of technical land was often used, as it was in a 1942 volume of *The Planners' Journal*, to discuss "technical land-use surveys." Equally common was the "important ... technical land appraisal work" that proceeded "from the standpoint of the valuation principle," as referenced in a 1930 job posting for a Principal Land Appraiser at the Interstate Commerce Commission.[3] The lexicon of technical land appeared in comparable ways in the closely linked discourse on landscape architecture during this historical moment. As stated in the journal *Landscape Architecture*, by 1916, and over the previous decade, jurisdictional transformations made possible "the application of specialized and technical knowledge to the problems of timber and forage production and utilization" in the United States.[4]

The language of technical lands can also be found across the broadly construed developmentalist literature of the second half of the twentieth century. It appears, for example, in the institutional documents of the United Nations' Food and Agriculture Organization (FAO) during the 1970s and, more specifically, in FAO's Soils Bulletin in 1974. In that document, the FAO encourages "the standardisation of land evaluation methods," as well as its systematic review of approaches "to the classification of agricultural land developed or adopted in the past by different countries or by different organisations throughout the world."[5] This late twentieth-century discourse on technical lands in the developmentalist sphere extends well beyond the domain of ostensibly "rural" lands and still lingers today. In more recent publications, one can just as readily find discussion of technical land regarding site reclamation and coal mining as the "effects of administrative land-use and technical land-form constraints on timber production at the landscape level."[6]

Premises and Positions

A critical engagement with technical lands, their histories, and their present contexts is generally available from several theoretical positions. Jason W. Moore's world-ecological framework represents a highly productive starting point. Moore's post-Cartesian understanding that capitalist crisis occurs due to the interlocking tension of overaccumulation and underproduction provides a valuable means for framing the historical emergence and rearticulation of technical lands over the *longue durée*. World ecology encourages us to ask: are technical lands a means of addressing the "insufficient flow" of capital's inputs "relative to the demands of value production?"[7] Or, how do technical lands relate to both the ontological dualisms of modernity—namely, the distinction between nature and society—*and* the process of valorization? On this second question, we also enlist a broad range of

[3] Bryant Hall, "How Much Land for Commerces," *The Planner's Journal* (1942), 7; see also, Personnel Classification Board, Preliminary Class Specifications of Positions in the Field Service. Field Survey Division (1930).

[4] E.A. Sherman, "The Forest Service and the Preservation of Natural Beauty," *Landscape Architecture* 6, no. 2 (1916): 115–19.

[5] Food and Agriculture Organization of the United Nations Soil Resources, Development, and Conservation, *Land Evaluation in Europe: Report on the Technical Consultation, Nitra, Czechoslovakia, 1–6 September 1975*, Food and Agriculture Organization of the United Nations (FAO), 1975.

[6] L. Karkkainen et al., "Effects of Administrative Land-Use and Technical Land-Form Constraints on Timber Production at the Landscape Level," *Scandinavian Journal of Forest Research* 26, no. 2 (2011): 120–27.

[7] Jason W. Moore, *Capitalism in the Web of Life: Ecology and the Accumulation of Capital* (New York, NY: Verso, 2015).

historical and geographical theorizations, including those more directly concerned with territory and land itself such as Stuart Elden's rigorous analysis of *The Birth of Territory*; Christine DeLucia's recent work on terrapolitics, relationality, and indigeneity; and Rob Nixon's writing on the conflicts that emerge when official landscapes are forced onto vernacular ones.

The works from Moore and his collaborators draw their own accounts and their relation to the problematics of technical lands. These include those closely linked to value theory discourses on unwaged social work, racial capitalism, and the continuance of the racialized hierarchy under capitalist accumulation and capital's tendency toward Karl Marx's "metabolic rift."[8] The work pursued by Tithi Bhattacharya, Silvia Federici, John Bellamy Foster, Ruth Wilson Gilmore, and Walter Johnson raises highly provocative questions relating to technical lands. These writings force us to consider the relationship between the designation and production of technical lands and the capitalist *value form*. Further still, they force us to contemplate whether the social ontologies or the normativity of these various "background spheres" have shaped and been shaped by technical lands across diverse spaces and times. They encourage us to consider the function of technical lands across distinct regimes of accumulation—including liberal, state-managed, and financialized-neoliberal capitalism.[9] What, for example, are the scopic regimes of the racialized "carceral landscapes" that defined the plantation economy, and what relation do they have to those that define the post-Fordist predatory economies of the contemporary United States?[10]

Recent work in the history of science and science and technology studies (STS) similarly provides a lens through which we might make sense of technical lands. Often highly attuned to biopolitics, socio-technical systems, and actor-network theory, this literature has productively demonstrated the importance of social imagination in making sense of urban infrastructures and the networked metropolis, as well as the centrality of circulation itself in the emergence of the urban as an ever-expanding "immunitary" biopolitical paradigm.[11] The ways in which design technologies shape consciousness and temporality raise epistemic, moral, and political questions.[12] Taken together, this literature provokes a range of questions: how might the growing scale, scope, and complexity of technical lands relate to Enlightenment understandings of the sovereign self? How do technical lands enable the biopolitical management of populations? Through what social imaginaries are technical lands conjured and produced? How might we read technical lands themselves as the accretion of multiple *durées*—as palimpsestic landscapes?

If an investigation of technical lands would benefit from a turn toward STS—due to its relation to the Foucauldian literature on biopolitics—it would also do well to turn to those closely linked theoretical discourses on necropolitics and biopolitical production. The former is especially pertinent given the relationship between technical lands and postcolonial contexts. Achille Mbembe, the author most closely associated with thinking on the

[8] For more on Marx's "metabolic rift," see John Bellamy Foster, "Marx's Theory of Metabolic Rift: Classical Foundations for Environmental Sociology," *The American Journal of Sociology* 105, no. 2 (1999): 366–405.

[9] See Nancy Fraser, "Rethinking the Public Sphere: A Contribution to the Critique of Actually Existing Democracy, *Social Text*, no. 25/26 (1990): 56–80.

[10] See Walter Johnson, "The Carceral Landscape," *River of Dark Dreams: Slavery and Empire in the Cotton Kingdom* (Cambridge: Harvard University Press, 2013): 209–43; and Ruth Wilson Gilmore, "Crime, Croplands, and Capitalism," *Golden Gulag: Prisons, Surplus, Crisis and Opposition in Globalizing California* (Berkeley: University of California Press, 2007): 128–80.

[11] Antoine Picon, "Urban Infrastructure, Imagination and Politics: From the Networked Metropolis to the Smart City," *International Journal of Urban and Regional Research* 42, no. 2 (2018): 263–275; see also, Ross Exo Adams, *Circulation and Urbanization* (London: Sage, 2018).

[12] John May, *Signal. Image. Architecture.* (New York, NY: Columbia University Press, 2019).

13 Achille Mbembe, *Critique of Black Reason* (Durham, NC: Duke University Press, 2017), 4.

14 See Malini Ranganathan, "Thinking with Flint: Racial Liberalism and the Roots of an American Water Tragedy," *Capitalism Nature Socialism* 27, no. 2 (2016) Crime, Croplands, and Capitalism, 17–33.

necropolitical, uses the term to think through postcolonial sovereignty—suggesting that Foucault's image of biopower is unable to make sense of those forms of postcolonial subjugation that submit life to the power of death and the "creation of death-worlds." For Mbembe, the necropolitical connotes a highly geographical condition: necropolitics moves through the construction of *spaces* that are effectively in-between life and death; it entails the creation of a "partition in time and an atomization of space."[13] This framework raises clear questions regarding the designation and production of technical lands in postcolonial geographies. What is the relation between technical lands and the specter and spatiality of necropolitics? What role do technical lands play—or what role have they historically played—in the subjection of some to premature death? How do technical lands function as a necropolitical technology *outside* of colonial and postcolonial political formations?[14] Finally, how do technical lands relate to the history—as narrated by scholars like Frank B. Wilderson III, Sylvia Wynter, and others—of blackness and the "genre of Man?"

The literature on biopolitical production diverges sharply from the necropolitical but similarly provokes constructive questions for thinking through technical lands. Insofar as the post-workerism or autonomous Marxist conceptual framework of biopolitical production is concerned with how post-Fordist capitalism is parasitic upon "the common"—in both its ostensibly "immaterial" and "natural" forms—it allows us to consider the relation between technical lands and extraction, or enclosure. For example, one might wonder how the more recent history of technical lands supports this literature's contention that sociality itself has become subsumed by the logics of accumulation, rendering the language of socially necessary labor time increasingly obsolete. Do technical lands contribute today to the subsumption of life itself? If so, what space do technical lands provide for political resistance—resistance that is constitutive of power itself?

Assemblages and Accumulations

Scholars involved in the discourse on "object-oriented ontology" (OOO), assemblage theory, and non-representational geography—radically distinct onto-epistemologies—also engage with issues relevant to technical lands. Insofar as it is concerned with contemplating the inaccessible and irreducible existence of objects (and, with rejecting "correlationism"), OOO might allow for a productive decentering of the human from thinking on technical lands. Assemblage theory, for its part, raises the question as to how technical lands are heterogeneously thrown together, composed, performed—and how they might be rearticulated or reassembled in a more just world. Further still, non-representational geography seems particularly useful if we are to think through the affective and phenomenological experience produced in and through an engagement with technical lands.

Following from OOO and assemblage theory—and these works' concern with issues of planetarity and flat ontology, respectively—one might more broadly say that technical lands demand a return to the longstanding problem of scale in human geography and its cognate fields. Here, the questions are relatively straightforward: How are technical lands—and the subjectivities that emerge through their production—relationally constituted? How do technical lands exist in relation to broader planetary geographies and flows, which are themselves "not the outside of place," nor "abstract" or "somehow 'up there' or disembodied?"[15] Does the history of technical lands demand a transcendence of the language of scale? Or do technical lands require a broader lexicon, encompassing scale as well as "territorialization, place-making, and networking?"[16] One might even use the frame of technical lands to return to fundamental questions in critical theory regarding the relationship between the concrete, the abstract, and real abstraction. How, for instance, do technical lands relate to "the treatment of labour as an abstraction?"[17] How should they be understood in relation to the concept of totality? And what relation do they have to abstract space?

Recent theorizations of extended or planetary urbanization have circled many of these same questions. Neil Brenner and Nikos Katsikis use the term "operational landscapes" to theorize the "hinterlands of the Capitalocene"—a concept that appears to be closely linked, if not overlapping, with the notion of technical lands.[18] For them, such landscapes confound traditional understandings of the city/country and core/periphery relation. They argue that these landscapes are implicated in variegated forms of hinterland-hinterland connection, extraction, waste management, and commodity production. Moreover, for some theorists of planetary urbanization and the planetary mine—such geographies of extraction productively demonstrate both the increasing robotization of labor and the contours of "resource imperialism after the West."[19] Here again, the questions are many: What is the precise relation between technical lands, planetary urbanization, and the "operational landscapes" of the Capitalocene? How do the history and presence of technical lands fit into narratives regarding long-term cycles of accumulation, territorial hegemony, and the shifting geography of core/periphery relations? And more broadly, how do technical lands shape capitalism's fixity/motion relation—or the "contradictory interplay" between capital's "need for territorial expansion" and its "equally foundational drive toward sociospatial restructuring?"[20]

Unsurprisingly, the study of technical lands would also benefit from a close engagement with the philosophical literature on "the political"—not least given the relation between technical lands and the state or declaration of exception. More precisely, and paradoxically, studies of technical land might do well to turn to the literature on *post*-politicization, which builds on the work of Giorgio Agamben, Carl Schmitt, and others. In reference to literature on post-politicization and the state of exception, the designation and production of technical lands is precisely *de*-politicizing rather than "necessarily political." In other words, the designation of technical lands can be understood as a practice to explicitly seek and enact the "total closure of the social" in a particular geography and establish a new form of hegemony, despite the impossibility of such a procedure.

[15] Doreen Massey, "Geographies of Responsibility," *Geografiska Annaler* 86, no. 1 (2004) Crime, Croplands, and Capitalism, 8.

[16] Neil Brenner, *New Urban Spaces* (Oxford: University of Oxford Press, 2019).

[17] Alex Loftus, "Violent Geographical Abstractions," *Environment and Planning D: Society and Space* 33, no. 2 (2015) Crime, Croplands, and Capitalism, 375.

[18] Neil Brenner and Nikos Katsikis, "Operational Landscapes: Hinterlands of the Capitalocene," *AD/Architectural Design* 90, no. 3 (2020) Crime, Croplands, and Capitalism, 22–31.

[19] Martín Arboleda, *Planetary Mine: Territories of Extraction Under Late Capitalism* (London: Verso, 2020).

[20] Neil Brenner, *New Urban Spaces* (Oxford: Oxford University Press, 2019), 53.

Aesthetics and Visualities

It is important to stress the fundamental insight that the literature on aesthetics and visual culture contribute to the study of technical lands. One might say these sites have an aesthetic, which have come together through "specific historical, economic, cultural, and discursive conjunctions."[21] It is impossible to imagine the forms of subjectification produced in and through technical lands without contemplating their aesthetics and the regimes of visuality they enlist. Therefore, what exactly is the aesthetic vocabulary of technical lands? In what sense do these lands exist in a broader relational field, a field of aesthetico-political and historical references? How and why do technical lands suggest modes or practices of "seeing (and not seeing)?"[22] How do the contemporary aesthetic and visual practices tied to technical lands "rhyme with other historical circumstances" and other modes of aesthetic production? What role does the "technological sublime" or "data sublime" play in the abovementioned forms of depoliticization that technical lands seek to produce?[23]

One might productively contemplate these questions with a turn to the emergent literature on critical cartography and countersurveillance, modes of inquiry and praxis that often seek to reflexively and taxonomically "reveal" technical lands and their implications, through what Trevor Paglen has called a "minoritarian empiricism."[24] Such work is instrumental in understanding that representation and visuality are never neutral. Under distinct regimes of visuality, the possibility for seeing otherwise is, while possible, highly circumscribed. When put another way, this work is highly attentive to the aesthetics and politics attendant to the production and representation of space and to those slippages that emerge in the performance and representation of "reality-as-it-is"; slippages that might open up discourse for new modes of seeing and becoming. How can we "orient our seeing and suggest practices in ways that suggest (even negatively) liberatory forms of being?"[25]

Each of these questions seems productive for thinking with and through technical lands. Moreover, they demand close consideration of the anti-visuality attendant to technical lands. Within geography and its cognate fields, this kind of dialectically emergent counter-visual praxis has already taken several forms, which might serve as reference points for future work. Here one finds several practical reflections, including Matthew Wilson's work on the "troubles of the map" and his attempt to "wallow in all the messes that trouble makes" in the realm of cartography; Eyal Weizman's forensic investigations at the "threshold of detectability"; Laura Kurgan's efforts to visualize carceral geographies and conflict urbanism; as well as Shannon Mattern's renunciation of any attempt to render cities as computers, to frame "the messiness of urban life as programmable and subject to rational [and thus aesthetic] order."[26] One might also note the relevance of closely allied efforts in critical archeological and anthropological practice to the study of technical lands. Here, the work of scholars like Jason De León and Amade M'charek is especially useful to consider, given that it seeks to

[21] Trevor Paglen, "Experimental Geography: From Cultural Production to the Production of Space," *The Brooklyn Rail: Critical Perspectives on Arts, Politics, and Culture* (March 2009); https://brooklynrail.org/2009/03/express/experimental-geography-from-cultural-production-to-the-production-of-space.

[22] Julian Stallabrass and Trevor Paglen, "Negative Dialectics in the Google Era: A Conversation with Trevor Paglen," *October* 138 (2011): 7.

[23] Stallabrass and Paglen, "Negative Dialectics," 3–14.

[24] Stallabrass and Paglen, "Negative Dialectics," 8.

[25] Stallabrass and Paglen, "Negative Dialectics,"14.

[26] See Matthew Wilson, "Quantified Self-City-Nation," *Mediapolis* 4, no. 3 (2018); and Eyal Weizman, "Violence at the Threshold of Detectability," *E-Flux* 64 (2015); see also, Shannon Mattern, "A City is Not a Computer," *Places Journal*, (2017), https://placesjournal.org/article/a-city-is-not-a-computer/.

make visible, with excruciating precision, the materiality of borderlands and the material cultures they produce. These borderland scholars have developed an intellectual *and* aesthetic counter-practice to think through both the material culture of the border and the possibility for care under prevailing conditions of "corporeal suffering."[27] What would an analogous practice look like in other types of technical lands?

[27] Jason De León, "Undocumented Migration, Use Wear, and the Materiality of Habitual Suffering in the Sonoran Desert," *Journal of Material Culture* 18, no. 4, (2013): 321–45.

Much as the problematics of technical lands link these distinct theoretical traditions, they also implicate a host of academic disciplines. The scholars gestured to and referenced above come from a range of fields across the critical humanities and social sciences. History, sociology, geography, anthropology, literature, science and technology studies, and political science are all represented, to name but a few. Theorists and historians of the design disciplines—architecture, landscape, and urban planning—sit at the cutting edge of this emerging area of inquiry. Thus, the critical study of technical lands represents a crucial opportunity to engage a broad, yet otherwise mainly siloed, group of scholars and research agendas.

This volume represents a modest beginning of that more ambitious project, as it gathers a coalition of distinct viewpoints from an extraordinary cohort of contributors. First among those is Peter Galison, whose leadership on this topic first indicated its potential. Galison's foreword situates the origins and implications of the topic. Shannon Mattern and Robert Pietrusko set the stage with the exploration of sense and sensation in the human subjects, spatial orders, and administrative surveillance of technical lands. Mattern's chapter introduces technical lands as perceived through the senses of human perception. Her contribution reveals the olfactory as a uniquely revelatory medium of an encounter between human subjects and the sites of technical lands. Pietrusko's chapter extends that concern with sensing through the distanced mediation of remote sensing, satellite reconnaissance, and the management of population measurement.

Matthew Wilson, Eric Huntley, and Richard Hindle describe the various instruments, individuals, and institutions responsible for maintaining and controlling technical lands. Wilson's chapter traces the essential role of technical lines in the administration and management of technical lands. Huntley's chapter introduces the occupation of technical lands as enabled by an essential new professional, the land technician. Hindle's chapter finds the status of technical lands as formed through the legal and financial instruments of technical patents. John Davis and Jay Cephas delineate the structures and infrastructures accommodating technical lands through the logic and logistics of fulfillment. Davis's chapter traces the armored edges of shipping ports across the Americas as unique case studies in technical lands. Cephas's chapter walks the long last mile of logistics landscapes and the technical lands they gather.

Neil Brenner, Swarnabh Ghosh, Nikos Katsikis, Florian Hertweck, and Marija Marić reveal the global flows of feed, food, and fuel that enable and demand the set-aside of technical lands. Brenner, Ghosh, and Katsikis's chapter explodes the metabolic monstrosity of the global feedlot matrix.

Hertweck and Marić's chapter reveals the petroleum economy refueling zone as a unique form of technical land embedded in and around urbanized areas in Europe.

Stephen Graham, Billy Fleming, and A L McCullough unearth the enormous reach of extraction economies claiming technical lands as well as their collateral societal, environmental, and human costs. Graham's chapter drills down on the technical lands of mining extraction as a form of vertical imperialism. Fleming and McCullough's chapter proposes the dismantling of the coalfield to prison industrial complex in contemporary Appalachia.

Caitlin Blanchfield and Desiree Valadares revisit the invention of conservation science and national reservations as technical lands and instruments of state formation. Blanchfield's chapter reveals the role of lands set aside for scientific knowledge production as a form of settler colonialism. Valadares's chapter conjures the invention of national parks and monuments as distinct forms of technical lands. Roi Salgueiro Barrio and Rania Ghosn pull back the camera to expand the collection's reach while articulating the role of design and technical lands in the construction of a planetary imagination. Salgueiro's chapter invokes technical lands as a lens through which to conceive a new cosmopolitical design practice. Ghosn's chapter extends the concern with design culture's role in visualizing forms of collective imagination despite our seemingly incongruously uncommon interests.

Like so many problems of the current condition, technical lands demand a transdisciplinary—or perhaps even *undisciplined*—approach. They represent an opportunity to forge new combinations and territorializations. In other words, none of the above theoretical frameworks can individually— nor in combination—comprehend technical lands, their histories, or their potentials. Given that the scale and complexity that attends to these lands has only increased in recent years, this volume begins an effort to theorize technical lands across borders and boundaries, and to make sense of their relation to the self, the social, and the ecological. It is this aspiration that *Technical Lands: A Critical Primer* proposes.

Scents of Spatial Order

Sensing Technical Lands

Shannon Mattern

Rigid lines of Douglas firs climb a mountainside. Arrays of calibration grids—like those you'd see at the optometrist's office but blown up for a satellite's eye—are sprinkled across the desert. Giant tractors till grooves into the Iowa prairie. A pastel patchwork of brine pools carpets the Atacama Desert. Eerily abandoned zones trap the ghosts of nuclear tests. Acres of dry lots enclose thousands of cows waiting to be shipped off for processing. Acres of solar panels and miles of gigantic wind turbines populate energy farms. Armies of pumpjacks pull oil to the earth's surface. Polychromatic stripes of tulips stretch out into the Dutch countryside as far as the eye can see, while polychromatic shipping containers cluster into metallic mountains on the Rotterdam docks. Deep gouges in the landscape mark the blasting or cutting away of limestone and marble. Putrescent ponds hold the tailings of nearby mines. Runways and rhizomatic airport terminals converge at odd angles, mediating between aerial and terrestrial logistics.

These scenes index "technical lands," which, as the editors of this volume explain, exemplify "sites where global knowledge practices and aesthetic categories have converged to literally transform the physical geography of the land." I've used a different term: "indexical landscapes." In 2015, I organized a symposium at ArtCenter College of Design, in Pasadena, CA, that examined how our "landscapes have long been shaped using techniques and technologies that render them 'intelligent' and intelligible—either to the people who inhabit them, or to the various tools we use to cultivate, navigate, and operationalize them." These terrains "index, materialize, and even render perceptible, the logics behind their own organization, management, and use."[1] Those logics encompass specific protocols of operation, legal codes, and systems of administration. The aforementioned spatial forms and aesthetics—the factory farms and container ports—also manifest epistemologies and ontologies that equate land with property, that reduce natural materials and living things to "resources" demanding exhaustive extraction and optimization, that regard geography as abstract space to be traversed as efficiently as possible.

We typically perceive the organizational and operational logics of technical lands through visual representation: maps and charts, photographs, and aerial imagery. Allan Sekula, Edward Burtynsky, Peter Goin, Richard Misrach, Trevor Paglen, Richard Mosse, Josh Begley, and Jenny Odell are among those who often deploy specialized imaging tools—including large-format and thermal radiation cameras, telephoto lenses, and cranes—as well as repurposed satellite images, to index the distinctive morphologies and colors of container ports, mines, nuclear test sites, border zones, top-secret military sites, maximum-security prisons, parking lots, and landfills.[2] Some of these sites, like satellite calibration targets and massive distribution centers, even function as images themselves; they're what Harun Farocki called "operational images": machine-readable images that do or effect things in the world, like tuning satellites or orchestrating robots.

This volume's editors argue that such technical or indexical terrains possess hypervisuality and susceptibility to surveillance, and, at the same

[1] Shannon Mattern, "Indexical Landscapes Symposium @ ArtCenter College of Design, October 29," wordsinspace.net, last modified 2015, https://wordsinspace.net/2015/10/06/indexical-landscapes-symposium-art-center-college-of-design-october-29/.

[2] John Beck, "The Purloined Landscape: Photography and Power in the American West," *Tate Papers* 21 (Spring 2014), https://www.tate.org.uk/research/publications/tate-papers/21/the-purloined-landscape-photography-and-power-in-the-american-west; Andriko Lozowy, "Picturing Industrial Landscapes," *Space and Culture* 17, no. 4 (2014): 388–97; Kerry Oliver-Smith, curator, "The World to Come: Art in the Age of the Anthropocene," Harn Museum at the University of Florida, September 18, 2018–March 3, 2019; Joshua Schuster, "Between Manufacturing and Landscapes: Edward Burtynsky and the Photography of Ecology," *Photography and Culture* 6, no. 2 (2013): 193–212.

time, opacity—a resistance to being seen and scrutinized. These lands, much like a cubist painting or glitchy digital image, are embodiments of the "scopic regime" of modernity and are works of art in their own right. And, as with much fine art, how we render these sites visible can contribute to their fetishization. In *Cartographies of the Absolute*, Alberto Toscano and Jeff Kinkle note "a tendency in the visual arts, and photography in particular, for a fixation with the symmetrical and homeomorphic properties of the logistical landscape"—all those transportation hubs and oil refineries and factory farms—"whose paradoxically photogenic character stems in many ways from its inadvertent mimesis of a modernist, minimalist geometry whose rules of representation are already deeply incorporated into the grammar of artistic form."[3] Literary scholar John Beck finds that this is especially true of landscape photographs of technical lands:

[3] Alberto Toscano and Jeff Kinkle, *Cartographies of the Absolute* (Winchester: Zero Books, 2015), 204.

> The landscape has been shaped according to the needs of the mode of representation, and the value of landscape photographs—a value transposed onto the terrain itself from its composition as images—so often lies in what they leave out: indigenous inhabitants, industrial devastation, military installations, prisons, toxic contamination, and the rest.[4]

[4] Beck, "The Purloined Landscape."

I'm particularly interested here in what these visual representations and ocular "operational" indices leave out—not what we don't see, but what other sensory dimensions are occluded. I want to examine what we can learn about technical lands by listening to and smelling them. We'll examine how these other senses also serve "operational" purposes by disclosing the functional logics and mechanisms driving technical lands, and by supporting diagnostic functions in case of malfunction; stench and clamor can signal inefficiencies and vulnerabilities. Sounds and smells can also manifest the broader environmental impacts of optimizing terrain while, at the same time, exposing the impacts on individual human and more-than-human bodies. These non-visual senses can help us appreciate how those bodies are integral parts of the technical apparatus—they work to ensure the smooth functioning of spatialized operations—while also often bearing the burden of their dysfunction. Yet sound and smell can also facilitate modes of resistance and divulge that which *escapes* the terrains' technical logics. In what follows, we'll examine the sounds and smells of two categories of technical lands—spaces of industrialized agriculture and spaces of extraction—and reflect on how broader sensory attunement could inform the design and governance of these terrains.

The Plantation, the Slaughterhouse, the Factory Farm

From the sugarcane fields in the Canary Islands of the fifteenth century to contemporary Indonesian palm estates and American prisons, the plantation has constituted a critical *dispositif* within the genealogies of industrialized agriculture and racial capitalism.[5] It's also an early example of a

[5] Katherine McKittrick, "Plantation Futures," *Small Axe* 42 (2013): 1–15; Sylvia Wynter, "Novel and History, Plot and Plantation," *Savacou* 5 (1971): 95–102.

technical land. As historian John E. Crowley (2016) notes, visual representations of slavery throughout the Atlantic world, from the mid-sixteenth to the mid-nineteenth century, "privileged machinery over people. This privileging largely took the work of slaves for granted and, intentionally or not, deflected attention from slavery."[6] By fetishizing the conventionally "technical" dimensions of technical lands, these images failed to capture the embodied agents central to their operation and to acknowledge that those bodies were themselves integral parts of the technical apparatus.

Yet sound gives voice and agency to these laboring subjects. Shane White and Graham White, in their canonical *The Sounds of Slavery: Discovering African American History through Songs, Sermons, and Speech* (2005), examine the bells and horns that commenced the workday, the crack of the master's whip, the songs of the field, the baying of hounds on the heels of a runaway—as well as the more reparative sounds audible *outside* of work, like the din of the Black marketplace, the celebratory clamor of the festival, and the performative dimensions of Black sermons.[7] Coded sounds, embedded in sermons and songs, could also serve as means of resistance.

Smell also exhibits and shapes the spatial logics and politics undergirding the plantation. In *The Smell of Slavery*, historian Andrew Kettler (2020) demonstrates how foul odor was associated with the racialized Other and racialized spaces—the slave ship and quarters, for example—and how that conditioned disgust justified the commodification and dominance of African bodies. Those prejudices also impacted the way plantation space was designed and inhabited. According to Kettler, the French ethnographer, architect, and slaveowner Monsieur Antoine-Simon La Page du Pratz warned plantation owners that enslaved people "ought not to be placed so near your habitation as to be offensive."[8] The slave camp should have a "bathing place formed by thick planks" and should be sited to the north or northeast of the plantation home, "as the winds that blow from these quarters are not so warm as the others," and are thus less likely to carry a foul odor from the camp.[9] Yet smell, like sound, could also be deployed as a tool or technique of resistance: the cooking of traditional foods could deter white masters from interfering in enslaved people's affairs, and decoy scents could be used to confuse a bloodhound in pursuit of a runaway.

The plantation's system of aesthetic governance laid the groundwork for future deodorized spaces of capitalist labor: "A stinking African, formed through hard labor and racist discourse, instituted capitalism by helping to create a later pecuniary system which truly did not smell, a system of numbers in space"—the kinds of actuarial, logistical, and "smart" landscapes we see everywhere today, and which we explored in my "Data Artifacts, Infrastructures, and Landscapes" class at The New School in 2020.[10] Literary scholar Hsuan L. Hsu explains how colonial practices of olfactory governance, many of which are still used today—valuing or suppressing particular smells, forcibly deodorizing foreign and abject bodies, distributing smells unevenly across spaces and populations, and subjecting particular bodies to noisome smells—can produce both deodorized spaces that

[6] John E. Crowley, "Sugar Machines: Picturing Industrialized Slavery," *The American Historical Review* 121, no. 2 (2016), https://doi.org/10.1093/ahr/121.2.403.

[7] Shane White and Graham White, *The Sounds of Slavery: Discovering African American History through Songs, Sermons, and Speech* (Boston, MA: Beacon Press, 2005).

[8] Andrew Kettler, *The Smell of Slavery: Olfactory Racism and the Atlantic World* (Cambridge: Cambridge University Press, 2020, Cambridge Core e-book), 90.

[9] Kettler, *The Smell of Slavery*, 91.

[10] Kettler, *The Smell of Slavery*, 22; Shannon Mattern, "Data Artifacts, Infrastructures, and Landscapes," Graduate Seminar, The New School (Spring 2020), https://datainfra.wordsinspace.net/spring2020/.

fig 1   Union Stockyards, Chicago, 1947.
John Vachon, public domain

"truly [do] not smell," as well as noxious atmospheres: two spatial conditions that, as we've observed and will continue to observe, often exist in tandem.[11]

Just two years after enslaved people were ostensibly liberated from the plantation, its spatial and sensory regime was reborn at the Union Stock Yard & Transit Co. in Chicago, in 1865. Here, Kettler's "numbers in space" are actualized. The stockyards, art historian Jason Weems writes, "materialized new conditions for the conceptualization of living bodies," both animal and human, "first rescaling them from the level of individual beings to that of the limitless multitude—whose primary markers were efficient mobility and extractable materiality—and then reconstituting them in the new industrial forms of commodity and capital."[12] The physical space embodied the logics of the accounting ledger.

fig 1

The sheer scale and sublime efficiency of the operation drew tourists, especially those who were in town for the 1893 Columbian Exhibition, and inspired the creation of various guidebooks and illustrated histories. The visualization techniques deployed in these venues were like those Crowley described with regard to the plantation, although here, in the stockyards, the "machinery" had grown to comprise the entire technical landscape: everything, animate and inanimate, within the frame was a cog in the machine. Typically, we'd see a bird's-eye photograph encompassing the entire spatial apparatus, ground-level photographs that aimed to cultivate a sort of "embodied" spectatorship, and a diagram depicting animals as assemblages of saleable meat parts: the body itself as a technical landscape. But Weems argues that "the vast and labyrinthine physical expanse of The Yards and its equally extensive and intricate system of operation" overwhelmed the viewer. Even The Yard workers depicted in the images were overwhelmed and diminished in comparison to the "towering steel apparatus."[13]

Tourists experienced "shock and revulsion," and guidebook readers experienced "psychological incongruities" upon confronting the "visual juxtaposition of piled, lifeless bovine bodies with the abstract, rationalizing diagrams of those same bodies viewed as commodities."[14] How to reconcile pain, sentience, and mortality with the stockyards' rationalization, depersonalization, and abstraction? Perhaps they're ethically and affectively irreconcilable. Guidebook readers and tourists simply couldn't comprehend "mortality at such a staggering scale."[15] Weems writes:

> The program that emerged for visualizing The Yards marked an attempt to simultaneously comprehend, celebrate, and disarm the massive-scale slaughtering system, and to rationalize its diminishment of living bodies (and beings) as inviolable wholes. The failure of the imagery to do so embodied, in drained blood and rendered flesh, the incommensurabilities of scale that existed between living bodies and industrial systems.[16]

Those "incommensurabilities" weren't merely of the scalar variety; they were sensory, too. Images of The Yards failed to convey the space's heat,

[11] Hsuan L. Hsu, *The Smell of Risk: Environmental Disparities and Olfactory Aesthetics* (New York, NY: New York University Press, 2020), 153.

[12] Jason Weems, "Scale, a Slaughterhouse View: Industry, Corporeality, and Being in Turn-of-the-Century Chicago," in *Scale*, ed. Jennifer L. Roberts (Chicago, IL: Terra Foundation for American Art, 2016), 111.

[13] Weems, "Scale," 122.

[14] Weems, "Scale," 129–30.

[15] Weems, "Scale," 118.

[16] Weems, "Scale," 111.

[17] Weems, "Scale," 115.

humidity, and stench. "The stockyards pushed the limits of the mind, soul, and, perhaps most strikingly, senses," Weems argues; visitors "described the pungency of excrement and offal, the piercing cries of stuck hogs and the hiss of knives passing through flesh, the clammy heat of the killing floors and the chill of the refrigerator rooms, and the slipperiness of blood under their feet."[17] Those visitors and guidebook readers sought to "see the yards," but their macro-scale visual order and assembly-line logistics simply couldn't contain the *other* sensory input that wafted through or pierced the air and bled across the floors, inciting repulsion, shock, and trauma.

Political scientist Timothy Pachirat, through his ethnographic work in a contemporary slaughterhouse, finds that the spatial partitioning of the plant into functional areas (each of which represents a different ontology of the animal), and into "dirty" and "clean" zones (distinguished by whether the animal on the line still has its hide), represents a modern, technical means of instantiating a deeply rooted social tendency. The history of civilization, he argues, echoing Norbert Elias and Alain Corbin, is "a process of quarantine and concealment, showing how a concern for classifying, confining, and segregating by smell" in historical societies later "came to be interpreted primarily as a reordering of the visual economy."[18] The visual order represents an attempt to tame, to deodorize, to dampen the more unruly senses—but they tend to resist containment, both within the plant and in the broader environment.

[18] Timothy Pachirat, *Every Twelve Seconds: Industrialized Slaughter and the Politics of Sight* (New Haven, CT: Yale University Press, 2013), 279–80.

Pachirat describes the plant's internal sound- and smell-scapes. On the kill floor, one hears the rhythmic "pffft, pffft, pffft" of "the knocker's" pneumatic bolt gun, used to stun the animal. This sound indexes the transformation of cow or pig into beef or pork. In the cooler, "the day is an interminable aural barrage, deep and throbbing. The cooling system is the constant background noise for everything that happens. The long, sharp cling, cling, cling of the half-carcasses straining with the force of gravity on their pulley wheels punctuates the dull background roar of the fans." On the kill floor, the smell "varies from place to place, but it is always organic, a combination of feces, urine, vomit, brain matter, and blood in various stages, from fresh to congealed."[19] In the cooler, smells, "dulled by the cooler ... are almost nonexistent."[20]

[19] Pachirat, *Every Twelve Seconds*, 40.
[20] Pachirat, *Every Twelve Seconds*, 39.

But outside, especially in the summer heat, the smells of death permeate the surrounding area. As Pachirat exits the interstate, heading toward the slaughterhouse's "olfactory kingdom," he encounters a roadside sign: "To Report Manure Spills or Odor, Call 444-4919." He continues:

[21] Pachirat, *Every Twelve Seconds*, 3.

An empty assertion of bureaucratic power over the unruliness of smell, it is one among numerous symptoms of the ongoing conflict between the messiness of mass killing and a society's—our society's—demand for a cheap, steady supply of physically and morally sterile meat fabricated under socially invisible conditions. Shit and smell: anomalous dangers to be reported to the authorities in an era in which meat comes into our homes antiseptically packaged in cellophane wrappings.[21]

These technical lands allow for the delivery of deodorized meat through the displacement of undesirable smells. Onsite odors can be "managed" by treating animal waste, filtrating smelly gases, or designing complex ventilation and oxidation systems. Following in the footsteps of La Page du Pratz, plant owners often consider atmospheric conditions, wind direction, and the proximity of commercial and residential development when choosing locations for their facilities.[22] Recognizing that the animal body itself, especially when subjected to the violent processes by which it is rendered into "meat," is bound to emit odors, the most packers can do is trap the foul odors in sealed zones, where only a largely immigrant workforce and terrified animals will have to smell them. The sensory segregation of the plantation persists.

The Foundry, the Refinery, the Chemical Plant

The local sensory-environmental politics around factory farms and meat-packing plants resemble those in extraction zones. Kettler, who earlier explained how olfactory politics justified the reduction of enslaved people's bodies to tools and commodities, has also examined how particular smells' ideological associations evolve over time, in relation to their cultural and political-economic contexts.[23] Prior to the Industrial Revolution, the presence of sulfuric smells was typically regarded as a sign of evil. After all, hell is made of fire and brimstone, which is simply an archaic name for sulfur. When coal became central to industrialization and its economic spoils, sulfur was newly associated with progress and profit.

fig 2

Through their 2012–16 fieldwork in the technical lands of the Peace River oil sands in Alberta, Canada, anthropologist Tristan Lee-Jones observed how such olfactory politics continued to play out both synchronously and locally. In Peace River, the smell of oil production, a mixture of "rotten eggs and freshly poured concrete," was differently perceptible and meaningful to different subjects.[24] Some, especially those regularly exposed to chemical vapors in their homes, described headaches, frequent bouts of nausea, watery eyes, and itchy skin, while others—including many oil workers and energy regulators—denied that the odors exist. "You can't smell it after you work with it for years," one of Lee-Jones's interlocutors proposed, imagining that her anosmatic neighbors have simply been desensitized to the stench.[25] Meanwhile, a local Métis elder worried that wildlife would be driven away by the odor and noise.[26] On a local Facebook forum discussion, some folks argued that:

> the smells were the product of nervous people's overactive imaginations. If emissions did exist, said others, surely industry could be trusted to ensure that there were no negative health impacts. Some wrote that industry had provided such tremendous economic benefits to the region that even to speak about potential contaminations could irrevocably damage the town's good relationship with industry.[27]

[22] Agency for Toxic Substances and Disease Registry, "Odor Control" (n.d.), accessed July 25, 2021, https://www.atsdr.cdc.gov/odors/odor_control.html; "Meat Processing Odor Control," Anguil, accessed July 25, 2021, https://anguil.com/case_studies/meat-processing-odor-control/.

[23] Andrew Kettler, "Queer Mineralogy and the Depths of Hell: Sulfuric Skills, Early Modern England, and the North American Frontier," *Journal of the Canadian Historical Association* 30, no. 1 (2019): 115–43.

[24] Tristan Lee-Jones, "Living and Dying Through Oil's Promise: The Invisibility of Contamination and Power in Alberta's Peace River Country," *Extracting Home in the Oil Sands: Settler Colonialism and Environmental Change in Subarctic Canada*, eds., Clinton N. Westman, Tara L. Joly, and Lena Gross, (London: Routledge, 2020), 73.

[25] Lee-Jones, "Living and Dying," 72; see also Warren Cariou, "Tarhands: A Messy Manifesto," *Imaginations* 3, no. 2 (2012), http://imaginations.glendon.yorku.ca/?p=3646.

[26] Lee-Jones, "Living and Dying," 73.

[27] Lee-Jones, "Living and Dying," 72.

fig 2   An oil field, between 1900 and 1920.
Detroit Publishing Co., Library of Congress

They had to practice rhetorical deodorization for the purposes of political-economic self-preservation.

In Sarnia, Ontario, oil refineries and foundries emerged in the mid-nineteenth century and were later joined by other petroleum-related production facilities and chemical plants. Before the area's transformation into "Chemical Valley," its Aamjiwnaang First Nation residents had experienced and understood their environment largely through smell—through plants and soils and foods and fire pits. "Each fragrance, in its time and season, characterized particular parts of the reserve and connected those places with specific events and practices important to community life," writes anthropologist Deborah Davis Jackson.[28] Initially, she acknowledges, the smells of industry would have carried positive connotations; as both Kettler and Lee-Jones describe, to many folks, emissions are olfactory indices of money. But as the community became more aware of the harmful environmental and health effects of industrial pollutants, local industrial smells became associated with disease and death.

Oil and gas development—especially hydraulic fracturing—also generates noise that can be deleterious to public health. The sounds of drills, pumps, compressors, flares, vents, and truck traffic can cause stress, disturb sleep, elevate blood pressure, and increase one's risk of heart disease. Wildlife, particularly songbirds, are affected, too. Strategies for mitigation are like those for odor: siting facilities to take advantage of natural noise barriers, like hills and trees; building perimeter sound walls; maintaining equipment to ensure that it's operating as efficiently and quietly as possible; using electric motors on that machinery; and limiting vehicle traffic.[29]

While the nineteenth-century arrival of these capitalist and settler-colonial extractive forces effected displacement by pushing human and more-than-human habitants from the land, Jackson explains that the ongoing transformation of the Aamjiwnaang smellscape (and, we can imagine, soundscape) has effected for its First Nations inhabitants continual "dysplacement," or a feeling of alienation and disorientation while still present in one's ancestral homeland.[30] One can be physically present yet sensorially and psychically removed. The smells of these extractive technical lands perform slow violences on those who live downwind, and their grand spatial order—rendered horrifically spectacular by photographers like Burtynsky and Mosse—belies the sensory injustices they exact on local bodies. As interdisciplinary scholar Macarena Gómez-Barris argues in *The Extractive Zone*, "the extractive view" manifested in such images, which deploy "the gaze of *terra nullius*, represent[s] Indigenous peoples as non-existent."[31]

Design And Sensory Attunement

Gómez-Barris proposes that early colonial modes of visualization, like the map, and newer visual technologies—including satellite images, LIDAR point clouds, and interactive maps—continue to "facilitate capitalist expansion, especially upon resource-rich Indigenous territories."[32] The state and the corporation map in order "to accumulate, to convert, and

[28] Deborah Davis Jackson, "Scents of Place: The Dysplacement of a First Nations Community in Canada," *American Anthropologist* 113, no. 4 (December 2011): 608.

[29] Ann Brody Guy, "Noise Pollution from Oil and Gas Development May Harm Human Health," *WVU Today*, December 22, 2016, https://wvutoday.wvu.edu/stories/2016/12/22/noise-pollution-from-oil-and-gas-development-may-harm-human-health; Earthworks, "Oil and Gas Noise," Earthworks (n.d.), https://www.earthworks.org/issues/oil_and_gas_noise/; Jake Hays, Michel McCawley, and Seth B.C. Shonkoff, "Public Health Implications of Environmental Noise Associated with Unconventional Oil and Gas Development," *Science of the Total Environment* 580 (2017): 448–56.

[30] Davis Jackson, "Scents of Place," 616.

[31] Macarena Gómez-Barris, *The Extractive Zone: Social Ecologies and Decolonial Perspectives* (Durham, NC: Duke University Press, 2017), 6.

[32] Gómez-Barris, *The Extractive Zone*.

33 Gómez-Barris, *The Extractive Zone*, 8; see also Candace Fujikane, *Mapping Abundance for a Planetary Future: Kanaka Maoli and Critical Settler Cartographies in Hawai'i* (Durham, NC: Duke University Press, 2021).

34 Gómez-Barris, *The Extractive Zone*, xv.

35 Gómez-Barris, *The Extractive Zone*, xx.

36 Gómez-Barris, *The Extractive Zone*, 15.

37 Shannon Mattern, "Ear to the Wire: Listening to Historic Urban Infrastructures," *Amodern* 2 (2013): https://amodern.net/article/ear-to-the-wire/; Shannon Mattern, "Sonic Archaeology," in *The Routledge Companion to Sound Studies*, Michael Bull (New York, NY: Routledge, 2018), 222–30; Shannon Mattern, "The Pulse of Global Passage: Listening to Logistics," in *Assembly Codes: The Logistics of Media*, eds., Matthew Hockenberry, Nicole Starosielski, and Susan Zieger (Durham, NC: Duke University Press, 2021), 75–92.

38 Hsu, *The Smell of Risk*, 20.

39 Daniel Fernández Pascual and Alon Schwabe, "Oranges Are Orange, Salmon Are Salmon," *The Paris Review*, August 17, 2020, https://www.theparisreview.org/blog/2020/08/17/oranges-are-orange-salmon-are-salmon/.

40 Daniel Fernández Pascual and Alon Schwabe, "ADS3: Refuse Trespassing Our Bodies—The Right to Breathe," Royal College of Art, 2019–20, https://www.rca.ac.uk/study/schools/school-of-architecture/architecture/ads-themes-2019-20/ads3/.

expand the global economy"—in part by turning Indigenous terrains into technical lands.[33] Given the limitations of standard modes of visualization, Gómez-Barris wonders, what might we learn about these terrains, about their alternative ontologies and genealogies, about possible modes of resistance, by questioning "what lies beneath the visible world of the extractive zone"?[34] How might we "seek out less perceivable worlds, life forms, and the organization of relations within them"? What new forms of representation or documentation or projection might help us "see, hear, and intimate the land differently? What do we really know about the invisible, the inanimate, and the nonhuman forms that reside as the afterlives of the colonial encounter?"[35] Gómez-Barris describes various techniques for inverting the gaze, for "peering below, above, and through"; for revealing "a submerged, below-the-surface, blurry countervisuality"; for listening to environmental agents.[36]

I want to pick up on her final provocation to ask what we might learn about technical lands—and what they once were, and what more they can be—by looking past visualization altogether, and instead by engaging with other senses. I've written elsewhere about what we can learn about infrastructures and the technical geographies of logistics by listening to them, and about how sound artists often help us auscultate these spaces and systems. I won't echo that discussion here.[37] But how might we engage with technical lands through smell? Hsu proposes that "to think with smell is not only to redistribute the sensible, à la Ranciere, "but to develop a sensory alternative to the system of Western aesthetics and its tendency to downplay invisible, environmental slow violence by framing the atmosphere as an empty space between (ocularcentric) subject and object rather than apprehending it as a material, biopolitical medium."[38] In other words, smelling technical lands reminds us that the atmosphere is part of their technical apparatus, and that environmental destruction is often a consequence of its technique or a manifestation of errors in its operational logics. Odors "sniff out" the inefficiencies and dysfunctions of technical lands.

How might thinking through smell inform the design of technical lands? We've already discussed how designers, engineers, and developers must be attuned to smell as they consider the labor conditions in, and environmental impacts of, these technical spaces. But how might an olfactory sensibility cultivate a deeper appreciation of the logics and politics undergirding the "design" of nuclear waste facilities, oil fields, and fish farms? Consider the work of Daniel Fernández Pascual and Alon Schwabe, who together form Cooking Sections, a research-design practice that thinks through food and its sensory and political geographies. Most recently, their work asks how the technical lands of orchards and fish farms have transformed oranges and salmon: the fruit, the fish, and their namesake colors.[39] Their 2019–21 studio at the Royal College of Art focused on the breath, pollution, contamination, and "how the built environment is entangled in biochemical pathways."[40] They sought to "incorporate metabolic thinking into architectural discourse" and to prompt designers to ask how we can remake "the world we now inhale, absorb, lick, sweat, and digest?" We can also look—or perhaps sniff—toward the work of artist Beatrice Glow, whose olfactory installations engage with the colonial geographies of spice.[41]

Spice is perhaps a useful synesthetic metaphor for thinking about and designing technical lands, which are so often represented through flat, abstracted maps, aerial photos, and diagrams. Spices adds sensory depth and texture that can unfold over time. As temporal media, they are used to preserve and embalm. Through their cultural histories, spices blend local terroir and global systems. And they, too, often emerge from technical lands—from plantations and factory farms—yet they remind us that these spaces of abstracted logic and visual order are atmospheric and reliant on organic bodies and ecologies, who are themselves, in turn, transformed by the technical apparatus that order them.

[41] Beatrice Glow, Selected Works, accessed July 25, 2021, https://beatriceglow.org/exhibitions/.

Census
and
Sensing

Robert Gerard Pietrusko

In May 1971, the University of Michigan hosted a two-week International Workshop on Earth Resources Survey Systems, during which US ambassador to the United Nations, George H. W. Bush, delivered the welcoming address.[1] Speaking as a representative of the State Department, and still basking in the success of NASA's Apollo program, Ambassador Bush highlighted the US government's promise to "share with the world community both the adventures and the benefits of space research."[2] Indeed, he continued, it was imperative to recognize that "space technology is a global tool," with which the world's countries—regardless of their overall level of economic or technological development—could collectively address "economic and social problems in search of practical solutions."[3] Referring to recent concerns about the state of the global environment, Bush's remarks set the tone for the following two weeks where a series of paper presentations were marked by an equal emphasis on the looming environmental crisis; an optimistic technological response; and the necessity for all countries to collaborate on the solution.

The workshop anticipated the launch of NASA's Landsat civilian satellite fourteen months later. From an altitude of 570 miles, Landsat's multispectral scanner produced continuous images of Earth and provided updated coverage for anywhere on the planet every eighteen days, indifferent to political borders.[4] During the workshop, scientists described techniques of satellite-based remote sensing—of which Landsat was a recent, civilian example—and emphasized its ability to identify and aid in the technical management of mineral resources, agricultural lands, and urban systems.

Though the presenters frequently described the workshop as an opportunity to share technical expertise with the global community, it was also implicitly a public relations event for US foreign policy. Eight federal agencies sponsored the event, which was attended by representatives of thirty-nine countries and fifteen international organizations.[5] During the plenary sessions, speakers repeatedly celebrated the international diversity of the audience before reaffirming the problems of environmental pollution, mineral depletion, and population growth that the whole world seemingly faced. With this framing, the organizers attempted to persuade foreign countries that NASA's civilian satellite program was a benevolent and valuable source of information. They also hoped to convince countries with "developing" economies to employ Landsat data to manage and share their natural resources.

The workshop predate more charismatic conferences on global environmental issues. The UN's Conference on the Human Environment in 1972, followed by the conference on World Population two years later, were commonly understood as watershed moments for the 1970s environmental movement.[6] And just as these later conferences would do, the workshop demonstrated how the rhetoric of global stewardship could be exploited for geopolitical purposes, in this case with an exceedingly technical bent. As Felicity Scott, Megan Black, and others have described, politicians adopted the language of the environmental movement and spoke passionately about

[1] National Aeronautics and Space Administration, *Earth Resources Survey Systems: Proceedings of an International Workshop Held at the University of Michigan on May 3–14, 1971*, (Washington, DC: US Government Printing Office, 1972).

[2] George H. W. Bush, "Welcoming Address," *Proceedings of The International Workshop*.

[3] Bush, "Welcoming Address."

[4] Pamela Mack, *Viewing the Earth: The Social Construction of the Landsat Satellite System* (Cambridge, MA: MIT Press, 1990).

[5] Homer Newell, "Chairman's Introduction," *Proceedings of The International Workshop*.

[6] Maurice F. Strong, "One Year After Stockholm: An Ecological Approach to Management," *Foreign Affairs* 51, no.4 (July 1973): 690–707; see Felicity D. Scott, *Outlaw Territories: Environments of Insecurity/Architectures of Counterinsurgency* (New York, NY: Zone Books, 2016).

[7] Scott, *Outlaw Territories*; Megan Black, *The Global Interior: Mineral Frontiers and American Power* (Cambridge, MA: Harvard University Press, 2018); Libby Robin, Sverker Sörlin, and Paul Warde, *The Future of Nature: Documents of Global Change* (New Haven, CT: Yale University Press, 2013); Elodie Vieille Blanchard, "Modelling the Future: An Overview of the Limits to Growth Debate," *Centaurus* 52, no. 2 (May 2010): 91–116.

[8] Sara Holiday Nelson, "Beyond the Limits to Growth: Ecology and the Neoliberal Counterrevolution," *Antipode* 47, no. 2 (March 2015): 461–80.

[9] Alison Bashford, *Global Population: History, Geopolitics, and Life on Earth* (New York, NY: Columbia University Press, 2014), 357.

[10] The Earth Resources Program was responsible for launching the Landsat satellite. The EROS data center made information derived from Landsat available to geographers, geologists, and policymakers.

[11] Neil M Maher, *Apollo in the Age of Aquarius* (Cambridge, MA: Harvard University Press, 2017), 92–136.

[12] Jeremy Walker and Matthew Johnson, "On Mineral Sovereignty: Towards a Political Theory of Geological Power," *Energy Research & Social Science* 45 (November 2018): 56–66.

[13] Nicolas King, *George Bush: A Biography* (New York, NY: Dodd Mead, 1980).

[14] For an indication of longstanding relations between Bush and the intelligence community, see "1963 F.B.I. Memo Ties Bush to Intelligence Agency," *The New York Times*, July 11, 1988.

"spaceship Earth," "the fragile biosphere," and a pending catastrophe awaiting future generations *if* global citizens did not properly and *collectively* manage the planet's resources.[7] The emphasis on a single borderless world and the branding of resources as belonging to Earth, rather than any single country, were used by Western governments to justify mapping, and later exploiting, developing nations that were mineral-rich, while also tying their economic stability to supply chains of the dominant capitalist countries.[8] This line of reasoning had biopolitical ramifications as well. As historian Alison Bashford describes, "By claiming 'the planet' as a space of operation, 'the world' and its people could also be claimed fairly easily—too easily— with seeming political neutrality."[9] Alongside minerals and soils, people were therefore also prominently and quantitatively framed by Landsat's imagery.

Therefore, projects like NASA's Earth Resources Program and the US Geological Survey's EROS data center were discussed in ambivalent terms.[10] On the one hand, they were celebrated as technological solutions to human-induced environmental issues, both sincerely and cynically.[11] On the other hand, they were criticized for violating the "mineral sovereignty" of other countries and enforcing imperial relations—both old and new.[12]

Bush embodied both aspects of the workshop's agenda and was an appropriately symbolic figure to deliver the welcoming address. Serving as a representative to the UN, Bush demonstrated support for tackling environmental issues, planetary resource management, and global cooperation; he also understood firsthand that US economic and political dominance was based on the persistent exploitation of mineral reserves in foreign landscapes—having only recently sold his shares in a global petroleum corporation he founded two decades earlier.[13] He was also symbolic in a third way. At the time of the workshop, he was five years from assuming the directorship of the Central Intelligence Agency (CIA) under President Ford.[14] When he spoke optimistically of Landsat's ability to scan foreign terrain to manage planetary resources, he also implicitly described a method for scanning urban areas and estimating foreign populations—a functionality that was not Landsat's primary goal but a secondary benefit that was not lost on the intelligence community that he would soon oversee.

Consequently, the environmentalist language in Bush's address obscured both Landsat's potential use for US mineral prospecting, as well as its possible use for gathering intelligence. On the one hand, Landsat's mere presence rendered the whole planet as a massive technical land and offered up Earth's surface as a domain to be rationally surveyed, managed, and extracted. But on the other hand, Landsat also made the planet technical in a deeper sense. Anything that could be quantitatively interpreted in its images was also treated as a signal that indicated unobservable processes or as an input for complex computational models of geopolitical dynamics.

Therefore, the International Workshop highlighted important technical and political dualities within the Landsat program. Technically, the presentations demonstrated how the scale and resolution of Landsat images thwarted direct interpretation and instead required an inferential mentality—anything seen could be and often was a proxy for something else.[15] Politically, the workshop's call for global environmental solidarity masked latent geopolitical ambitions for which the satellite was optimized to fulfill despite, or perhaps because of, its civilian status.[16] Alongside the main discussion of natural resources at the International Workshop, several papers were devoted to problems of urban development and growth.[17] These were presented by researchers from the US Geological Survey's Geographic Applications Program (GAP). Relative to the EROS data center, the GAP played a secondary and short-lived role in NASA/USGS's remote sensing program.[18] Its projects, however, demonstrated how geopolitical concerns, when mediated through remote sensing technology, influenced the creation of geographic categories.[19]

As an example, this chapter will explore Landsat's technical and political dualities and how these affected the representation of cities within land-use and land cover datasets created by the GAP during the 1970s. Though established to publicly demonstrate Landsat's applicability to urban problems in the US, the GAP also privately studied Landsat's ability to collect intelligence over foreign territories. Using urban photographic patterns as proxies for population and US cities as proxies for international ones, the program reflected US anxieties about population growth and political instability in developing countries. Through this analysis method, cities were translated into spatially bounded containers of population counts that conformed better with computational models used by CIA analysts than with more robust theories of urban processes. At a time when the environmental movement imagined the material and social aspects of cities within a complex ecological totality, the USGS's resultant classification scheme unexpectedly offered "urban" as a monolithic, undifferentiated polygon whose size was treated as more important than its connectivity or internal organization.[20] The legacy of the program's original intentions remains embedded in contemporary land cover datasets and subtly naturalizes views of the city as a spatially bounded, quantitative surrogate for urban populations.[21]

Civilian Reconnaissance

Throughout the 1960s, there were multiple collaborations between the US Geological Survey (USGS) and the CIA, where projects that tested novel forms of reconnaissance also had potential usefulness for domestic applications.[22] In fact, the interaction between intelligence agencies, the USGS, and other civilian departments was so active that by the end of the 1960s, a committee was initiated within the CIA to manage the frequent exchanges of information.[23] It is in this general environment that the Geographic Applications Program (GAP) was established and funded by NASA in 1966. Program director Arch C. Gerlach clearly stated his ambition to continue these collaborations. While planning the program, "[Gerlach] had contacted key individuals in the Central Intelligence Agency and Defense Intelligence Agency and had received tentative assurance that one or more experts

[15] For a foundation of this sensibility within remote sensing, see Robert Gerard Pietrusko, "Ground Cover," *LA+ Journal of Landscape Architecture* 12 (Fall 2020): 12–19.

[16] Black, *The Global Interior*, 183–214.

[17] See papers by Robert H. Alexander, James R. Wray, Frank E. Horton, and James R. Anderson published in *The Proceedings of the International Workshop*.

[18] Mary E. Graziani, *Geographic Research in the US Geological Survey* (Reston, VA: US Department of the Interior, Geological Survey, 1982).

[19] The relationship between geopolitical concerns, cartography, and geographic categories from an earlier moment in the Cold War are explored in Mathew Farish, *The Contours of America's Cold War* (Minneapolis, MN: University of Minnesota Press, 2010).

[20] On the relationship between urbanism and ecology as understood in the early 1970s, see Howard T. Odum, *Environment, Power, & Society* (New York, NY: John Wiley & Sons, 1971).

[21] Viewing the city as merely the spatial concentration of population has had broad social, cultural, and political ramifications. For an incisive description, see Neil Brenner and Christian Schmid, "The Urban Age in Question," *Implosions / Explosions: Towards a Study of Planetary Urbanization*, ed. Neil Brenner (Berlin: Jovis, 2015), 310–37.

[22] For instance, a 1963 study that used infrared cameras to detect underground volcanic heat sources in Hawai'i was designed in collaboration with photo-intelligence officers who hoped that the technology would allow them to detect nuclear weapons hidden in Cuba. See Dino Brugioni, "The Serendipity Effect," *Studies in Intelligence* 14, no. 1 (Spring 1970): 60.

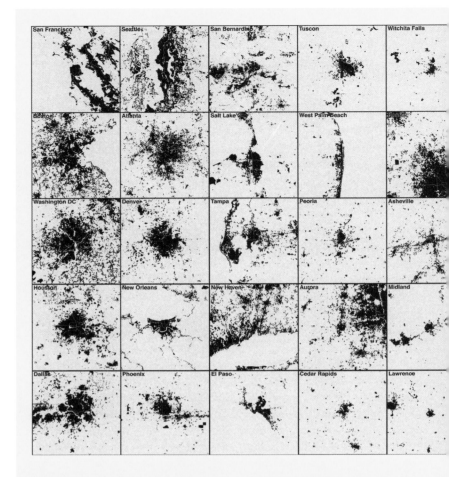

fig 1   Twenty-Five Census Cities test sites.
Robert Gerard Pietrusko

working on classified projects will assist in planning geographic research projects."[24] Shortly after the program's official launch, the CIA's deputy director of basic and geographic intelligence was appointed to the GAP's advisory committee.[25]

Like the dualities in the more extensive Landsat program, the GAP created remote sensing techniques used for gathering intelligence across the globe that *might be useful for civilian applications*. They hoped to convince US academics, urban planners, and policymakers that Landsat data was helpful in the management of urban areas.[26] They reasoned that a demonstration of domestic uses for remote sensing at home—and their adoption by US municipalities—might reduce foreign apprehension about satellites invading their airspace and photographing their cities.[27] A 1965 conference on the use of spacecraft in geographic research created the GAP blueprint and acknowledged its international implications. "The fact that many of the sensors were developed and perfected for purposes of military reconnaissance," the organizers wrote, "is a psychological disadvantage."[28] After a series of collaborative missteps in Vietnam with the Department of Defense, NASA was also struggling to establish Landsat's civilian relevance and assure foreign nations that the program was not, in fact, a covert military operation.[29] Therefore, when Robert Alexander, head of GAP research, described the program's ambition "to improve the habitability of this planet by monitoring surface environmental conditions and changes," he aligned the GAP with NASA's PR campaign for the Earth Resources program more generally.[30]

Through the 1970s, GAP researchers created several pilot projects to demonstrate Landsat's capabilities. Among these was the Land Use and Land Cover (LULC) Classification System for Use with Remote Sensors, a taxonomy for translating the tones and textures of Landsat images into discrete land-use classes.[31] In accordance with the program's focus on natural resources and urban analysis, its designers argued that the lack of land-use information in cities resulted in chaotic urban growth; new development, when not properly planned, might cover subsurface mineral deposits or negatively impact fertile agricultural soils.[32]

The system was conceived ahead of Landsat's launch in 1971. It contained nine general land-use categories that were updated and republished after five years of study by the GAP.[33] The categories were intended to be deployed over the entire earth, disciplining its surface variation into a single technical system of comparable polygons, whose relative areas could be measured, tabulated, aggregated, and analyzed for a variety of managerial purposes. GAP researchers assessed the efficacy of the categories during several pilot projects, and many alterations were proposed in the process. Notably, the categories were not evaluated for their representational correspondence to land uses as they might appear on the ground.[34] Instead, researchers evaluated how easily the categories could be deciphered within satellite images or how smoothly they articulated specific practices of urban and territorial analysis. Consequently, the *meaning* of the categories was determined by

[23] "Minutes of the ARGO steering committee meeting of 10 June 1968," General CIA Records Collection, doc., CIA-RDP80T01137A 000200060034-6, CIA FOIA Reading Room, accessed June 1, 2021, https://www.cia.gov/readingroom/document/cia-rdp80t01137a 000200060034-6.

[24] "Minutes of the forty-first meeting of the Committee, Dec 16–17, 1965," Archives of the National Academy of Sciences, Division of the National Research Council (DNRC), Earth Sciences, Committee on Geography Advisory to the Office of Naval Research.

[25] Deputy Director, Basic and Geographic Intelligence, "Memo: Participation on a National Academy Advisory Committee, 13 September 1967," General CIA Records Collection, doc., CIA-RDP79-01155A000300020115-8, CIA FOIA Reading Room, accessed June 1, 2021, https://www.cia.gov/readingroom/document/cia-RDP79-01155A000300020115-8.

[26] NAS-NRC Committee of Geography, Advisory to the ONR, *Spacecraft in Geographic Research* (Washington, DC: National Academy of Sciences and National Research Council, 1966); NAS-NRC, *Useful Applications of Earth-Oriented Satellites*. (Washington, DC: National Academy of Sciences and National Research Council, 1969).

[27] For an in-depth treatment of the transfer of aerial sensing technology from military to civilian applications, see Jennifer S. Light, *From Warfare to Welfare: Defense Intellectuals and Urban Problems in Cold War America* (Baltimore, MD: Johns Hopkins University Press, 2005).

[28] NAS-NRC Committee of Geography, *Spacecraft*, 20.

[29] Neil M. Maher, *Apollo in the Age of Aquarius* (Cambridge, MA: Harvard University Press, 2017), 54–91.

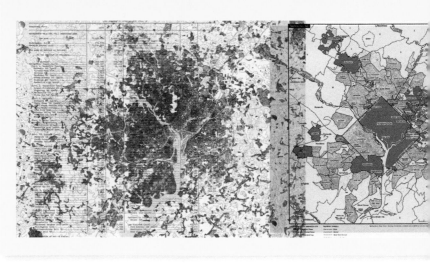

fig 2   Washington, DC test site, remotely
sensed by NASA's ERTS-1 satellite. Robert Gerard
Pietrusko

fig 3   Washington, DC test site, urba
as determined by remotely sensed image
official municipal boundaries, respectively
Gerard Pietrusko

technical workflows within the pilot projects used to assess them. As I will show in the following section, studies like the 1970 Census Cities Project reduced the category "urban" to a quantitative measurement of changing population density.

fig 1

Urban Change Detection

The Census Cities Project (also called the Census Cities Experiment in Urban Change Detection)[35] was directed by geographers Robert Alexander and James Wray. Their goal was a "combined use of sensors and census" through which changes in land use and population density could be measured over time.[36] Tracking these changes, they argued, would provide rapid information to urban planners about the status of their city's economic development and populace.[37] In 1970, the GAP commissioned NASA airplanes to gather high-altitude imagery over twenty-six US cities, or "test sites." Using GAP's LULC scheme, the team classified the images into land-use categories and drafted the boundaries onto mylar maps for easy measurement and analysis. As Robert Alexander described, the map was only part of the final product; more important was what the land-use categories indicated—and what an analyst could infer *through* them. The patterns within the images and the categories assigned to them were proxies for other urban information that was of the genuine interest of the researchers.[38]

fig 2

fig 3

Interpreters analyzed the patterns of urban form but not in their own right; instead, what interested them was what these patterns indicated— urban population density. The GAP and NASA timed the photo missions to be contemporaneous with the 1970 decennial census. The simultaneous collection of aerial imagery and statistical data allowed researchers to make visual-numeric correlations between land-use patterns in the photographs and demographic enumerations on the ground. Once the land uses had been mapped, they were associated with the underlying census information—most notably, the population counts. The result was a baseline from which future aerial images could be visually interpreted and quantitatively described. They developed this approach anticipating Landsat's frequent overflight, which captured images of the cities every eighteen days. They reasoned that the repetitive coverage would allow them to detect small changes in photographic patterns over time. Since these photo patterns were associated with land uses, researchers could measure the area of an observed change and calculate a new population estimate. Up-to-date information would then flow into urban management practices that were seemingly made more efficient as a result.

Despite the project's stated goals, it was indifferent to the specific conditions of US urbanization in the 1970s. For example, New York, Chicago, and Los Angeles were omitted from the study despite their large extents, dynamic land uses, and complex planning issues.[39] The project also had an a priori assumption of remoteness; it was seemingly most useful for

[30] Robert H. Alexander, "Geography Program Review and Integration," *Second Annual Earth Resources Aircraft Program Status Review, NASA Manned Spacecraft Center, Houston, TX, September 16–18 1969, National Aeronautics and Space Administration* (Washington, DC: US Government Printing Office, 1969), 322–23.

[31] James R. Anderson, E. E. Hardy, J. T. Roach, and R. E. Witmer, *A Land Use and Land Cover Classification System for Use with Remote Sensor Data* (Reston, VA: US Geological Survey, 1976).

[32] Anderson et al., *Land Use and Land Cover*, 1–2.

[33] It also contained thirty-six subcategories, but these were intended for images gathered at roughly 40,000 feet, far below Landsat's altitude; Anderson et al., *Land Use and Land Cover*, 2.

[34] Anderson et al., *Land Use and Land Cover*, 5; see Robert Gerard Pietrusko, "The Surface of Data," *LA+ Journal of Landscape Architecture* 4 (Spring 2016): 78–85.

[35] James R. Wray, "A Preliminary Appraisal Of ERTS-1 Imagery for The Comparative Study of Metropolitan Regions," *Earth Resources Technology Satellite-1 Symposium Proceedings, Goddard Space Flight Center, Greenbelt, MD, September 29, 1972* (Washington, DC: US Government Printing Office), 95–99.

[36] James R. Wray, "Census Cities Project and the Atlas of Urban Regional Change," *Proceedings of The International Workshop vol. 2*, 343.

[37] Wray, "Census Cities Project."

[38] Robert H. Alexander, *Central Atlantic Region Ecological Test Site, Final Report Vol. 1* (Reston, VA: US Geological Survey, 1979), 251.

[39] US Census Bureau, *1970 Census—Population and Land Area of Urbanized Areas for the United States, PC(S1)-108* (Washington, DC: US Census Bureau, 1979).

40 For instance, the GAP's first publication on land-use classification presented a scheme stating that the only source of information would be remotely sensed imagery. James R. Anderson, "Land-Use Classification Schemes," *Photogrammetric Engineering* 37 (April 1971): 379–87.

41 Harry F. Lins Jr. and James R. Wray, *Urban and Regional Land Use Analysis: Carets and Census Cities Experiment Package: Monthly Progress Report* (April 20, 1974).

42 At the 1971 International Workshop, for instance, Wray presented a speculative proof-of-concept that mapped changes at a detailed urban scale. See Wray, "Census Cities Project and the Atlas of Urban Regional Change."

43 Lins and Wray, *Urban and Regional Land Use Analysis*, 3.

44 Alexander, *Central Atlantic Region Ecological Test Site*, 291.

45 Brian J. L. Berry and Donald C. Dahmann, "Population Redistribution in the United States in the 1970s," *Population and Development Review* 3, no. 4 (December 1977): 443–71; US Census Bureau, *1980 Census of Population—United States Summary, PC80-1-A1* (Washington, DC: US Department of Commerce, Bureau of the Census, 1984).

46 Office of Research and Development (ORD), Central Intelligence Agency, *Some Likely Key Intelligence Questions for the 1980s* (July 1974); see Nick Cullather, *The Hungry World: America's Cold War Battle against Poverty in Asia* (Cambridge, MA: Harvard University Press, 2010).

47 In 1970 alone, there were nearly eighty articles about population concerns in the popular American press, followed by a nearly equal number in 1974. For instance, the September 1974 issue of *Scientific American* was devoted solely to population studies and concerns, see "The Human Population" *Scientific American* 231, no. 3 (September 1974); John R.

physically inaccessible cities.[40] Researchers did not consider implementations of the project where land-use categories were confirmed on the ground or connected to specific planning processes.

Two years after Landsat's launch, Alexander and Wray's results confirmed these assumptions and the project's poor fit for US cities. Using Landsat's high-altitude imagery, they could not identify "intra-urban land uses" or detect their changes.[41] From the standpoint of an urban management strategy, these identifications were a necessary precondition, and the project was seemingly a failure.[42] However, these findings were not presented as detrimental within the project report. Instead, they implied a different use of the technology. Though changes internal to a city could not be detected, Wray wrote, the pattern of urban *growth* could be, and this allowed them to successfully "define urban expansion, project future population densities, and assess the environmental impact resulting from gradual and catastrophic changes."[43] As a result, no land-use changes were measured, only the size of a generalized urban condition, and most notably, those that appeared to be growing. But within a US context, this too was an unnecessary use of the technology. Once describing the importance of the project, Alexander cautioned that "there is a finite limit to the number of people who can be accommodated in any given region without causing an irreversible change in either the environmental or the supporting social systems."[44] Despite the alarming language, it was a poor description of US cities in the 1970s when metropolitan areas rapidly lost people to the suburbs. Even Washington, DC—the main site of their study—shrank by 118,117 people between 1970 and 1980.[45] While seeming evidence of a poor understanding of US cities, the misalignments between the GAP's stated goals and the project's domestic usefulness communicates something else entirely: the Census Cities project was intended to be used in locations other than the census cities themselves. Therefore, it was not *urbanization*—with all its complexity and specificity—that the Census Cities Urban Change Detection Project monitored, it was "urban" as a nominal label that quantitatively indicated a density of bodies. This result pointed away from domestic uses of the technique and instead towards foreign countries now accessible through Landsat imagery, where growing populations were seen as potential risks for US national security.

Modeling the Population Bomb

In an era of Cold War détente, intelligence analysts believed that the movement of troops, missiles, and other weapons were not the only factors to assess for national security; intelligence on the stability of developing countries was becoming equally important.[46] Alongside various UN committees and the participants of the global environmental movement, the US intelligence community was also influenced by warnings about world population growth appearing in academic circles and the popular press during the 1960s and 1970s.[47] For political and economic analysts within the CIA, there was a belief that population growth and depleted resources might lead to the toppling of developing democracies. Especially worrisome was the possibility that political instability could occur in countries with mineral resources that were important for US industries. And these concerns were reflected in internal intelligence planning documents; for example, a 1959 CIA report on the relationship between authoritarianism and underdevelopment cited the findings of sociologist Kingsley Davis on the exacerbating effects of population growth:[48] "Caught in the predicament of having an ever-larger share of the world's people and an ever-smaller share of the world's resources, they will be driven to adopt revolutionary policies ... obvious possibilities (include) ... the transformation of the economy by totalitarian methods."[49]

Davis, who was credited with coining the term "population explosion" with all its ballistic connotations, was the leading public intellectual during the 1950s and 1960s, connecting neo-Malthusian views of third-world population dynamics with Cold War geopolitical tensions.[50] Intelligence analysts were receptive to this general narrative. With the later publication of books like Paul Ehrlich's *Population Bomb* and *The Limits to Growth* by Donella Meadows, concerns about population continued through the 1970s.[51] For example, population growth—and the associated strain from uneven access to food—were listed as the most pressing problems facing global stability according to an internal CIA forecast on what issues were expected to affect geopolitics in the 1980s.[52]

In response, the intelligence community began deploying new quantitative tools for modeling future trends attempting to make sense of this increasingly complicated global picture. In 1974 a classified report titled "A Survey of the Community's Use of New Analytical Methods" described the expansion of advanced techniques to all branches of the CIA. Though "sophisticated analytical methods" had long been used to study military forces and weapons, they were now applied to "political, economic and cartographic research."[53] In particular, economic analysts began working with dynamic systems models that researchers Danella and Dennis Meadows had used to predict the population explosion and ultimate collapse of world resources in *The Limits to Growth*. Their primary simulation tool, "The World Model," visualized a system of connected differential equations that represented causal interactions among the world's ecology, economy, and population over time.[54] The model didn't merely represent the world; it inverted the relationship between reality and simulation. Analysts measured populations, economic indicators, and characteristics of the Earth's surface to create input parameters that increased the model's predictive capabilities. In the process, they rendered the whole planet as a massive technical object that could be known only through the characteristics of differential equations, specifically, rates of change and growth.

After the book's publication in 1972, the CIA established the Systems Development and Analysis Center and consulted directly with Dennis Meadows and Jay Forrester on training materials for the analysts who would soon be working with their models.[55] Therefore, *The Limits to Growth* did not only alter analysts' outlook on what challenges faced US national interests,

Wilmoth and Patrick Ball, "The Population Debate in American Popular Magazines, 1946–90," *Population and Development Review* 18, no. 4 (December 1992): 631–668.

[48] James S. Lay Jr, "Secret Memorandum for the National Security Council: Political Implications of Afro-Asian Military Takeovers, May 22, 1959," General CIA Records Collection, doc., at CIA-PDPB86T0026 8R000400110002-6, CIA FOIA Reading Room, accessed June 1, 2021, https://www.cia.gov/readingroom/document/cia-PDPB86T00268R000400110002-6.

[49] Kingsley Davis, "The Other Scare: Too Many People," *The New York Times Magazine*, March 15, 1959, 108.

[50] Kingsley Davis, "Analysis of the Population Explosion," *The New York Times*, September 22, 1957, 226, 257–58; Ernest Weissman, "The Urban Crisis in the World," *Urban Affairs Quarterly* 1 (1965): 65–82; Georg Borgström, *Too Many: A Study of the Earth's Biological Limitations* (New York, NY: MacMillan, 1969); see Björn-Ola Linnér, *The Return of Malthus: Environmentalism and the Post-War Population Resource Crisis* (Isle of Harris: White Horse Press, 2003).

[51] Paul R. Erlich, *The Population Bomb* (New York, NY: Ballantine Books); Donella H. Meadows, D. L. Meadows, J. Randers, and W. W. Behrens, *The Limits to Growth: A Report for the Club of Rome's Project on the Predicament of Mankind, 2nd Edition* (New York, NY: Universe Books).

[52] ORD, *Some Likely Key Intelligence Questions for the 1980s*, 1.

[53] "A Survey of the Community's Use of New Analytical Methods, 1974," General CIA Records Collection, doc., CIA-RDP83M00171R001800110002-5, CIA FOIA Reading Room, accessed June 1, 2021, https://www.cia.gov/readingroom/document/cia-RDP83M00171R001800110002-5.

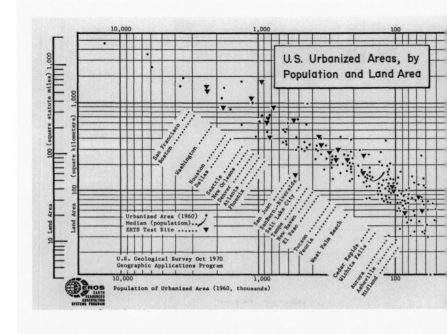

fig 4   Correlation between land area and
1960 population in US cities. Geographic Applications
Program, U.S. Geological Survey, 1971

but it also changed their ontology of global processes. Complex political and economic dynamics were now framed in the language of systems models—stocks, flows, and rates of change. With a mindset that population was a ticking bomb and that density led to political instability, urban populations—and their expression as model parameters—were viewed as quantities to be constantly tracked, both in their total counts and in their spatial distributions.[56] The demands for dynamically updated population estimates placed new pressures on aerial reconnaissance, image interpretation, and cartography. As CIA photo-interpreter Dino Brugioni described, this made mapping by conventional means difficult: "In less than 30 years," he wrote, "the world's population will double, and experts generally agree that urbanization will occur faster than the world can be mapped. It can be readily seen that the present cartographic effort is much too slow."[57] Therefore, from the standpoint of the US intelligence community, new techniques of urban analysis were necessary to gather cartographic and demographic information appropriate for the dynamic models that analysts were now using. The CIA's report "New Analytical Methods" also described research for "exploiting satellite photography," conducted with external, academic, and industrial partners. Detecting "urban change" was seen as a new and vital technique. In the future, the report explained, the Office of Geographic and Cartographic Research intended to "extend the use of these methods to such other subjects as world population and food problems."[58]

Alexander and Wray's Change Detection project was an overt gesture to this overlap of civilian and intelligence research. The phrase "change detection" had a military significance to the early remote sensing audience. It first appeared in 1963 during a symposium on military photo interpretation. A paper by two engineering psychologists described techniques for intelligence analysts to contend with the flood of imagery generated by CIA reconnaissance satellites.[59] The direct connection to CIA-sponsored projects continued throughout the decade.[60] Yet the term "change detection" was not applied to a civilian project until the early 1970s when it was used to describe urban analysis projects sponsored by the Geographic Applications Program. By Wray's own account, before the 1970s, urban analysis within the discipline of photographic interpretation was seemingly underdeveloped relative to the analysis of natural resources. This, however, was a fallacy. In fact, the city had always been a research topic for photo interpreters, but it was most frequently conducted within classified settings for military purposes. And it was through a military or intelligence framework that the city was now understood. "There would be no urban photo interpretation," Wray wrote, "without military photo interpretation."[61] And in the 1970s, seemingly civilian concerns like tracking the growth of urban areas took on military importance.

fig 4

The correlative technique developed within Wray and Alexander's change-detection project could be applied to cities other than the original test sites, even where no information was gathered beforehand. This indicated

[54] The World Model was created by the MIT engineer Jay Forrester.

[55] "Conferences with Dennis L. Meadows, Pugh-Roberts, and Jay W. Forrester regarding Systems Dynamics, 3 August 1973," General CIA Records Collection, doc., CIA-RDP82M00531R 000400120022-8, CIA FOIA Reading Room, https://www.cia.gov/readingroom/document/cia-RDP82M00531R 000400120022-8.

[56] On the "conflation of information with transparency," and how computation creates worlds (and world views) rather than represents them, see Wendy Hui Kyong Chun, "On Software, or the Persistence of Visual Knowledge," *Grey Room 18* (January 2005): 26–51; see Paul N. Edwards., *The Closed World: Computers and the Politics of Discourse* (Cambridge, MA: MIT Press, 2010).

[57] Brugioni, "The Serendipity Effect," 54.

[58] "A Survey of the Community's Use of New Analytical Methods, 1974," 20–22.

[59] Conrad S. Kraft and C. L. Klingberg, "Factors Affecting Change Discrimination," *Proceedings of Symposium on Human Factors Aspects of Photo Interpretation, The Rome Air Development Center, 7–8 November 1963* (New York, NY: Griffiss Air Force Base), 61–85. On satellite imagery as a "flood" or "deluge," see Tomas Dvorak and Jussi Parikka, "Introduction: On the Scale, Quantity and Measure of Images," *Photography Off the Scale: technologies and theories of the Mass Image,* eds. Tomas Dvorak and Jussi Parikka (Edinburgh: Edinburgh University Press, 2021).

[60] James R. Shepard, "A Concept of Change Detection," *Photogrammetric Engineering* 30 (July 1964): 648–51.

61 James R. Wray, "Photo Interpretation in Urban Area Analysis," *Manual of Photographic Interpretation,* ed. Robert N. Colwell (Washington, DC: American Society of Photogrammetry, 1960), 669; William T. Walsh, "Strategic Target Analysis," *Photogrammetric Engineering* 14 (1948): 507–12.

62 Wray, "Census Cities Project and the Atlas of Urban Regional Change."

63 NAS-NRC, *Useful Applications,* 9.

how the project might inform reconnaissance over foreign territory. The project's twenty-six test sites were chosen based on abstract—and narrowly framed—urban parameters: statistical population count and municipal land area. The largest and most populous were San Francisco, CA, Boston, MA, and Washington, DC; the smallest were Midland, TX and Asheville, NC, with the remaining sites distributed between these extremes. The researchers justified the sites using a logarithmic diagram. With land area on the y-axis, and population on the x-axis, they mapped the remaining US cities as points; the test sites themselves were highlighted as well-distributed representatives of the complete set.[62] The diagram implied that visual-numerical correlations arrived at within the test sites could be applied to adjacent cities, even in cases where visual-statistical baselines for those cities had not or could not be established. It also implied that the XY space could be easily filled with cities beyond US borders—all urban areas were commensurable. Any correlations developed in the test sites could be directly applied to similar cities elsewhere. During a 1969 conference hosted by the National Academy of Sciences, Alexander and Gerlach made this purpose clear: "In many underdeveloped nations census data are inadequate or lacking," they wrote, "Synoptic coverage coupled with ground samples will permit highly improved census estimates over large areas of the earth, and thus simplify calibration and verification of analytical models of geographical growth and diffusion."[63] Consequently, the Census Cities Project was not a study about managing cities through Landsat images but about abstracting and estimating unobservable urban populations, regardless of where they were located, and making them available for analytical models.

The project's diagram had another benefit as well. Systems models had a core ontology that represented all processes as quantities (stocks) and rates of change (flows). Likewise, the Urban Change Detection Project implicitly turned cities into visual patterns representing populations as bounded containers (stocks). And from Landsat's repetitive coverage, changes in the visual pattern could be detected and associated with population growth at a particular rate (flows). Therefore, cities abstracted into area and population counts could easily supplement the CIA's analytical models.

GAP researchers did not have CIA systems models explicitly in mind or imagined cities as simple population containers. Instead, a network of factors mutually reinforced this image of urbanism and transformed it into a quantitative and representational object within their work. Those factors included: 1) the need to deploy change detection over foreign territories produced an a priori assumption of physical remoteness; which, 2) reduced urban analysis to photo analysis; and therefore 3) required inferential approaches—informed by the history of military photo interpretation—to associate visual patterns with meaningful and quantitative values. Bounded in space and numerically tagged, this image of the city was then further reinforced by 4) sociologists warning of a population explosion who used the urban-municipal boundary as their unit of analysis. And since the *visual* pattern of urban growth could be numerically associated with population, it was easily translated into 5) the stock and flow ontology of systems models that intelligence analysts were newly deploying. These factors continually resonated with each other during the early years of Landsat and asserted the validity and usefulness of this urban representation. The result was an unchallenged de facto understanding of the city as a monolithic and spatially bounded entity that could be visually interpreted as a proxy for population.[64]

The GAP's civilian-intelligence duality meant that the specific context of their projects directly informed the land cover classification scheme published by the USGS in 1976. Since its release, the LULC system has provided the template for every land cover classification scheme designed by US agencies over the following fifty years.[65] It was, therefore, the GAP's most important project. If not thoroughly scientific, its taxonomy of cover types was presented as indifferent and practical. But the trace of a reconnaissance mentality is encountered throughout. For instance, six of its ten classification criteria are concerned with the reliability of interpretation, and one asserts that the categories should act as surrogates. None mention any representational correlation with things on the ground.[66] The resultant categories, like "urban," now circulate globally and are disconnected from their original production sites. Though seemingly neutral representations, they reinforce an interpretation of the urban as a spatially bounded technical object rather than a social or ecological process.

[64] On the mediation of the environment through remote sensors and the sensory results, see Ryan Bishop, "Felo de se: The Munus of Remote Sensing" *Boundary* 2 45, no. 4 (2018): 41–63.

[65] J. D. Wickham et al., "Thematic Accuracy of the NLCD 2001 Land Cover for the Conterminous United States," *Remote Sensing of Environment* 114, no. 6 (2010): 1286–96; Suming Jin et al., "Overall Methodology Design for the United States National Land Cover Database 2016 Products," *Remote Sensing* 11, no. 24 (December 2019):2971.

[66] Anderson et al., *Land Use and Land Cover*, 5.

Technical *Lands* *and* Technical Lin*es*

Matthew W Wilson

One tendency in the discipline of geography is to consider the difference between technical and interpreted representation in stark contrast: objective or subjective, scientific or artistic, descriptive or analytical, observed or derived, innovated or calculated. In this essay, I speculate on the conceptual space between a line derived by technical means and a line derived through interpretation. Both demand discipline and yet are capacious, even if only in brief moments of creativity and intuition. Departments of geography in US universities have historically doubled down on these differing capacities in their course offerings, reflected by the different training necessary for technically drawn lines and interpreted ones. By the late twentieth century, textbooks like *Map Use* (1978), *Map Appreciation* (1988), and *The Language of Maps* (1996) represented an established notion that techniques in map literacy were differently developed than techniques in map production.[1]

Over the last twenty-five years, course offerings on the topic of map interpretation have dwindled. This has mostly gone unnoticed, thought to be an inevitable effect of the rise of courses on the use of GIS.[2] At the University of Kentucky, a course on map interpretation ran from 1980 to 2013. This course on map interpretation was designed by Karl Raitz, a cultural-historical geographer with expertise in the American landscape. It emerged out of his training at the University of Minnesota, where he completed a similar course by Philip W. Porter in 1965. Then, as in the 1980s, the transition to more technically advanced forms of symbolism in geographic representation begins with the more tactile sensation of reading Erwin Raisz's *Landforms of the United States*. This famous map, produced through six revisions from 1939 to 1957, provided users with a hand-drawn, continental view of the United States. The processes of map generalization that produce a sense of relief make bare the signature style of Raisz. However, Raisz attributed the development of this method to his colleagues and professors at Columbia University: Armin Lobeck (1886–1958) and Douglas Johnson (1878–1944).[3] The issue, perhaps, was how to represent the truth of nature. Indeed, as Lorraine Daston and Peter Galison argue in their discussion on a transition between eighteenth- and nineteenth-century atlas makers, there are "different epistemic ways of life made for different diagnoses of the sources of variability."[4] Examining the traditions in the representation of relief in cartography is instructive. As suggested by Jill Desimini and Charles Waldheim, "These mark a transitional moment of greater measure and precision in topographic representation, when surveying and drawing techniques advanced to better reflect the geographic location of key physical features."[5]

Raisz understood the physiographic method that produced his *Landforms* as addressing a problem in cartography's "depiction of the scenery of large areas on small-scale maps."[6] According to Raisz, William Morris Davis's method had initial application in the mapping of Europe for military purposes. Careful to indicate the scientific provenance of what seems to be an artistically driven illustration, Raisz argued that this method was "a *systematic application of a set of symbols* ... [rather than] a bird's-eye view of a region."[7] Indeed, the viewpoint is oblique, but the symbols are physiographical—not

[1] Green et al., (2008) provide an overview of these textbooks, including an analysis of declining course offerings on map interpretation in US institutions. See Jerry E. Green, David U. Burns, and Toby P. Green, "The Enigmatic Enrolment Trend in US Map-Interpretation Courses," *Cartographica* 43, no. 3 (2008): 221–26; Phillip C. Muehrcke and Juliana O. Muehrcke, *Map Use: Reading, Analysis, and Interpretation* (Madison, WI: JP Publications, 1978); Mark S. Monmonier and George A. Schnell, *Map Appreciation* (Englewood Cliffs, N.J.: Prentice-Hall, 1988); Philip Gersmehl, *Language of Maps, Pathways in Geography Series, 15th ed.* (Indiana, PA: National Council for Geographic Education, 1996).

[2] Here, Green et al. (2008) discuss that while courses on remote sensing, air-photo interpretation, and cartography remained largely stable in the 1980s and early 1990s, the rapid growth in course offerings in GIS might help explain some of the redistribution of students out of map interpretation courses.

[3] Douglas Johnson trained under William Morris Davis (1850–1934) at Harvard, who also developed methods of relief representation. See Erwin Raisz, "The Physiographic Method of Representing Scenery on Maps," *Geographical Review* 21, no. 2 (April 1931): 297–304.

[4] Lorraine Daston and Peter Galison, *Objectivity* (New York, NY: Zone Books, 2007), 113.

[5] Jill Desimini and Charles Waldheim, *Cartographic Grounds: Projecting the Landscape Imaginary* (New York, NY: Princeton Architectural Press, 2016), 73.

[6] Raisz, "Physiographic Method," 297.

[7] Raisz, "Physiographic Method," 299, emphasis original.

mathematical. While elevation and slope cannot be directly measured on these maps, the choice of symbol is a scientific understanding of landforms, Raisz insisted. He continued the assessment,

> On the other hand, in addition to the basic importance of the type of information yielded by the physiographic method, the map appeals immediately to the average [person]. It suggests actual country and enables [them] to see the land instead of reading an abstract location diagram. *It works on the imagination*.[8]

[8] Raisz, "Physiographic Method," 303, emphasis added.

That these landform maps work on the imagination is perhaps their rationale for continued use today in modules in map reading. According to the course designed in the latter half of the twentieth century by Karl Raitz, these landform maps provide an on-ramp to the more mathematical expressions of relief. Students learned to read USGS quadrangles and other techniques for topography.

Importantly, landform maps are not only meant in appreciation of the landscape. The method of interpretation of these maps is best utilized in classrooms where students are also required to draw these physiographic symbols. Raisz continued:

> Finally, it may be said that to produce a physiographic map requires not only the best knowledge of the physiography of the region in question but also a certain ability in drawing. The importance of the latter, however, should not be exaggerated. Almost every student in the author's class in cartography was able to draw satisfactory mountains after a little practice. It is easier and more natural than to draw contours or hachures.[9]

[9] Raisz, "Physiographic Method," 303.

A half-century after Raisz's course, classes in map interpretation require aspects of drawing that connect hand to eye in the practices of map literacy. Raisz was well known for his ability in the classroom to draw physiographic maps and cross-section diagrams by memory. These diagrams were drawn at the front of a classroom, where Raisz would, from memory, depict a cross-section of the South American continent for his students, carefully noting urban centers, elevations, predominant food crops, as well as the geologic system that produced the dominant landforms. Reportedly saved by his students,[10] these drawings mark a moment in geographic education where an understanding of human-environmental relations was sutured to the practices of drawing and representation.

[10] Personal correspondence with Joseph Garver, then curator (now emeritus) at the Harvard Map Collection, July 2, 2014.

[11] Indeed, we might think the interpretative work of map reading to "emancipate potentials", as James Corner suggests in "The Agency of Mapping: Speculation, Critique, and Invention," *Mappings*, ed. Denis E. Cosgrove. (London: Reaktion Books, 1999), 213.

This way of understanding geography through map interpretation was thought as both the development of techniques to receive information *and* an active practice of imagination, applied perspective, and the tactile work of drawing.[11] Raisz understood it required practice to identify landforms, the geological processes that produced them, and the cultural landscapes that developed across them while communicating these features as small-scale representations. He realized these efforts as differently scientific than the precise mathematical calculations that derived slope from contour intervals.

If, as Raisz suggested, the development of techniques in map interpretation is aided by the development of techniques in map drawing, how might we think about the space between technical and interpreted lines? Both are productive as tools of a representational regime, as they may operate to constitute worlds (or none at all). Both are bound to each other, at times like two sides of the same coin, at different times, like a Möbius strip—the trace of the interpretative fingertip precedes and prefigures the cut of the wood-block.[12] Indeed, while the technical line is drawn, the force of the pen against paper is not a purely mechanical relation but born of little fictions—moments of imaginative projection. These moments are buttressed by expertise and experience, granting a veneer of objectivity and even obviousness to technical lines. Technical lines that are "well-drawn" may be considered when the drafting marks belie the creator or their creation. The role of interpretation then is partially forensic and archaeological: who did it *and* what does it represent? But these approaches demand an understanding of drawing techniques and the scopic grammars within a representational regime.

Here, we might recall Jacque Bertin's notion of generalization as drawing features through structural and conceptual transformations.[13] Consider the simple example of the drawing of a river. The river and its winding bends are structurally transformed into a represented line with no bends. The structure is altered. This technical line can be conceptually generalized into a dashed line, representing a river with several bends.

Suppose the work of map generalization is thought of as the exercise of technique that anticipates the interpretative work of map literacy. In that case, there remains a possibility that the technical line goes too far—that it exceeds its capacity to be interpreted as intended. This reasoning follows Bernard Stiegler's concern in *Taking Care of Youth and the Generations*.[14] Toxicity, understood as when the cure becomes poisonous, reminds me to think carefully about techniques of representation that may reduce or block the potential for care, attention, regard, curiosity, etc. For instance, when the technical line defies the ability to understand its making, might this be described as a *successful* or *complete* reification? How might this reification convince the map reader of the objectivity of a technically drawn line, thereby making the interpretative frame more rigid? Understood in this way, geovisualization and mapmaking are practices that produce a technical line that anticipates its interpretation and, as such, forwards a conundrum or contradiction. To generalize well enough is to excel at the mechanics of a technically drawn line that carries the interpretative trace. This process may also remove the audience from the conditions of its creation and the various scopic grammars necessary to be interpreted well enough.

Why, then, might revealing the conditions of creation in a technically drawn line provide some checks against this potential for toxicity? Why should the scopic grammars of representation be known by an audience of map readers? Should the mapmaker and their craft not continue to be

[12] Franz Grenacher, "The Woodcut Map: A Form-Cutter of Maps Wanders through Europe in the First Quarter of the Sixteenth Century," *Imago Mundi* 24 (1970), 31–41.

[13] Jacques Bertin, *Semiology of Graphics* (Madison, WI: University of Wisconsin Press, 1983), 301.

[14] Bernard Stiegler, *Taking Care of Youth and the Generations*, Meridian: Crossing Aesthetics (Stanford, CA: Stanford University Press, 2010).

shrouded in expertise (as mystery and magic)? To understand conditions is to begin again on some shifting ground—where should we mark the original flashpoint of the drawn line? At least three generations of critical cartographers have cut their teeth on thinking about the military and colonial and capitalist co-implications of the technically drawn line (that precedes technical lands). And yet, the technical and interpretive traditions continue, albeit with caveats and radical appropriations and resistive responsibilities and modules on "ethics."[15] There are, of course, "conditions" beyond the purely historical that require our attention. These might include the affective conditions of the drawn line. For instance, the pressure of the pen to paper is both a physical relationship *and* born of the projective force that links past to present to future. This effective mode/condition of the technical/interpreted line produces the movement of the static drawing. How then to understand these scopic grammars as productive of these affective modes, especially when these movements are not always perceptible/accessible to an audience of map readers?

It is instructive to consider how the prevailing thoughts on map use might reflect some distinctions captured in the technical/interpreted line. The enormous wake created by Alan MacEachren's scholarship—specifically by his book *How Maps Work*—continues to propel academic cartography toward a further refined and tested characterization of map use.[16] His well-known cartography cube (or cart3) is a heuristic volume for identifying map uses. However, the intended effect seems to draw us toward a diagonal that stretches between two conditions: 1) an audience of the general public, wherein the map is presenting known things about the world with a low amount of interaction between humans and the map, and 2) an individual engaging with a map in highly interactive ways to reveal something yet unknown about the world.

This diagonal is the fold created within the volume, a fold that stretches between visualization map uses and communication map uses,[17] expressed as exploration, confirmation/analysis, synthesis, and presentation.[18] Ideally, we are told that map uses that encourage higher levels of interaction between the user and the map might constitute more effective forms of spatial-visual thinking. However, is human-map interaction (as perhaps the ultimate "dimension" of the cartographer's craft) so easily bound within this secured volume? Are there other wiggling and rambunctious and fractal and branching lines that might constitute other, even *ideal*, map uses?

According to Arthur Robinson, what remains outside the cart3 volume stays elusive, perhaps even "essentially subjective."[19] The bounds on the volume are far squishier; the corners can be pinched to draw them toward each other. They also stretch outward and inward, producing new juxtapositions and reducibility. The volume is entirely situated in this reimagined cart3, not floating in a static void. Instead, the cube is suggestable. It moves as force is applied. But what forces are used to draw these corners toward each other? What remains outside the volume and yet impacts the interior and its expression? Perhaps how maps work cannot be fully captured inside

[15] Sarah A. Elwood and Matthew W. Wilson, "Critical GIS Pedagogies Beyond 'Week 10: Ethics,'" *International Journal of Geographical Information Science* 31, no. 10 (2017), 2098–116.

[16] Alan M. MacEachren, *How Maps Work: Representation, Visualization, and Design* (New York, NY: Guilford Press, 1995).

[17] MacEachren, *How Maps Work*, 358.

[18] Robert E. Roth, "Cartographic Interaction: What We Know and What We Need to Know," *Journal of Spatial Information Science* 6 (2013): 71.

[19] Arthur Howard Robinson, *The Look of Maps: An Examination of Cartographic Design* (Madison, WI: University of Wisconsin Press, 1952), 73.

the volume. Other forces operate, yet the conventional cart3 volume does not further epistemological investigation. The volume remains epistemologically sealed. How do we account for the structural forces that operate on and through maps if we choose theoretical frames that foreclose their recognition?

Even a most basic consideration of the ideology of the map—well known by the time MacEachren designed the cube—is missing.[20] As a result, the most basic question around who benefits from a map is forced outside the volume. Further inquiries into the economy, labor, identity and subject formation, privacy and surveillance, or any notion of politics (beyond public or private) remain conspicuously absent. These questions are then cast outside the bounds of behavioral cartography, wherein the concern is with the more practical operation of the map: creating an environment that best visualizes or communicates the subject matter. The impact of this Robinsonianism on the field cannot be overstated. The concern with how maps work becomes a function of the technical craft and interpretative experience. However, understanding the regimes within which maps operate and produce is not to suddenly put away the drafting table. "But do you actually *do* GIS?" marks such a boundary, evoked by this epistemological gatekeeping.[21] Rather, the technical/interpreted line is simultaneously inside and outside the cart3. It is responsive *and* responsible. Responsibility is not an afterthought—ideally—but is bound up in the fabricating work of the drawn line (a drawn line that already anticipates the trace).

I conclude with more questions than answers. How might responsibility and responsiveness be better sutured in drawing a line? How might technical lands be bound to, determined by, these technical lines? Recall the Möbius strip of the drawn line that is simultaneously a trace. Drawing a line down the center of this one-sided surface would eventually encounter itself. Or was this technical/interpreted line always there, emerging from scopic grammars of literacy and fluency or the tactile memories of place, and the tactical capacities of movement? Perhaps, this "encounter" is emblematic of the work of tracing bound up in drawing itself. The line's cut anticipates the tracing with fingertips—a whole mechanics of interpretation that informs the crafting of a visualization. Herein we might place greater notions of responsibility in the drawn line, for mechanics of interpretation should be about the effectiveness of the visualization (its responsiveness) and the possible outcomes (its possibilities). To be clear, it is much easier to study and control for responsiveness. The cart3, tightly bounded, is one such frame to tame the map—how it works is much more slippery, how it requires different frames—not a rejection of the necessary techniques of responsiveness, but a widening of that responsiveness to account for its possibilities (by taking responsibility in the act of drawing/tracing the technical/interpreted line).

[20] For instance, John Brian Harley's path-defining work to deconstruct the map would challenge thought on how maps operate. See J. Brian Harley, "Silences and Secrecy: The Hidden Agenda of Cartography in Early Modern Europe," *Imago Mundi* 40 (1988): 57–76; Harley, "Deconstructing the Map," *Cartographica* 26 (1989): 1–20.

[21] Matthew W. Wilson, *New Lines: Critical GIS and the Trouble of the Map* (Minneapolis, MN: University of Minnesota Press, 2017).

Land Technicians

Eric Robsky Huntley

Introduction

I began by mapping the mines. With colleagues, I had acquired a tantalizingly large dataset containing cross-sectional descriptions of active, retired, and exploratory mining operations, including productivity measures, historical weather conditions, and dozens of other attributes.[1] We could use these to expose the mining industry: the scars, the damage, the tailing ponds, the affected communities—we'd take it to the public to expose malfeasance. In short, we could produce an extensive critical mapping project by providing cartographic evidence of the violence of extractive capital.

I set to it. I wrote a script that would produce an aerial image of each pit, gash, and speculative site.[2] Images began to multiply in front of me as the God's eye of my desktop moved across the surface of Earth, telling me what I already knew: the ravages of the extractive industries were widespread and awe-ful. I hyphenate deliberately—the visual effects of the commodified planet were, in their way, sublime. I found my eye drawn to the immensity and form of the pits, these technical lands aestheticizing their sheer number and scale.

fig 1

I write this from my apartment in Somerville, Massachusetts, on unceded Wampanoag and Massachusett land. The temperature recently topped 100 degrees Fahrenheit. On multiple evenings these past several weeks, the Boston skyline was obscured by a haze of wildfire ash that had blown in from California. Here! On the East Coast of the United States, I smelled the incinerated fragments of the West. Wildfires are now bicoastal; my neighbors' lungs are now threatened by conflagrations thousands of miles away.

I stopped the script. One more exercise decrying the outcomes of mining— and a superficial one at that—felt dizzyingly inadequate. Of course, there are good reasons to monitor the ecological impacts and conflicts over labor, land, and territory that accompany the so-called mining cycle in a given place.[3] But why pursue an exercise that gave the impression of a coffee table book heroizing ecological devastation? Why render its perpetrators sublime, muscular, and prolific? These spectacular mines, "technical lands," multiplied over and over affected me. Awe, dread, a sense of scale and enormity, a shimmer of what Julian Stallabrass calls the "data sublime." The magnitude of the gashes produced what Jenny Rice calls an "epistemic aesthetic," insisting on their own vitality through their sheer enormity.[4] As nineteenth-century viewers in the colonizer nations may have been emotionally moved by paintings of seascapes or mountains, I found myself similarly moved: to awe but to little else.

fig 2

I loaded a different table, one which located firms' headquarters instead of mining sites. Imagery began to appear again, but the feeling was different. In the place of violently exposed subsurfaces, there was a parade of postmodern skyscrapers in Toronto, rococo McMansions in Metro Detroit, and office parks in Victoria (figure 2). Topographically far from—but topologically next door to—the depths of mining operations were the architectural

[1] The dataset in question is produced by Mining Intelligence, an industry data broker.

[2] Discussion of scripting in this essay refers to code that is available at https://gitlab.com/-/snippets/2210740.

[3] These efforts can be supported by data science. For example, see Victor Maus, Stefan Giljum, Jakob Gutschlhofer, Dieison M. da Silva, Michael Probst, Sidnei L. B. Gass, Sebastian Luckeneder, Mirko Lieber, and Ian McCallum, "A Global-Scale Data Set of Mining Areas," *Scientific Data* 7, no. 1 (September 8, 2020): 289, https://doi.org/10.1038/s41597-020-00624-w.

[4] Julian Stallabrass, "What's in a Face? Blankness and Significance in Contemporary Art Photography," *October* 122 (2007): 71–90, https://doi.org/10.1162/octo.2007.122.1.71. See also Jenny Rice, *Awful Archives: Conspiracy Theory, Rhetoric, and Acts of Evidence* (Columbus, OH: Ohio State University Press, 2020).

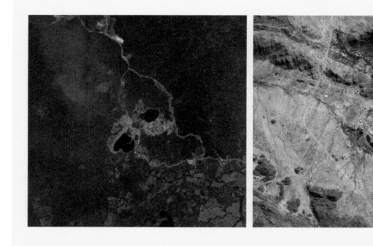

fig 1   A mine in Panama, owned by Petaquilla
minerals; a platinum mine in South Africa, owned
by Anglo American Platinum. Google Earth

fig 2   Petaquilla minerals in Vancouv[
Columbia; Anglo American Platinum in Jo[
burg, South Africa. Google Earth

artifacts of extractive capital. In at least one sense, I had moved to an analytical antipode. Instead of the places of extraction, I was inventorying the places of their extractors.

From site to relation. From pit to digger. From landscape studies to political ecology. Mapping, even as it is a primary mining technique, can be put in service of projects that trace outward from the mine site and its engineered, increasingly automated landscape[5]—an example of technical land, by anyone's definition—to the land's technicians.

My interests here are two-fold. First, I encourage scholars to think, draw, and map the making of technical lands relationally and topologically, simultaneously leveraging a rich stream of contemporary geographic thought and devising means of representing far richer spatial ontologies than those predicated on the Cartesian plane. Secondly, I suggest that tracing technical expertise through its networks will place technical lands within a political economy and set of historical and material circumstances. Building on a growing interest in the political economy of mapping and "location intelligence," land technicians will yield insights into spatial technologies in multiple industrial contexts and include a broader range of actors. I will point expressly to opportunities to expand geography's "geological imagination" through studies of spatial data science's role in the extractive industries.

In both cases, there is a broader point in play—our interest in technical lands might yield heightened interest in holding technicians accountable. By insisting on lands as technical, we already imagine them produced and productive. For that reason, we might spend more time examining the techniques and technologists etching their imperatives into the landscape than in the bare fact of the landscape itself. In some sense, this should be taken as a call to attempt the arduous work of digging into the offices of prospectors, mineral developers, even financial institutions—land technicians, all— where data is scarce, proprietary, and underexamined.

Technical Lands in Relation

Thinking of the land as technical draws our eye to landscapes that are the objects of technicians.[6] As Galison suggests, technical lands encourage an aesthetic materialism that directs our attention. The combination of waste and wilderness found in, for example, a disused tailing pond begs the question: how did things come to be the way they are?[7] In the key of Jane Bennett, we could understand technical lands as a kind of enchantment with the terrain given over to engineers and engineering, without which we could not care.[8]

To this point, thinking technical lands resonates with contemporary theorists of waste. Vittoria di Palma, for example, describes how a "wasteland"—often a disused technical land—is culturally constructed through the feeling of disgust. We see the land and render a simultaneously emotional and aesthetic judgment: we are repulsed. Accompanying Traci Brynne Voyles further, we might examine how we can glimpse longer processes of colonial erasure through wastelands.[9] Technical lands lend themselves to a

[5] For more on the automation of mining landscapes, see the discussion of the "Fourth Industrial Revolution" in Martín Arboleda, *Planetary Mine: Territories of Extraction under Late Capitalism* (London: Verso Books, 2020).

[6] To suggest that landscape is the object of technicians is not to grant them absolute agency over any given landscape; I hew to J.K. Gibson-Graham's caution against critical approaches that establish the critiqued as totalizing and all-powerful. See *The End of Capitalism (As We Knew It): A Feminist Critique of Political Economy* (Minneapolis, MN: University of Minnesota Press, 1996). Rather, I mean object in the more modest sense of a ground worked with through drawing and speculative techniques, à la Robin Evans, "Translations Drawing to Building," *Translations from Drawing to Building and Other Essays*, (London: Architectural Association, 1986, reprinted 1997), 152–93.

[7] Galison's discussion of the subject can be found in "What Are Technical Lands?" *Technical Landscapes: Aesthetics and the Environment in the History of Science and Art* (Cambridge, MA, 2017), https://www.youtube.com/watch?v=NnFgnEwNIFU&t=2441s; Jeffrey S. Nesbit builds on the relationship between waste and wilderness in "Spaceport: Technical Lands for Departing Earth," Harvard University, 2020, http://nrs.harvard.edu/urn-3:HUL.InstRepos:42689380.

[8] Jane Bennett, *The Enchantment of Modern Life: Attachments, Crossings, and Ethics* (Princeton, NJ: Princeton University Press, 2001).

[9] Vittoria di Palma, *Wasteland: A History* (New Haven, CT: Yale University Press, 2014); Traci Brynne Voyles, *Wastelanding: Legacies of Uranium Mining in Navajo Country* (Minneapolis, MN: University of Minnesota Press, 2015). I am grateful

to my former students, Tess McCann and Michelle Mueller Gámez, for calling my attention to the work of di Palma and Voyles through their own lively engagements.

10 This work was supported by an International Workshop Award from the Antipode Foundation.

11 Christopher Alton, "The Lower Athabasca Regional Plan's Future Is History," *Critical Planning* 23 (2017): 129–53, https://doi.org/10.5070/CP8231038131.

12 Rob Nixon, *Slow Violence and the Environmentalism of the Poor* (Cambridge, MA: Harvard University Press, 2011); Shannon Elizabeth Bell, *Fighting King Coal: The Challenges to Micromobilization in Central Appalachia* (Cambridge, MA: MIT Press, 2016); Shannon Elizabeth Bell, *Our Roots Run Deep as Ironweed: Appalachian Women and the Fight for Environmental Justice* (Champaign, IL: University of Illinois Press, 2013); Thea Riofrancos, *Resource Radicals: From Petro-Nationalism to Post-Extractivism in Ecuador* (Durham, NC: Duke University Press, 2020); Gabrielle Hecht, *Being Nuclear: Africans and the Global Uranium Trade* (Cambridge, MA: MIT Press, 2012).

13 For more on the visuality of mining at PDAC, see Christopher Alton, Eric Robsky Huntley, and Zulaikha Ayub, "Conjuring the Planetary Mine: Counter-Mapping the Heart of Extractive Capital," *Thresholds* 50: 239–55, https://doi.org/10.1162/thld_a_00765.

linkage between the symbolic and the material, the aesthetic and the administrative, the affective and the active.

So why should we, in a critical primer on technical lands, move our gaze away from the lands themselves—from the conditions of labor on the ground, as it were—and towards their managers, administrators, and speculators? Following all the above rhymes and resonances, technical lands provide a productive starting point. Imagine one node in an origin-destination pair or—better—a spider-chart. In other words, if studies of technical lands leave us digging in the landscape, sitting amidst the bunkers, tailing ponds, server rooms, and launchpads, we will have missed an opportunity to trace outwards from the land and examine its relational production. I would hope to encourage work that traces lines outward into the networks of power and expertise whose sites are scattered and frequently distant from the forms that dot and fill the landscapes: the offices and conference rooms of, for example, the extractive industries.

As February turned to March 2020, my colleagues and I found ourselves in downtown Toronto, Ontario, at the annual meeting of the Prospectors and Developers Association of Canada (PDAC), one of the largest annual gatherings of extractive industry representatives. My small band of researchers joined 23,144 others in wandering conference floors of small cubic booths, suits, swagger, and high-tech graphics demonstrating what deep learning, AI, and innovations in old-fashioned drill bits promised the industry. Our interest was different from most attendees. Most were there to seek or reproduce their fortune by buying and selling properties on the promise of their mineral content or buying and selling technologies that might improve predictability and profitability. In contrast, we had organized a counter-conference, direct actions, and a set of critical corporate research workshops alongside activists with the Mining Injustice Solidarity Network and the Beyond Extraction Collective at York University.[10]

Walking through the convention center, the walls were bedazzled with maps, plans, and deep sections of speculative sites. It struck me on later reflection how thoroughly the iconography of mining is tied to the blasted mountaintop, the tailing pond, the lumbering, increasingly driverless crawlers moving up and down the concentric rings of the pit. These are technical landscapes—sites of exclusion and limited access well on their way to becoming wastelands—aesthetic products with dubious prospects for reclamation, no doubt worthy of our attention.[11] Many have documented the slow violence associated with mining and the powerful resistance it has engendered.[12] But I also wondered about the images that flashed on the screens: of eerie-blue, disembodied network iconography, data-rich cartography, and carefully modeled subsurfaces. Who made these? How has the introduction of geographical information systems (GIS) and spatial data science into mining reconfigured the practice (and vice versa)?[13]

Standing in the PDAC exhibit hall, multiple stories beneath the CN tower, there was a pervasive feeling of betweenness, perhaps attributable to the palpable mixture of jetlag and hangover that characterizes so many big-tent industry events. However, here, among the land technicians, selling, conjuring, investing, and speculating, I could not help but feel that I was in the middle of multiple sites of action: the property and the location of its developer; colonized and colonizer; extraction site, extractor, and seller.

On PDAC's exchange floor, one becomes aware of space as relational, as topological. The physical distance between site and speculator is collapsed by property relations, by the immediacy of visualizations, maps, and sections. This type of relation, in which physical distance is bent, collapsed, and skewed (or simply not the salient measure of relatedness), has been the subject of a great deal of interest in geographical theory. Feminist critics have detailed the masculinist assumptions that support Cartesian spatialities, associated with the aperspectival, unmarked view from nowhere; feminists are also at work developing new representational techniques more attuned to embodiment and relation, and context and labor.[14] Geographers have queered the map and mapped queer lifeworlds, developing a new and profoundly relational language to evoke the trajectories and constellations of queer life.[15] Spatial theorists have given us the means to think of space as relational and topological, which says that "here" is not only related to "there" but folded up in it, maintaining that relation even under changing conditions.[16]

fig 3

What does this mean for the mines? Rather than mapping the mine or the developer, we might devise new ways to draw relations that do not amount to simple spaghetti maps. For example, we might move literally, visualizing the mine within the metro and vice versa. We might visualize the relatedness of technical land to the land technician through simple superimposition. In such a visualization, the literal Cartesian relation between the two points—the single line drawn on the globe's surface—is less salient than depicting the grounds intertwined and even in conflict. The Cartesian visuality of GIS need not limit inquiry into technical lands—we can visualize them within webs of relation and in topological networks, and in so doing devise software innovations that support what Bergmann and Lally call "geographical imagination systems" (GIS), answering spatial questions anew through relational and topological understandings of proximity.[17]

The Geological Imagination

Geography's geological imagination is highly constrained, partly because barriers to information about the uptake and use of GIS in the mining sector are incredibly high.[18] One does not need to look far to find instances where geospatial techniques have developed alongside innovations in the mining industry. Bill Rankin, for example, demonstrated the well-known but little examined relationship between geostatistics and the practices of mineral exploration. Megan Black weaves a history of what she calls "space-age globalization," identifying the complex questions of mineral sovereignty raised by the launch of the Landsat program in the 1970s.[19] Several tantalizing asides in Martín Arboleda's *Planetary Mine* point to the ongoingness of these relations, outlining how the introduction of GIS, AI, and more

[14] Classic statements are Gillian Rose, "Situating Knowledges: Positionality, Reflexivities, and Other Tactics," *Progress in Human Geography* 21, no. 3 (1997): 305–20, https://doi.org/10.1191/030913297673302122; Donna J. Haraway, "Situated Knowledges: The Science Question in Feminism and the Privilege of Partial Perspective," *Feminist Studies* 14, no. 3 (1988): 575–99, https://doi.org/10.2307/3178066; Meghan Kelly, "Mapping Bodies, Designing Feminist Icons," *GeoHumanities* 7 (2021): 529–557, https://doi.org/10.1080/2373566X.2021.1883455; Meghan Kelly, "Mapping Syrian Refugee Border Crossings: A Feminist Approach," *Cartographic Perspectives*, no. 93 (2019): 34–64, https://doi.org/10.14714/CP93.1406; Catherine D'Ignazio and Lauren F Klein, "Feminist Data Visualization," *IEEE Vis Conference*, 2016.

[15] Jen Jack Gieseking, *A Queer New York: Geographies of Lesbians, Dykes, and Queers* (New York, NY: New York University Press, 2020).

[16] Lauren Martin and Anna J. Secor, "Towards a Post-Mathematical Topology," *Progress in Human Geography* 38, no. 3 (2014): 420–38, https://doi.org/10.1177/0309132513508209; Anna J. Secor, "Topological City," *Urban Geography* 34, no. 4 (2013): 430–44, https://doi.org/10.1080/02723638.2013.778698.

[17] Luke Bergmann and Nick Lally, "For Geographical Imagination Systems," *Annals of the American Association of Geographers* 111, no. 1 (2021): 26–35, https://doi.org/10.1080/24694452.2020.1750941; Nick Lally and Luke Bergmann, "Enfolding: An Experimental Geographical Imagination System (gis)," in *A Place More Void*, eds. Paul Kingsbury and Anna J. Secor (Lincoln, NE: University of Nebraska Press, 2021), 167–80. For further examples of what such analysis might look like (and the plethora of forms it might take), see Garrett Dash Nelson and

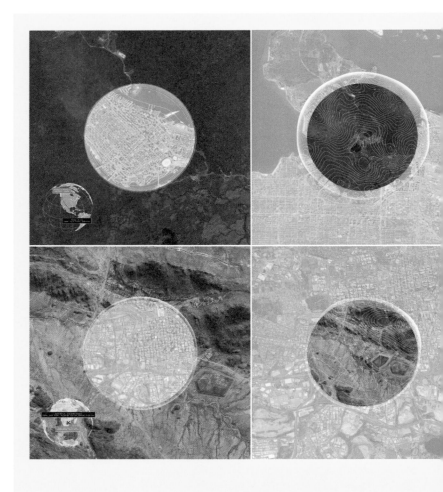

fig 3 Grid of images depicting topological relations between mines in Panama and South Africa and mining industry headquarters in Seattle, Washington, United States and Johannesburg, South Africa. Eric Robsky Huntley

sophisticated subsurface modeling tools has transformed the viability of low-grade ore.

Even fundamental market analysis, though, is hard to come by. Setting out to answer a broad but simple question (what is the extent of the mapping industries' participation in mining?), the researcher will hit (pay)walls. In industry documents, one frequently sees unsourced statements about the scale of the involvement. One report by geospatial data annotation firm iMerit suggests that the "resource extraction sector has become the biggest consumer of GIS and geospatial data," and that the sector has "in recent years become an ever-hungrier consumer of GIS and other geospatial data ... few industries are as closely connected to spatial data as mining." No figures or citations are provided.[20] The evidence supporting this claim is often hidden in industry reports of a type rarely purchased by academic libraries.[21]

Currently, calls for a more robust political economy of GIS abound even as that economy's entanglements shift rapidly.[22] This is urgent; our existing critical histories hew tightly to critiques of military and academic actors while failing to recognize many other lines that feed their "mangle"; elaborating upon the "killing fields" has taken precedence over resource exploitation.[23] Elaborating upon the fate of the discipline has elided its relationship to its associated industries.[24] Here, I gesture to geological politics, but we could multiply the lines.

Mines are made through a highly speculative process involving immense geological and spatial expertise carried out by industry actors in the exploration and development sector. The mine is not yet a mine; there are no pit or tailing ponds. It is, instead, "conjured" to use Anna Tsing's phrase.[25] The process is simultaneously analytical and occult, taking place in centers of calculation distinct from the land itself. Technical lands give us an opening to investigate those industries and technologies that support mineral development: the techniques of the land technicians.

To focus on the extractive industries might also require us to step outside of the visual repertoires and scopic regimes of geography and cartography. "The map," as an artifact, is not what is at stake, but the model, the diagram, the visiotechnical means through which ground is produced as a speculative zone for extractive exploration: more-than-cartographic grounds, as it were.[26] Similarly, tracing relations between technician and site requires novel representational interventions, specifically means of figuring relationality and topology.

Conclusion: Map Up (and Down, and Around)

I have held that technical lands are most generatively understood in relation to their technicians. Technical lands are cyborg things, impossibilities in the absence of human technicians. (Though to some degree, any landscape is already a cyborg, made and remade by a human implement in collaboration with nonhumans.) A technical land wraps up the whole web of relations: owners, dissident claimants, regulators, speculators, residents (humans and other critters) and leaves us to identify salient lines and

Alasdair Rae, "An Economic Geography of the United States: From Commutes to Megaregions," *PLOS ONE* 11, no. 11 (2016): e0166083, https://doi.org/10.1371/journal.pone.0166083; Laura Kurgan, *Close up at a Distance: Mapping, Technology, and Politics* (New York, NY: Zone Books, 2013).

[18] Here, I riff on Susan Schulten's *The Geographical Imagination in America, 1880–1950* (Chicago, IL: University of Chicago Press, 2002) and Derek Gregory's *Geographical Imaginations* (Malden, MA: Wiley-Blackwell, 1994). Promising sources for a "geological information" include Rosalind Williams's *Notes on the Underground: An Essay on Technology, Science, and the Imagination* (Cambridge, MA: MIT Press, 2008) and Carolyn Merchant's *The Death of Nature: Women, Ecology, and the Scientific Revolution* (San Francisco, CA: Harper San Francisco, 1990).

[19] William Rankin, "The Accuracy Trap: The Values and Meaning of Algorithmic Mapping, from Mineral Extraction to Climate Change," *Environment and History*, August 2021, https://doi.org/10.3197/096734020X15900760737275; Megan Black, "Prospecting the World: Landsat and the Search for Minerals in Space Age Globalization," *Journal of American History* 106, no. 1 (2019): 97–120, https://doi.org/10.1093/jahist/jaz169.

[20] "GIS Data Annotation for Mining," iMerit, n.d., https://imerit.net/whitepapers/gis-data-annotation-for-mining/.

[21] See *Markets and Markets*, "Geographic Information System Market by Offering (Hardware (GIS Collector, Total Station, LiDAR), Software, Services), Function (Mapping, Surveying, Telematics and Navigation, Location-Based Service), Industry, Region—Global Forecast to 2025"; *Markets and Markets*, February 2020—retailing for $4,950. Or *Grand View Research*, "Geographic Information System Market Size, Share &

Trends Analysis Report By Component (Hardware, Software, Services), By Usage, By Application (Transport, Agriculture, Construction, Mining, Aerospace), By Device, By Region, And Segment Forecasts, 2018–2025"; *Grand View Research*, November 2017—also $4,950; StrategyR, "Geographic Information Systems (GIS): Global Market Trajectory and Analysis"; StrategyR, April 2021—as of this writing, priced at $5,450.

22 Agnieszka Leszczynski, "Situating the Geoweb in Political Economy," *Progress in Human Geography* 36, no. 1 (2012): 72–89; Jim Thatcher and Laura Beltz Imaoka, "The Poverty of GIS Theory: Continuing the Debates around the Political Economy of GISystems," *The Canadian Geographer / Le Géographe Canadien* 62, no. 1 (2018): 27–34, https://doi.org/10.1111/cag.12437; Jim Thatcher, Luke Bergmann, Britta Ricker, Reuben Rose-Redwood, David O'Sullivan, Trevor J. Barnes, Luke R. Barnesmoore, et al., "Revisiting Critical GIS," *Environment and Planning A* 48, no. 5 (2016): 815–24, https://doi.org/10.1177/0308518X15622208; Jen Jack Gieseking, "Operating Anew: Queering GIS with Good Enough Software," *The Canadian Geographer / Le Géographe Canadien* 62, no. 1 (2018): 55–66, https://doi.org/10.1111/cag.12397.

23 On GIS and the "killing fields," see Neil Smith's critique of theoretical critiques of GIS, "History and Philosophy of Geography: Real Wars, Theory Wars," *Progress in Human Geography* 16, no. 2 (1992): 257–71; On the military-industrial "mangling" of geography, see Trevor J. Barnes, "Geography's Underworld: The Military-Industrial Complex, Mathematical Modelling, and the Quantitative Revolution," *Geoforum* 39, no. 1 (2008): 3–16, https://doi.org/10.1016/j.geoforum.2007.09.006; Matthew J. Barnes and Matthew W. Wilson, "Big Data, Social Physics, and Spatial

trajectories. The lines to follow are those that situate land technologies in a political economy that includes but is broader than that of GIS and "location," and that pushes our thought to consider technical lands as relationally and topologically constituted.

However, there is a broader point here. In encouraging studies of technical lands looking outwards, I encourage us to *map up*. Because being situated on the ground encourages us to look around, a more satisfying image will come into focus if we direct our eyes upwards. In other words, to study technical lands can be a critical, radical project, but only if we cultivate a culture of research more interested in holding power to account than in demonstrating, over and over again, the scars left in the earth and our communities by the malfeasance and malign neglect of unaccountable interests. I have been recently thinking on the work of Laura Nader, who, decades ago, wrote that anthropologists have been too slow to use their anthropological tools to study the powerful. As Nader asks, "What if, reinventing anthropology, anthropologists were to study the colonizers rather than the colonized, the culture of power rather than the culture of the powerless, the culture of affluence rather than the culture of poverty?"[27] The widely recognized dimension of this argument is that by emphasizing the study of marginalized people, social scientists inadvertently made it easier to speak of marginality as a problem rather than identifying and focusing on the real problem of exploitation. By centering on the effects of exploitation, we are studying the symptom rather than the cause. We can also point to contemporary sympathizers with this perspective, whether it be Eve Tuck's powerful call to resist research (and researchers) more interested in demonstrating damage and brokenness in Indigenous communities than in holding the settler nation state to account, D'Ignazio and Klein's forceful rebuke of deficit narratives in feminist data science, or the range of researchers who are explicitly renewing interest in Nader's work.[28] But I'm drawn to Nader's argument for an additional reason.

> If anthropology were reinvented to study up, we would sooner or later need to study down as well. We aren't dealing with an either/or proposition; we need simply to realize when it is useful or crucial in terms of the problem to extend the domain of study up, down, or sideways.[29]

Extend the domain of study and do so from a perspective. The diagram implied by "up," "sideways," and "down" reminds us that the would-be inquirer into technical lands has a position, a perspective, and an orientation towards their object. To look up at something implies a change in the angle of the head, a change in the direction of the eyes, and an adjustment of their focal depth. I contend that, even as our eyes are drawn to sites around us, even as we attend to technical lands (and look down to their subsurfaces), we should not forget to hold technicians accountable for what their techniques produce.

Analysis: The Early Years," *Big Data & Society* 1, no. 1 (2014): 1–14, https://doi.org/10.1177/20539517 14535365; and John Cloud, "American Cartographic Transformations During the Cold War," *Cartography and Geographic Information Science* 29, no. 3 (2002): 261–82, https://doi.org/10.1559/15230400278 2008422.

24 Eric Robsky Huntley and Matthew Rosenblum, "The Omega Affair: Discontinuing the University of Michigan Department of Geography (1975–1982)," *Annals of the American Association of Geographers* 111, no. 2 (2021): 364–84, https://doi.org/10.10 80/24694452.2020.1760780.

25 Anna Tsing, "Inside the Economy of Appearances," *Public Culture* 12, no. 1 (2000): 115–44, https://doi.org/10.1215/08992363-12-1-115. See also Christopher Alton, Zulaikha Ayub, and Eric Robsky Huntley, "Conjuring the Planetary Mine: Counter-Mapping the Heart of Extractive Capital," *Thresholds* 50, forthcoming.

26 Jill Desimini and Charles Waldheim, *Cartographic Grounds: Projecting the Landscape Imaginary* (New York, NY: Princeton Architectural Press, 2016).

27 Laura Nader, "Up the Anthropologist: Perspectives Gained from Studying Up," *Reinventing Anthropology*, ed. Dell Hymes (New York, NY: Pantheon Books, 1972), 289.

28 Eve Tuck, "Suspending Damage: A Letter to Communities," *Harvard Educational Review* 79, no. 3 (2009): 409–28, https://doi.org/10.17763/haer.79.3.n0016675 661t3n15; Catherine D'Ignazio and Lauren F. Klein, *Data Feminism* (Cambridge, MA: MIT Press, 2020); Chelsea Barabas, Colin Doyle, J. B. Rubinovitz, and Karthik Dinakar, "Studying Up: Reorienting the Study of Algorithmic Fairness around Issues of Power," in *ACM Conference on Fairness, Accountability, and Transparency, January 27–30, 2020, Barcelona, Spain* (New York, NY: ACM, 2020), https://doi.org/10.1145/3351095.3372859; Luis L. M. Aguiar and Christopher J. Schneider, *Researching Amongst Elites: Challenges and Opportunities in Studying Up* (New York, NY: Routledge, 2016).

29 Nader, "Up the Anthropologist," 292.

Technical Lands

A Patent Perspective

Richard L Hindle

Patents and physical geography have paralleled each other for more than six centuries. The systems, modules, instruments, strategies, material processes, and devices disclosed in patents transform landscapes, construct sites, and are integrated into the everyday environment. Patent law, and the bureaucratic infrastructure that supports the global patent system, also have geographical dimensions through the management of sequential innovation, transfer of technology, and strategic initiatives at the intersection of innovation and environment. The agency of patent law and patented technology is particularly relevant today, as environmental systems and the infrastructure of urban landscapes become more technologically advanced, networked, logistical, and integrated, simultaneously expanding the disciplinary scope of environmental design and planning disciplines while challenging conventions of representation and praxis. This chapter explores the geographical dimension of patents, representations of technology and environment in patent documents, and the patent system's role in creating knowledge infrastructure and anticipatory governance for future planetary management. Together these interconnected themes and histories offer a critical reflection on the history of environmental innovation and a framework for designing technical lands.

Geographical Dimensions

In 2018 the European Patent Office launched the Y02A patent classification scheme to facilitate the diffusion, transfer, and implementation of "Technologies for Adaptation to Climate Change," covering the cross-sectoral innovations in coastal and riverine technology, flood control, mapping, sensing, human health, infrastructure, etc.[1] The 457,748 patents currently tagged in the Y02A classification suggest the emergence of a new stratum of environmental technology for adaptation to climate change—describing technical lands and their geographies ranging from sediment bypass systems and artificial reef datacenters to automated systems to map glacial retreat and farm arid regions.

fig 1

The special "Y02" designation was developed by the European Patent Office following the 2015 Paris Agreement to tag climate change mitigation technologies and develop a clearer picture of the capacities of existing and future technologies.[2] A subsequent report, "Invention and Global Diffusion of Technologies for Climate Change Adaptation: A Patent Analysis," published by the World Bank in 2020 notes that among the sectors experiencing rapid growth in the Y02A scheme, flood protection is experiencing the most growth "by far."[3] The notable uptick in patenting flood-mitigation technologies is not surprising as "natural" disasters often catalyze innovation. This trend will likely continue as climate change scenarios are further impacted by social-ecological-technical systems.[4]

The establishment of the Y02A classification scheme is not the first time the patent system was operationalized to help develop technologies with geographic, urban, and environmental dimensions. However, it may be the

[1] A summary of the Y02A classification scheme and information on related patents can be found at the European Patent Office's patent search website, https://worldwide.espacenet.com/patent/cpc-browser#!/CPC=Y02A.

[2] Stefano Angelucci, F Javier Hurtado-Albir, and Alessia Volpe, "Supporting Global Initiatives on Climate Change: The EPO's 'Y02-Y04S' Tagging Scheme," *World Patent Information* 54 (2018): 85–92.

[3] Antoine Dechezlepretre et al., "Invention and Global Diffusion of Technologies for Climate Change Adaptation," World Bank, 2020.

[4] Qing Miao and David Popp, "Necessity as the Mother of Invention: Innovative Responses to Natural Disasters," *Journal of Environmental Economics and Management* 68, no. 2 (2014): 280–95; Ariel E Lugo, "Effects of Extreme Disturbance Events: From Ecesis to Social–Ecological–Technological Systems," *Ecosystems* 23, no. 8 (2020): 1726–47.

US010524395B2

(12) **United States Patent**
Cutler et al.

(10) Patent No.: **US 10,524,395 B2**
(45) Date of Patent: **Dec. 31, 2019**

(54) **ARTIFICIAL REEF DATACENTER**

(71) Applicant: **Microsoft Technology Licensing, LLC,** Redmond, WA (US)

(72) Inventors: **Benjamin F. Cutler**, Seattle, WA (US); **Norman Ashton Whitaker**, Seattle, WA (US); **Spencer G. Fowers**, Duvall, WA (US); **Jeffrey Alex Kramer**, Redmond, WA (US)

(73) Assignee: **Microsoft Technology Licensing, LLC,** Redmond, WA (US)

(*) Notice: Subject to any disclaimer, the term of this patent is extended or adjusted under 35 U.S.C. 154(b) by 315 days.

(21) Appl. No.: **15/167,755**

(22) Filed: **May 27, 2016**

(65) **Prior Publication Data**
US 2016/0381835 A1 Dec. 29, 2016
US 2018/0352680 A9 Dec. 6, 2018

Related U.S. Application Data

(63) Continuation of application No. 14/752,669, filed on Jun. 26, 2015, now Pat. No. 9,801,313.
(Continued)

(51) **Int. Cl.**
H05K 7/20 (2006.01)
A01K 61/00 (2017.01)
(Continued)

(52) **U.S. Cl.**
CPC *H05K 7/20836* (2013.01); *A01K 29/005* (2013.01); *A01K 61/00* (2013.01); *F25D 1/02* (2013.01); *F28D 1/022* (2013.01); *F28D 15/00* (2013.01); *G06F 1/20* (2013.01); *G08B 13/2491* (2013.01); *H05K 7/2079* (2013.01);

H05K 7/20236 (2013.01); *H05K 7/20263* (2013.01); *H05K 7/20709* (2013.01);
(Continued)

(58) **Field of Classification Search**
CPC A01K 29/005; A01K 67/033; A01K 61/70; F28D 1/022
USPC 119/221, 219
See application file for complete search history.

(56) **References Cited**

U.S. PATENT DOCUMENTS

1,757,174 A 6/1930 Douglas
2,870,729 A 1/1959 Shannon et al.
(Continued)

FOREIGN PATENT DOCUMENTS

CN 0040651 A1 12/1981
CN 101048055 A 10/2007
(Continued)

OTHER PUBLICATIONS

Kramer, Dr. Sharon. "Final Technical Report: Evaluating the Potential for Marine and Hydrokinetic Devices to Act as Artificial Reefs or Fish Aggregating Devices." May 12, 2015.*
(Continued)

Primary Examiner — Magdalena Topolski
Assistant Examiner — Morgan T Barlow

(57) **ABSTRACT**

Examples of the disclosure provide for an apparatus for actively promoting marine life. The apparatus includes a datacenter implemented in a body of water and coupled to a network, a pressure vessel that houses the datacenter, and one or more components coupled to the pressure vessel and adapted to actively promote reef life and sustain a surrounding ecosystem.

20 Claims, 7 Drawing Sheets

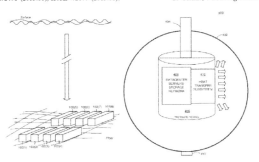

fig 1   US Patent 10,524,395, "Artificial Reef Datacenter," granted to Microsoft Technology Licensing, LLC, on December 31, 2019. United States Patent and Trademark Office

first with a planetary scope. In 1421 the Florentine government issued the first actual patent to the eminent architect Filippo Brunelleschi for a ship designed to move heavy materials on the River Arno to construct the Duomo of Florence, helping to solve one of three engineering challenges associated with the building project and establishing a legal precedent for the "patent bargain" between inventors and the state.[5] Fifty-three years later, the Venetian State formalized patent law with the Venetian Patent Statute of 1474, codifying the patent bargain to incentivize the sharing of new inventions in exchange for protection of intellectual property within Venetian territories.

Venetian patent rights were highly sought after, catalyzing innovation among Venetian citizens and the transfer of foreign technological know-how to the lagoon city. The effects of the patent statute were widely realized, leading to innovations in the broader economy, territorial development, and advances in urban and environmental infrastructure. This included "mud" technologies used for ground stabilization, reclamation, drainage, and dredging.[6] Perhaps the grandest and most conspicuous features of the urban landscape resulting from this process are the canals of Venice, built-in part with innovative technology developed in partnership with private inventors through the granting of patent rights.[7] The operationalization of the patent system in public works meant that innovative technologies could be tried and tested as Venice urbanized the lagoon, revealing the distinct agency of the patent system in the production of technical lands, and situating environmental innovations in a specific location with a "distinctly local and immediate notion of utility"[8]

As a political act, the Venetian patent statute decoupled invention from privilege, class, and guilds, liberating inventor and democratized ingenuity to allow broad constituencies to engage the processes of innovation as anyone could be granted a patent for their invention. According to Mario Biagioli, a leading scholar of law, science, and technology, this paralleled "the demise of political absolutism, the development of liberal economies, and the emergence of the modern political subject."[9] These ideas spread through Europe and the Americas were later constitutionalized. Some legal scholars even argue that all patent law is only an amendment to the original Venetian patent statute.[10] The conflation of invention and democratic principles gives modern patent rights hybrid vigor—leading to their universal adoption in early Western legal traditions. As Buckminster Fuller states of this historical development, "The necessity of invention and growth were highly apparent to the budding democracies, for had not invention itself forwarded [hu]man to the possibility of emergent DEMOCRACY?"[11] This political sentiment echoed in his Guinea Pig B design experiments and twenty-eight patented inventions.[12]

In the United States, patents and the patent system were again intertwined with nation-building, statecraft, territorialization, and physical geography. Prior to the American Revolution, patents and monopolies for manufacturing issued in the American colonies mirrored pieces of European, and more commonly English, patent law. They were, therefore, dependent on

[5] Frank D. Prager, "Brunelleschi's Patent," *J. Pat. Off. Soc'y* 28 (1946): 109.

[6] Salvatore Ciriacono, *Building on Water: Venice, Holland and the Construction of the European Landscape in Early Modern Times* (New York, NY: Berghahn Books, 2006).

[7] Roberto Berveglieri, *Le Vie Di Venezia: Canali Lagunari e Rii a Venezia: Inventori, Brevetti, Tecnologia e Legislazione Nei Secoli XIII–XVIII* (Cierre, 1999).

[8] Mario Biagioli, "Patent Republic: Representing Inventions, Constructing Rights and Authors," *Social Research* (2006): 1129–72.

[9] Biagioli, "Patent Republic."

[10] Craig Allen Nard and Andrew P. Morriss, "Constitutionalizing Patents: From Venice to Philadelphia," *Review of Law and Economics* 2, no. 2 (2006): 223–321.

[11] Richard Buckminster Fuller, *Nine Chains to the Moon* (London: Feffer & Simons, 1938).

[12] Richard Buckminster Fuller, *Inventions: The Patented Works of Buckminster Fuller* (New York, NY: St. Martins Press, 1983).

[13] P. J. Federico, "Colonial Monopolies and Patents," *J. Pat. Off. Soc'y* 11 (1929): 358.

[14] Edward C. Walterscheid, "Charting a Novel Course: The Creation of the Patent Act of 1790," *AIPLA QJ 25* (1997): 445.

[15] Karl Raitz, "Making Connections via Roads, Rivers, Canals, and Rails," *North American Odyssey: Historical Geographies for the Twenty-First Century*, eds. Colten and Buckley (Lanham, MD: Rowman & Littlefield, 2014), 117; United States et al., *Report of the Secretary of the Treasury on the Subject of Public Roads and Canals Made in Pursuance of a Resolution of Senate of March 2, 1807* (Washington, DC: Printed by R.C. Weightman, 1808).

[16] Henry Barrett Learned, "The Establishment of the Secretaryship of the Interior," *The American Historical Review* 16, no. 4 (1911): 751–73.

[17] United States Congress, "State Papers on the Patent Office and Arguments for Creation of a Home Department," *American State Papers: Documents, Legislative and Executive, of the Congress of the United States* (Washington, DC: Gales and Seaton, 1834), 187–91, https://books. google.com/books?id=MhV-FAQAAMAAJ.

[18] R. N. L. Andrews, *Managing the Environment, Managing Ourselves: A History of American Environmental Policy* (New Haven, CT: Yale University Press, 1999), https://books.google.com/books?id=yxzcMhK9HdYC.

European institutions for enforcement.[13] American independence necessitated the creation of a new patent system, helping to chart an independent technological trajectory in the United States premised on political sovereignty. Article 1, Section 8, Clause 8 of the US Constitution gives Congress the power "to promote the progress of science and useful arts by securing for limited times to authors and inventors the exclusive right to their respective writings and discoveries." The establishment of patent rights was codified within the newly formed government, charting a liberal, egalitarian approach to invention.[14] Arguably, the new patent system was so integral to the American domestic agenda that it served as the foundation for technologies that would define the colonies and western territories as infrastructural space. Pieces of this early history can be found throughout the patent archive and across the American landscape, from boundary fences demarcating homesteads to Gallatin's infrastructure plan (1807) that envisioned interstate transit and trade using canals and newly invented steamships.[15]

The interconnection between patent innovation and nation-building is also evident in the organizational structure of the Patent Office itself. From 1790 to 1849, the Patent Office was operated by the Department of State. At the time, the Department of State was primarily concerned with domestic affairs and development, including managing innovation. The increasing rate of patent submissions and an explosion of domestic concerns overwhelmed the State Department and led to the creation of the Department of Interior in 1849. Congress first considered creating a "Home Department" in the early decades of the nineteenth century to alleviate Patent Office caseloads from the Department of State's ever-expanding portfolio.[16] Arguments supporting the restructuring were elaborate, but in essence, reflected the sentiment that innovation was integral to nation-building. A congressional report supporting the Patent Office's relocation states, "Progress of the arts of civilization keep pace with each other; the arts are favorable to civil liberty; they alone give rise to internal improvements; and that nation is of all others the most certain of prosperity by which these principles are well understood and put into practice."[17] The Department of Interior was eventually formed through a strategic reorganization of the USPTO, General Land Office, Census Bureau, and Bureau of Indian Affairs and charged with managing domestic affairs, including wilderness areas and new US territories. The combined interests of the Department of Interior made it the de facto department of the West, playing a vital role in the expansion and development of western states. Richard Andrews, an environmental policy scholar, has argued that in an ideal world, the integration of interior, patent, land, and census departments might have provided the "foundation for integrated planning and management of the nation's environment."[18]

Inclusion of the Patent Office within the Department of Interior was strategic, following a track record of progress in infrastructure and innovation internal improvements. The Patent Office's early role in managing sequential innovation in these sectors is documented in Class 9 of the patent classification scheme (1790–1847) related to inventions of "Civil engineering and architecture, comprising works on rail and common roads, bridges, canals, wharves, docks, rivers, dams, and other internal improvements, buildings, roofs, etc.," which chronicles core infrastructure of a developing nation as well as technologies employed in environmental transformation.[19] Notable examples include the Superintendent of Western River Improvements, Henry Shreve's patented snag boat "Heliopolis," which was used to open the Mississippi River to shipping and Oliver Evans' steam engine used to power *Oruktor Ampihibolos* (amphibious digger), which was driven around the streets of Philadelphia before diving into the Schuykill River where it aimed to clear sandbars and build docks, thereby timestamping the advent of the world's first amphibious vehicle.[20]

The agency of the patent system and incentives of patent rights in infrastructure delivery was clear and sometimes utilized by the US Congress to procure, test, and prototype innovative urban and environmental technologies. For example, in 1821, Congress waived the residency requirement to grant Englishman Thomas Oxley a patent for his "American Land Clearing Engine," which promised to hasten development. In 1844, while pondering interstate communications, Congress passed acts to construct an experimental telegraph line from Washington to Baltimore following Samuel Morse's patent. Similarly, in 1845, Congress approved the creation of a panel of experts to test an experimental dredge machine, patented by J. R. Putnam for the removal of sandbars at the mouth of the Mississippi River.[21] And, in 1847, James Crutchett was commissioned to prototype and test his experimental gaslight in the US Capitol, proving the viability of artificial lighting in the urban landscape.[22]

The US Patent Office was also actively engaged in geographical, atmospheric, and technological initiatives. The first meteorological studies in the United States were commissioned jointly by the Patent Office and Smithsonian Institute in 1855, helping to promote advances in agricultural technology and the science of climate.[23] The data, standards, and instrumentation developed by the Smithsonian Institute during this venture led to creating the formal national weather system known as the Signal Service (1870–1891).[24] The Patent Office's involvement in this meteorological research venture was also fruitful, building upon a track record of agricultural innovation that eventually led to the creation of an independent Department of Agriculture in 1862 and the publication of pioneering works of agrometeorology such as "Meteorology and its Connection with Agriculture" in 1857.[25] The US Patent Office began collecting agricultural germplasm in the early nineteenth century, distributing the seeds, along with knowledge of agricultural innovations, essentially defining the future role of the Department of Agriculture.[26] In this expanded role, we see a patent office broadly concerned with the technology and data that would transform western states into a vast agricultural territory. During these early days of discovery, the Patent Office also served as the National Botanical Garden (c. 1942), storing and accessioning the botanical findings of Charles Wilkes's voyage to the Pacific West Coast of the American continent. In a subsequent exhibition, the

[19] United States Patent Office, *List of Patents for Inventions and Designs: Issued by the United States, from 1790 to 1847, with the Patent Laws and Notes of Decisions of the Courts of the United States for the Same Period* (Printed by J. & G. S. Gideon, 1847), https://books.google.com/books?id=oHq0AAAAMAAJ; Heather J. E. Simmons, "Categorizing the Useful Arts: Part, Present, and Future Development of Patent Classification in the United States," *Law Libr. J.* 106 (2014): 564.

[20] Edith S. McCall, *Conquering the Rivers: Henry Miller Shreve and the Navigation of America's Inland Waterways* (Baton Rouge: Louisiana State University Press, 1984).

[21] James R. Putnam, *J. R. Putnam's Plan for Removing Bars at the Mouth of the Mississippi River and Other Harbors on the American Coast and Interior. With a Full Description of His Patent Ploughing and Dredging Machine, Invented by Him for That Purpose, with Drawings, Etc.* (New Orleans: Bulletin Office, 1841).

[22] John B. Miller, *Principles of Public and Private Infrastructure Delivery* (New York, NY: Springer US, 2013).

[23] United States Patent Office, Bishop, William D., Henry, Joseph, Hough, Franklin B., Coffin, James H., Smithsonian Institution., *Results of Meteorological Observations, Made Under the Direction of the United States Patent Office and the Smithsonian Institution from the Year 1854 to 1859, Inclusive, Being a Report of the Commissioner of Patents Made at the First Session of the Thirty-Sixth Congress, Vol. I–II: Pt. 1* (Washington, DC: US Government Printing Office, 1861).

[24] Joseph M. Hawes, "The Signal Corps and Its Weather Service, 1870–1890," *Military Affairs* 30, no. 2 (Summer 1966): 68–76.

[25] Joseph Henry, *Meteorology in Its Connection with Agriculture* (Washington, DC, 1857), 455–492, 419–|552; 461|–524 incl. diagrs., illus. tables, //catalog.hathitrust.org/Record/012307539.

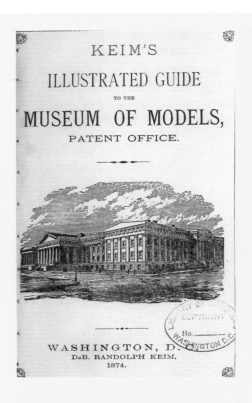

fig 2   Keim, De B. R. *Keim's Illustrated Guide of the Museum of Models, Patent Office* (Washington, DC: Be B. R. Keim, 1874). Library of Congress

Patent Office symbolically displayed discoveries from the nation's distant and prospective territories right alongside the Declaration of Independence, George Washington's War Tent, and a trove of other patent models and drawings.[27] By 1925, the Patent Office found its permanent administrative home in the US Department of Commerce (where it remains), signaling a shift in the organizational structure and the economy.

The frontiers of climate change and planetary urbanization will necessitate the geographical dimensions of patented technology. Collectively, the global patent system will remain integral to the invention of adaptation technologies and the production of future technical lands. In response to this global imperative, the YO2A classification scheme was created by the European Patent Office to leverage sociotechnical aspects of inventions and increase the pace of diffusion. We see elements of a Venetian model for environmental innovation revised through six centuries of precedent incentivizing innovation, building knowledge infrastructure, and serving as an anticipatory form of governance. Notably, the patent documents tagged by the YO2A scheme disclose technologies with the capacity to construct, construe, and manipulate the environment across scales and geographies in response to the wicked problem of climate adaptation—foreshadowing the emergence of new strata of innovation.

fig 2

Invention, Representation, and Environmental Imaginaries

This technological stratum's invention, representation, diffusion, and implementation have environmental, urban, and social implications. A patent is, in essence, a textualized and visualized representation of an invention, operating simultaneously as a legal document disclosing the nature of an invention and projection of a future potentiality. Of course, the invention process is more than representational and requires research and development of specific novel technologies. But in the context of patent law, the boundary line between invention and representation is sometimes opaque, enabling the projection of future technologies and environmental imaginaries without the invention being realized (that is, reduced to practice). This peculiarity creates a significant epistemological loophole in the inventive process, simultaneously facilitating the projection and disclosure of leading technology and exploitation through misrepresentation and fallacy. Irrespective of the tension between fact and fiction, the representation of technology in patent documents is integral to managing sequential innovation and the disclosure of new inventions. This is fascinating to ponder as we approach and project a future in which natural and cultural systems are more integrated, networked, sustainable, and technologically advanced.

Modern representational standards for patents originated in the United States and later France in the latter part of the eighteenth century.[28] The US Patent Act of 1790 states that grantees shall deliver to the Secretary of State, Secretary of War, and Attorney General "a specification in writing, containing a description, accompanied with drafts or models, and explanations and models (if the nature of the invention or discovery will admit of a model) of

[26] Alfred Charles True, *A History of Agricultural Experimentation and Research in the United States 1607–1925 Including a History of the United States Department of Agriculture* (Washington, DC: US Government Printing Office, 1937).

[27] Henry, *Meteorology in Its Connections;* United States Patent Office, et al., *Results of Meteorological Observations.*

[28] Biagioli, "Patent Republic: Representing Inventions, Constructing Rights and Authors."

29 US Government, "United States Patent Act" (1790).

30 Timothy Lee Wherry, "Patents in the New World," *Science & Technology Libraries* 17, no. 3–4 (1999): 217–22.

31 Teresa Riordan, "Patents," *New York Times*, February 18, 2002.

32 William Rankin, "The 'Person Skilled in the Art' Is Really Quite Conventional: US Patent Drawings and the Persona of the Inventor, 1870–2005," *Making and Unmaking Intellectual Property: Creative Production in Legal and Cultural Perspective*, eds., Mario Biagioli and Peter Jaszi (Chicago, IL: University of Chicago Press, 2015).

33 Richard Hindle, "Prototyping the Mississippi Delta: Patents, Alternative Futures, and the Design of Complex Environmental Systems," *Journal of Landscape Architecture* 12, no. 2 (n.d.): 32–47, https://doi.org/10.1080/1862 6033.2017.1361084.

the thing or things, by him or them, invented or discovered."[29] If the invention was found to be new and valuable by the cabinet secretaries and the Attorney General, the patent was granted and signed, bearing the "teste" (witness) of the President. In that manner, the government and inventors coevolved the technological substrate of "the arts" towards unforeseen ends through future projections and representation of innovative technology—a process so integral to the founding of the country that Thomas Jefferson, the first Secretary of State and Patent Commissioner, is rumored to have slept with newly submitted patents in special boxes under his bed.[30] Through time, models and drawings of new inventions curated by the Patent Office amassed. By 1870 the Patent Office, designed by the architect Robert Mills and situated between the Capitol Building and the White House in L'Enfant's plan, was the busiest tourist destination in Washington, DC, surpassing the Washington Monument and the White House, effectively consolidating a grand tour of American innovation in a single location.[31]

fig 3a, 3b, 3c

Fusion between representation and invention unlocked ingenuity and hastened the rate of patent submissions, allowing American inventors to project forward a new technological sublime designed for the new nation. Critics argue that drawings of patented technology using patent conventions of plan, section, axonometric, diagram, data, and text determine the types of technology that can be invented, leading to a kind of banal standardization.[32] Yet, patent drawings and the inventions they represent do have the capacity to construct, construe, and transform the environment across scales and geographical contexts. Take, for example, attempts to build permanent navigable channels at the southwest pass of the Mississippi River. Three distinct technological scenarios were developed and patented by leading engineers, with two leading prototypes in other locations.[33] We know of these proposals through archives at the US Patent Office, documentation in *Scientific American*, their inclusion in Acts of Congress, and through the impact once implemented on the geomorphology of the Mississippi's bird-foot delta. The site-specificity of these inventions dissolves the boundary between technology and environment, simultaneously designating the delta as technical through the patent's representational standards and leveraging the patent system's bureaucratic procedures in service of environmental transformation.

fig 4

Other environmental imaginaries exist in patents, ranging from early biomorphic coastal structures and vegetated facades to oyster architecture and polyfunctional flood infrastructure strategies. Like other patents, these environmental technologies are disclosed using requisite representational standards to describe the nature of the module, typological configuration, material assembly, logistics, and processes. Interestingly, some environmental patents also include uncommon modes of technological representation, including perspectival and cartographic drawing types that position an invention in a place, space, and context. Although the inclusion of perspectives, maps, and other spatial drawing types is by no means universal, they do help situate an invention in context, revealing the instrumentality and effect of the proposed technology. Briefly consider a recent patent by Keith Van de Riet, Jason Vollen, and Anna Dyson known as a "Method and apparatus for coastline remediation, energy generation, and vegetation support."[34] The patent drawings include technical specifications and models, with mappings that show the ecological extents of the invention. Spatial context is also provided through perspectival images, such as in Stanley Hart White's patent for a "Vegetation Bearing Architectonic Structure and System."[35]

fig 5a, 5b

The history of perspectival representation of patented technology can be traced back to Venice through the work of Cornelius Meijer. He arrived in Venice from the Netherlands in 1674, bringing news of a mighty chain dredger. He received a patent in 1675 and the title of engineer in exchange for his knowledge and drawings of the new method. Historians note that a similar chain dredger was invented in Holland decades earlier, but the technology was new to Venice, and the patent was granted.[36] A drawing of the technique and machinery used reveals a system of massive scrapers tethered to ships designed to scour the bottom of a water body. Meijer is noteworthy in the history of science and technology, not just for inventions but also for his drawings of technology, many of which use the representational technique of perspective to site distinct environmental technologies.[37] In the broader history of science and technology, this situates Meijer among greats such as Alexander Von Humbolt and Leonardo Da Vinci, who validated their discoveries "not only with trustworthy eyewitnesses and elaborate verbal descriptions, but precise, lifelike, and attractive visual representations" that could represent their "newly discovered worlds convincingly to those who were not there."[38] In this context, Alexander Von Humbolt's theory of plant biogeography is particularly relevant as the geologic cross-sections and cataloging of the biological world were fundamental, validating the theoretical premise through the visual representation of plants situated in specific locales and climatic zones.

fig 6

Cartographic modes of representation are another technique used in environmental patents to situate an invention. The direct correlation between the configuration and function of a novel invention and a specific location, landscape, or environmental condition is atypical. However, a unique subset of patents includes texts and images that suggest site-specificity within intellectual property claims, collapsing the boundary between technology and geography. The potentiality of these technical lands creates a unique hybrid in which an invention is associated with a site, giving the proposed technology scale, scope, and context while simultaneously instrumentalizing the landscape. Early examples include proposals for the removal of ice from New York Harbor and the East River; a passive dredge system for Galveston Bay; and a hydroelectric plant for Niagara Falls that

[34] Keith Van de Riet, Jason Vollen, and Anna Dyson, "Method and Apparatus for Coastline Remediation, Energy Generation, and Vegetation Support," US8511936, 2013.

[35] Stanley Hart White, "Vegetation-Bearing Architectonic Structure and System," US2113523, 1938.

[36] Karel Davids, *The Rise and Decline of Dutch Technological Leadership: Technology, Economy and Culture in the Netherlands, 1350–1800*, vol. 2 (Boston: Brill, 2008), 288.

[37] Cornelis Meijer, *L'arte di restituire à Roma la tralasciata navigatione del suo tevere* (Rome: Nella Stamperia del Lazzari Varese, 1685).

[38] Klaas van Berkel "Cornelius Meijer Inventor et Fecit': On the Representation of Science in Late Seventeenth-Century Rome," in *Merchants and Marvels: Commerce, Science, and Art in Early Modern Europe*, eds. Pamela Smith and Paula Findlen (London: Routledge 2002), 277.

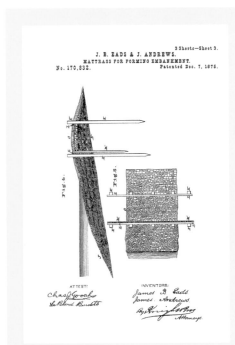

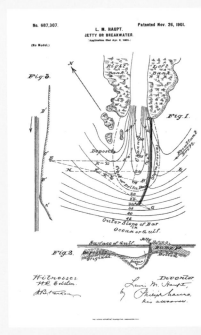

fig 3   J. B. Eads and J. Andrews, "Mattrass for Forming Embankment," US 170,832; Lewis M. Haupt, "Jetty of Breakwater," US 687,307; and Juan Bautista Medici, "System for Formation of Permanent Channels in Navigable Rivers," US 658,795.
United States Patent and Trademark Office

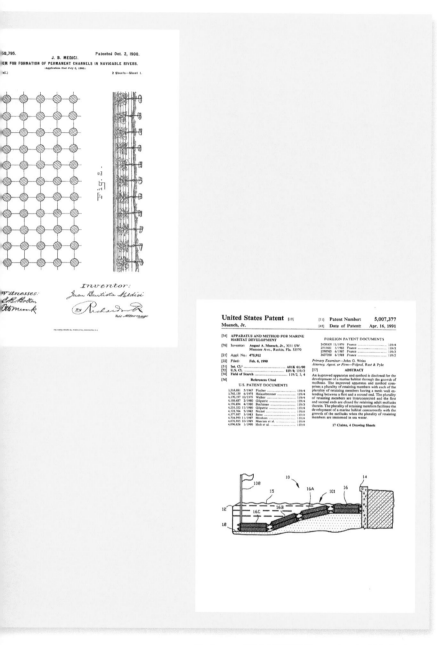

fig 4   US 5,007,377, "Apparatus And Method
For Marine Habitat Development," granted to
August A. Muench Jr. on April 16, 1991. United States
Patent and Trademark Office

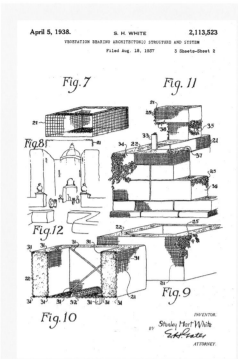

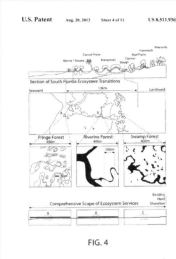

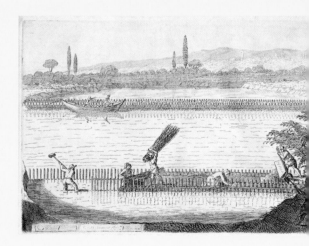

fig 5   Stanley Hart White, "Vegetation bearing architectonic structure and system," US 211,523; Keith Van de Riet, Jason Vollen, and Anna Dyson, "Method and apparatus for coastline remediation, energy generation, and vegetation support," US 8,511,936B2. United States Patent and Trademark Office

fig 6   Cornelius Meijer's perspectiv are significant in the history of science a were often used by the inventor to situat new technologies within an environ. In Me *restituire* (Rome: Nella Stamperia del Lazzari Va Getty Images

preserves scenery and produces power.[39] Following this line of inquiry, the relationship between patented technology and cartography is further confounded by the existence of cartographic devices and methods disclosed in patents that also contain mappings. Prime examples of this are the Dymaxion map and mapping system patented as "Cartography" by Buckminster Fuller and the more recent patent for "Glacial Geomorphic Mapping" by Andreas Laake.

fig 7

Of course, the relationship between patented technology and cartography is more than a representational anomaly or rhetoric. Patents for cartographic inventions span centuries and include technological domains ranging from printing and folding large maps to surveying equipment and global positioning systems.[40] Today the most rapid growth in cartographic technology is in systems that support autonomous vehicles or those integrated with smartphones. However, early warning technology for natural disasters is also in rapid development. Technologies tied to weather forecasting, the mapping of climate change scenarios, remote sensing, and environmental imaging are organized by the Y02A 90/10 patent subclass for innovations that indirectly contribute to climate adaptation and resilience.

fig 8a, 8b

Environmental Knowledge, Infrastructure, and Anticipatory Governance

Patent documents have been archived for six centuries globally and provide a valuable dossier of technological knowledge in every sector of the known *technosphere*—existing simultaneously as a robust form of knowledge infrastructure and a framework for anticipatory governance.[41] The global patent archive now contains approximately 110 million searchable documents. The primary function of this vast repository is the bureaucratic management of sequential innovation in support of legal rights for inventors. But the patent archive also provides deep insights about contemporary inventions, past discoveries, and future trends through its capacity of search, metadata, citation networks, language translation, image, and ever-evolving classification systems that organize extents of human ingenuity disclosed in patents. As a form of knowledge infrastructure, the archiving of patents facilitates discovery and provides information that may be utilized and translated in legal, technical, and non-technical domains alike. As a form of anticipatory governance, the patent system helps predict future trends and gain insights regarding technological trajectories. These core functions of the patent system are integral to the invention and diffusion of environmental technology, including the emerging sectors such as climate adaptation and resilience covered by the Y02A classification scheme and the technical lands they represent.

Paul Edwards defines knowledge infrastructure as "robust networks of people, artifacts, and institutions that generate, share, and maintain specific knowledge about the human and natural worlds."[42] In essence, knowledge infrastructures are complex networks of information intertwined

[39] Peter Voorhis, "Improved method of obstructing ice in rivers and harbors", US63968, 1867; Daniel Spangler, "Submarine wall", US325127, 1885; Christian Zeitinger, "Device for utilizing the water-power of falls", US442000, 1890.

[40] Mark Monmonier, "Patents and Cartographic Inventions: A New Perspective for Map History," 2017, http://public.ebookcentral. proquest.com/choice/public-fullrecord.aspx?p=4832532.

[41] *Technosphere* refers to the technological component of earth systems created by humans, comprising "our complex social structures together with the physical infrastructure and technological artifacts supporting energy, information, and material flows that enable the system to work." For an expanded discussion and additional references, see Jan Zalasiewicz et al., "Scale and Diversity of the Physical Technosphere: A Geological Perspective," *The Anthropocene Review* 4.1 (2017): 9–22.

[42] Paul N. Edwards, *A Vast Machine: Computer Models, Climate Data, and the Politics of Global Warming* (Cambridge, MA: MIT Press, 2010).

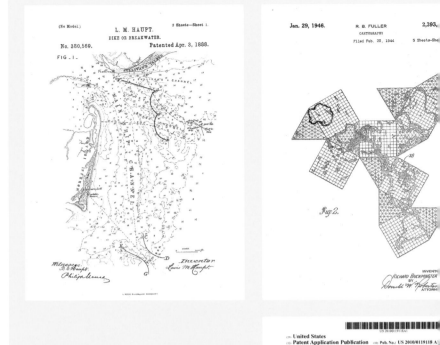

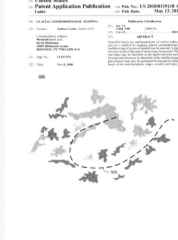

fig 7   Patent for "Dike or Breakwater (US 380,569, April 3, 1888) by Lewis M. Haupt uses precise bathymetry and technical specifications to describe a self-dredging "reaction" breakwater system. United States Patent and Trademark Office

fig 8   Dymaxion Map, patent for "Ca phy" (US 2,393,676, January 29, 1946) by minster Fuller; "Glacial geomorphic mapp 8,280,116B2) by Andreas Laake. United Sta and Trademark Office

with social, technical, and environmental systems and therefore have radical implications for the way society perceives and manages the world. As methods of the Anthropocene, knowledge infrastructures are also linked to planetary processes. Through the evolution of the technosphere, they can contribute to "large-scale, long-term, anthropogenic environmental change," making them essential for future planetary management.[43] The global patent archive exists as one such form of knowledge infrastructure built on the disclosure and representation of new technology by inventors, and the management, archiving, and legal protection of sequential innovation by government institutions—a process complicit in the creation of the extractive economies of the past but also the networked, resilient, and adaptive ecologies of today.

The word "infrastructure" implies that these knowledge systems serve as substructures supporting other systems and are enmeshed with society, economy, energy, material use, politics, and the management of a complex environment. Climate change data, for example, reveals the ongoing relationship between the technologies used to map and model the environment and our understanding of a changing planet. The interrelation of data, technology, science, and society represents the "climate knowledge infrastructure" that shapes our environmental management. Similarly, in the allied fields of environmental design, planning, and engineering, geographical knowledge infrastructure is essential and widely integrated with research and praxis. Geographical knowledge infrastructure, such as geographical information systems (GIS), spatializes data and is also the necessary infrastructure for building smart cities and territorial intelligence, etc.[44] These dynamics operate at multiple scales, from the individual actor/organization to vast territorial networks.[45]

The global patent system is a knowledge infrastructure created to stimulate innovation. The system's core capacities of archiving, searching, categorizing, and citing also serve as an infrastructure that supports other uses.[46] As a form of innovation-knowledge infrastructure, the patent archive is essential in tracking progress in technical fields. It chronicles developments and establishes a precedent of prior art, archiving specifications, claims, and drawings while providing metadata for research, interpretation, and discovery. Beyond merely describing a particular invention, a patent is theorized to serve as a "carrier" of innovation, leaving "footprints" for the development of new technology through a combinatory process that evolves through knowledge of prior inventions in a specific sector.[47] In emergent sectors such as climate adaptation and resilience, this combinatory process is precious.

A general theory of invention suggests that searching is the essential framework for discovery, often involving the iterative and recursive stages of stimulus, net casting, categorization, linking, and discovery.[48] It is hypothesized that in the process of searching, inventors gather information inside and outside of their domains to create mental schemas to link ideas, build context, and make discoveries. As Eugene Furgeson argues in "Engineering

[43] Paul N. Edwards, "Knowledge Infrastructures for the Anthropocene," *The Anthropocene Review* 4, no. 1 (2017): 34–43.

[44] Robert Laurini, *Geographic Knowledge Infrastructure: Applications to Territorial Intelligence and Smart Cities* (Amsterdam: Elsevier, 2017).

[45] Frank Moulaert and Abdelillah Hamdouch, "New Views of Innovation Systems: Agents, Rationales, Networks and Spatial Scales in the Knowledge Infrastructure," *Innovation: The European Journal of Social Science Research* 19, no. 1 (2006): 11–24.

[46] Yo Takagi, "WIPO's New Strategies on Global Intellectual Property Infrastructure," *World Patent Information* 32, no. 3 (2010): 221–28.

[47] Hyejin Youn et al., "Invention as a Combinatorial Process: Evidence from US Patents," *Journal of the Royal Society Interface* 12, no. 106 (May 2015).

[48] Patrick G. Maggitti, Ken G. Smith, and Riitta Katila, "The Complex Search Process of Invention," *Research Policy* 42, no. 1 (2013): 90–100.

US 20100252648A1

(19) **United States**
(12) **Patent Application Publication**   (10) Pub. No.: **US 2010/0252648 A1**
    Robinson   (43) **Pub. Date:**   **Oct. 7, 2010**

(54) **CLIMATE PROCESSOR**

(76) Inventor: **Nicholas Paul Robinson**,
                   Cottingham (GB)

    Correspondence Address:
    Nicholas Paul Robinson
    17 West End Road
    Cottingham, E. Yorkshire HU16 5PL. (GB)

(21) Appl. No.:   **12/698,848**

(22) Filed: **Feb. 2, 2010**

(30)   **Foreign Application Priority Data**

    Aug. 21, 2007   (GB) 0716285
    Oct. 17, 2007   (GB) 0720463
    Feb. 19, 2008   (GB) 0802955
    Aug. 20, 2008   (GB) .... 2 452 152 A

Publication Classification

(51) Int. Cl.
    A01G 15/00   (2006.01)
(52) U.S. Cl. 239/14.1

(57)   **ABSTRACT**

A climate processor having virtual estuaries which enable large strips of land to act like real water estuaries thereby providing a means of climate control overhead. Said estuaries are also used to prevent polar isotherm migration, melting ice shelves, vortical storm formation and migration from lateral coastal airflow. Said estuaries are formed between two parallel-laid thermal belts formed from artificial surface whitening and jet contrails. The surface whitening can be laid down as a foam or gel and deployed overhead as a high level aviation propellant. The belts may be applied daily and dissipate as the day progresses and subsequently warms. Commercial aircraft flights may be readjusted based on the placement of the artificial estuaries. Also claimed are an aerial deployment system for the foam, a high-level aviation propellant system, a carbon trading system for commercial airlines, a "Russian Doll" gas mixing device and a range of suitable foams.

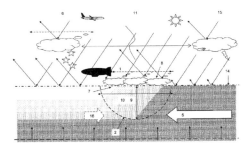

fig 9   The "Climate Processor" (US Patent Application 20100252648A1) by Nicholas Paul Robinson archives, categorizes, cites, and publishes the invention helping to map and organize the extents of the technosphere. United States Patent and Trademark Office

and the Mind's Eye," this complex process involves not only the interpretation of data, text, and equations but also the visual communication of ideas from which new ideas and technologies can be developed. Furgeson points out that Edison's automatic-printing telegraph was simultaneously an invention and a drawing, each integral to the communication of his idea and the establishment of a new sector.[49] Because the allied fields of environmental design and planning address broad questions of climate adaptation and resilience, a vast visual and technical repository exists within the patent archive for the technologies to structure, build, sense, and design adaptive and resilient landscape systems. This knowledge infrastructure can serve both heuristically to help problem-solve and as a technological database to develop frameworks for innovation. For example, during the 2017 Resilience by Design Bay Area Challenge, the Common Ground Team coupled patent-innovation studies with a heuristic process to develop innovative strategies for coastal resilience. Each landscape condition was linked to an innovation citation network of patented technologies that might structure the site. In certain instances, specific site assemblies were suggested and integrated into the design, showing how each technology would impact the site and future scenarios for the region. The team adapted existing technologies to the design framework and then made informed suggestions for future needs based on these innovation studies. This led to novel design strategies at the site-detail and regional scales while linking geographical contingencies to a technological dossier.[50]

Anticipation of the future has become a common theme in governance, especially in the context of science and development of sociotechnical fields dependent on anticipatory copractices between inventors, intuitions, and broader societal assemblages.[51] Theorists claim that in an ideal world,

[anticipatory governance] would register and track events that are barely visible at the horizon; it would self-organize to deal with the unexpected and the discontinuous; and it would adjust rapidly to the interactions between our policies and our problems. In anticipatory governance, systems would be designed to handle multiple streams of information and events whose interactions are complex rather than linear.[52]

Beyond the technological, anticipatory governance is integral to social-ecological resilience and suggests that effective management of this process can increase ecological knowledge.[53]

A central tenant of anticipatory governance is the recognition of values associated with emergent technologies and their role in society in sectors ranging in scale from nanotechnology to geoengineering.[54] Foresight is integral to anticipatory governance as institutions establish future trajectories for investment and innovation.[55] Technological innovation and patent trends offer distinct insights about future environmental scenarios while simultaneously revealing the patent system's role of adaptive governance

[49] Eugene S. Ferguson, *Engineering and the Mind's Eye* (Cambridge, MA: MIT Press, 1993).

[50] "Common Ground_The Grand Bayway_Final_Design_Roadmap.Pdf – Google Drive," accessed April 4, 2019, https://drive.google.com/file/d/1rigcTd_IHx-0WnCvKeJCqtTJmtfsbr2ci/view.

[51] Carla Alvial-Palavicino, "The Future as Practice: A Framework to Understand Anticipation in Science and Technology," *TECNO-SCIENZA: Italian Journal of Science & Technology Studies* 6, no. 2 (2016): 135–72.

[52] Leon Fuerth, "Operationalizing Anticipatory Governance," *Prism* 2, no. 4 (2011): 31–46.

[53] Emily Boyd et al., "Anticipatory Governance for Social-Ecological Resilience," *Ambio* 44, no. 1 (2015): 149–61.

[54] Risto Karinen and David H. Guston, "Toward Anticipatory Governance: The Experience with Nanotechnology," *Governing Future Technologies* (Heidelberg: Springer, 2009), 217–32; Rider W. Foley, D. Guston, and Daniel Sarewitz, "Towards the Anticipatory Governance of Geoengineering," *Geoengineering Our Climate*, 2015.

[55] Jose M. Ramos, "Anticipatory Governance: Traditions and Trajectories for Strategic Design," *Journal of Futures Studies* 19, no. 1 (2014): 35–52.

and new knowledge infrastructures. Knowledge and anticipation of these trajectories have planetary implications, as evident in evolving discourse and debate on geoengineering. Few laws or government entities are in place in the emerging geoengineering sector to manage developments given the extraterritorial nature of the proposals and global impact, making foresight of future trends imperative. According to a recent paper on the subject, "in the absence of a governance framework for climate engineering technologies such as solar radiation management (SRM), the practices of scientific research and intellectual property acquisition can de facto shape the development of the field."[56] In this speculative technological space, new frameworks for patent law are also being proposed, including patent pools that ensure the free use and diffusion of technologies to "save the planet."[57] Irrespective of the validity of existing geoengineering technology, it is interesting to take note, just in case these projections of future climate solutions take shape.

fig 9

Conclusion

Leveraging the distinct agency of patented technology and the patent system offers one strategy for the invention and production of technical lands, engaging broad sociotechnical processes and bureaucratic infrastructure in the transformation of sites and geographies. The systems, modules, machines, sensors, materials, and maps that will be invented have significant implications for future planetary management through their integration with urban sites and large-scale environmental systems. A reliance on technology to solve future environmental problems has its limits and is inherently paradoxical, as innovations of the past have contributed widely to environmental decline, as is evident today. However, as environmental systems and designed urban landscapes become more technologically advanced, networked, logistical, and integrated, a cohesive strategy is required for the allied disciplines of environmental design, planning, and engineering to engage the processes that produce the technical lands of the future.

Patents and the patent system will play an increasingly important role in this space by managing sequential innovation, developing knowledge infrastructure, projecting future imaginaries, and transferring technology in this emerging sector. Significantly, these processes may be leveraged to help build a more sustainable, adaptive, and equitable environment. Like other landscape strategies, the operationalization of the patent system represents "a highly organized plan (spatial, programmatic, or logistical) that is at the same time flexible and structurally capable of significant adaptation in response to changing circumstances."[58] Many questions remain regarding the invention, prototyping, testing, and implementation of the future's environmental technologies. Nevertheless, this work is imperative, and these questions must be answered. If the allied profession of environmental design and planning does not invent and project the new technological strata that define the sites and geographies of tomorrow, who will?

[56] Paul Oldham et al., "Mapping the Landscape of Climate Engineering," *Philosophical Transactions of the Royal Society A: Mathematical, Physical and Engineering Sciences* 372, no. 2031 (December 2014).

[57] Anthony E. Chavez, "Exclusive Rights to Saving the Planet: The Parenting of Geoengineering Inventions," *Northwestern Journal of Technology and Intellectual Property* 13 (2015): 1.

[58] James Corner, "Not Unlike Life Itself: Landscape Strategy Now," *Harvard Design Magazine* 21 (2004).

Finding the Technical Edge

John Dean Davis

When the French ship *Grandcamp* detonated in Galveston Bay, Texas, in 1947, the explosion flung an anchor weighing three-and-a-half tons nearly two miles inland. A 2,000-foot-tall mushroom cloud rose over the Texas wetlands, and two small planes unlucky enough to be flying overhead at the time were blasted out of the sky. The resultant fire triggered the explosion of another sulfur- and fertilizer-laden ship, which set a Monsanto chemical plant and the crude storage tanks at a nearby refinery on fire. The disaster's scale points to substantial chemical force in a concentrated area. The destruction of most of the shoreline buildings in Texas City, an industrial hub located about ten miles north of Galveston, similarly revealed a hellish sort of proximity of several volatile industrial systems. The Texas City Disaster, as the event has come to be known, happened because of friction at the edges of two large-scale technical landscapes. The *Grandcamp* held 2,300 tons of ammonium nitrate, a potent fertilizer produced in the US interior that had made its way to the Texas coast where it was bound for France. Under the Marshall Plan, the tonnage joined millions more, enriching agricultural fields in the reconstruction of Europe. Texas City was its on-ramp to the world of maritime logistics, a knotted confluence of infrastructural facilities at the intersection of different industrial, agrichemical, and transit systems.[1]

[1] Hugh W. Stephens, *The Texas City Disaster, 1947* (Austin, TX: University of Texas Press, 1997), 1–6.

fig 1

The two worlds that collided that day in the Texas shallows represent two of the larger technical projects of industrialized modernity: agricultural intensification and global supply chains (both enabled by fossil-fuel energy). The dynamics of these technical "fields" and the various ways we might describe them could fill several volumes; the thickness of infrastructures and embodied technical knowledge in each of the realms presents an opportunity for ongoing comparative study. Galveston Bay, however, is an engineered edge that is more mechanism than zone and offers a different way of looking at the "field condition" of technical landscapes. Some technological landscapes, such as proving grounds, military reserves, or wildlife study areas, are best conceptualized by their ability to use space to produce isolation. The phenomena of technical study are most revealed, so the logic goes, in sparse context. Remote specialized sites stand little chance of interference and consequently collect data with less risk of contamination. However, the hard edge at Galveston is perhaps a better way to see the inner workings of the two technical realms that intersected to produce it. The engineering involved describes an outline of technical function and gives a glimpse of the complexity of the convergent landscapes it handles.

Nevertheless, the *form* of these structures, which we usually believe to be aloof constructions, operates symbolically. When considered diachronically alongside the currents of capital and imperialism, these facilities reveal aspirations as they develop over time. When we assess the meta-goals of engineers or technocratic colonial administrators, we have to also consider dimensions of the design that may be irrational or even imagistic.

The Caribbean and Gulf of Mexico ports underwent significant engineering upgrades in the late nineteenth and early twentieth centuries. Each of

fig 1   Slip #2 and destroyed ship in the aftermath of the Texas City Disaster, 1947. University of
Houston Libraries

fig 2   Port cities of the Caribbean ar
Mexico basins considered in this study. Jo
Davis

the ports became something like a hydraulic machine, a large-scale attempt to bend the landscape to accommodate the hull dimensions of oceangoing ships. The Caribbean (in which this chapter includes the Gulf of Mexico for practical purposes) presents unique technical problems whose expensive and laborious resolution indicates the intense pressure colonial and capital interests have put on the region. For centuries, the Caribbean was the heart of the colonial extractive enterprise and the site of capitalism's foundation. Its ports were where the "open veins" of the Americas were concentrated, materials shipped to the Old World, and the place where untold millions of enslaved Africans were pushed into the colonial-technical landscape. The stakes of lubricating these exchanges were essential to the modern project. The Caribbean is a relatively shallow sea, and the low volume of water in the region translates to low tidal action at wharves and quays. Engineering practices of the time looked to harness as much of this gravitational energy as possible in stacking and pushing coastal water, so when the cities of the Caribbean needed to improve their ports, the engineering structures proved significant to amplify the forces present at the coast. These port machines are records of technical knowledge gathering and describe contours of flows in vast territories both inland and seaward.

fig 2

At their heart, technical landscapes use some preexisting characteristic or set of conditions. The engineers recognized the Caribbean port zones were landscapes of action. They worked to intensify and calcify some of that preexisting dynamic to increase the effectiveness of the technical project in a larger territory. It would seem straightforward, as Sara Ahmed has described in her fascinating study on utilitarianism, to "make use of use to explain the acquisition of form" in the cases of these and many other engineering structures.[2] In contrast, I am interested in engineering form as it emerges (and maintains a remarkable consistency in objective) available to a *longue durée* study over more extensive geography than is typical of project-based history. A long-term, genealogical, or diachronic study of engineering practice records the shifting ideas of what constitutes "use" and registers vestiges and remains about how problems were conceived and solved. Use, usage, intentions, consequences, and changes over time can reveal much about technical praxis and attitudes toward landscape if we adapt a looser idea of causality and consequence. The tendency toward the hardening of technical structures reflects a similar inclination in our thinking about their embedded landscapes. Ahmed describes an accumulation of use as a sort of theoretical, mental hardening, where "possibilities become restricted, how histories become concrete, hard as walls," participating in condemnation of entire landscapes to our perception, effectively assigning "function as fate."[3] Similarly, the functions of technical structures and landscapes need to be understood as a zone or territory of heterogeneous parts and actors.[4] Technical modernization under capitalism is essentially a story of the atomization and disintegration of many of the older analysis models. As one sociologist described, the spatial phenomena that crop up around

[2] Sara Ahmed, *What's the Use?: On the Uses of Use* (Durham, NC: Duke University Press, 2019), 8.

[3] Ahmed, *What's the Use?*, 212, 133.

[4] See Christopher Jones, *Routes of Power: Energy and Modern America* (Cambridge, MA: Harvard University Press, 2016).

[5] Zygmunt Bauman, *Liquid Modernity* (Malden, MA: Polity, 2000), 1–14.

[6] Martín Arboleda, *Planetary Mine: Territories of Extraction under Late Capitalism* (London: Verso, 2020), 15–16.

[7] "Report of the Chief of Engineers Accompanying the Report of the Secretary of War, 1867" (Washington, DC: Government Printing Office, 1867), 363; N. A. Cowdrey to William Belknap, July 11, 1870, Box 5, Entry 71, Correspondence of the River and Harbor Division, Letters Received 1871–1886, Record Group 77, Records of the Office of the Chief of Engineers, National Archives, Washington, DC (hereafter referred to as "NA77-71"); Howell to Andrew A. Humphreys, June 24, 1872, Box 21, NA77-71; Zealous Tower to Humphreys, January 1874, Box 46, NA77-71.

[8] David G. McComb, *Galveston: A History* (Austin, TX: University of Texas Press, 1986), 152.

[9] For a complete account of the dispute, see Martin Reuss, "Andrew A. Humphreys and the Development of Hydraulic Engineering: Politics and Technology in the Army Corps of Engineers, 1850–1950," *Technology and Culture* 26, no. 1 (1985): 1–33.

[10] Elmer Lawrence Corthell, *A History of the Jetties at the Mouth of the Mississippi River* (New York, NY: J. Wiley & Son, 1881), 60.

infrastructures, particularly in the extractive, colonial or neocolonial locations, are read as constantly shifting fluids.[5] Maritime infrastructures, particularly those that alter tidal patterns and move enormous volumes of water, produce fragmented, disjointed, and drastically reorganized landscapes around them. The hard edges of port structures represent what Martín Arboleda calls the "functional integration" wrought by global capital that subsumes and subjugates the ecological and social territories that existed around them but are nontechnical.[6]

To illustrate this process, we return to the Texas coast. In the second half of the nineteenth century, Galveston became an important shipping hub and commercial destination for much of its bay's watershed. Galveston officials and commercial interests drew rail lines out through the wetlands to a terminus on the barrier island where the city lay and lobbied the federal government to improve their harbor. In the years after the Civil War, Galveston capitalists had made significant investments in docking facilities for deepwater ships, no easy feat in the shallow and protean Galveston Bay. In the 1870s, both government and private hydro-engineering efforts focused on maintaining channels that ocean-going vessels could navigate and ensuring they reached the city docks and were within reach of the inland railroad network. The US Army Corps of Engineers took up a full-scale survey of the bay in 1867 when the naval survey party initially assigned to the area had to abandon the task due to yellow fever. The Corps made scant progress over the next decade, making plans to cut a channel through the muck of Buffalo Bayou up to the sleepy town of Houston, to build a canal through to Sabine Lake on the Louisiana border, and, most importantly, to fortify the Bolivar Pass with parallel jetties to control the tidal discharge.[7]

However, these large-scale plans to make the bay navigable would be technically and politically complex. Galveston had competitors who sought to divert the limited amount of federal funding available for engineering toward their own projects, especially as the century ended. A shipping magnate from Duluth named August B. Wolvin created Texas City from whole cloth, buying 7,000 acres of prairie in 1890 that he saw, correctly, as having commercial potential because of its proximity to a natural channel and poised to compete with the more weather-vulnerable Galveston.[8] Houston, similarly, smelled opportunity, and agents of the railroad men and land speculators sought copies of the government hydrography work, looking to promote their railroad terminus and bypass the stranglehold Galveston held on the Gulf of Mexico's shipping lanes. The Corps of Engineers also had competitors who sought to tap into the artery of federal dollars the military controlled. James Eads, the famed submariner and salvage diver from St. Louis, had very publicly embarrassed the US military engineers in a dispute over the best way to maintain a channel at the mouth of the Mississippi.[9] In 1874, Eads had proposed replicating the parallel jetty system he had seen in a recent visit to the engineering works on the mouth of the Danube.[10] With a few minor design tweaks, his parallel jetty system defeated the sandbar in the Mississippi's South Pass, a phenomenon that had confounded all efforts, government and private, up to that point. Eads became famous and extremely rich and pressed both to his advantage. Perhaps a better self-promoter than a scientist, Eads used his public relations coup to leverage further privatization and capture of public works expenditures, eventually extending his desire to head a dominant international construction syndicate.

A decade after their embarrassment in Louisiana, the Corps struggled to piece together enough funding to tackle the problems presented by bringing navigation to Houston. Eads saw an opportunity for another payday. Using his political connections, Eads arranged to have a public congressional hearing in 1884 where officers of the Corps of Engineers could be present but were barred from speaking. In this theater, he proposed what amounted to a moderate change to the Corps's design but would have contractually obligated the US to pay him $1,000,000 for each additional foot of depth achieved.[11] Congress balked at paying Eads a fee that amounted to seven times the construction cost had it been undertaken as a public project. Eventually, a group of Houston businessmen assembled an amalgam of private capital, state bonds, and federal appropriations to build the Houston Ship Channel from the Gulf of Mexico through Buffalo Bayou to Houston's city docks. More than a mere stretch of deep water, this infrastructural corridor has become the spine around which the largest accumulation of petrochemical refining, research, and technical expertise in the world has gathered.[12] The "Houston Plan," as its enabling financing scheme came to be known, became the template for massive harbor projects in the future.[13] The shared arrangement perhaps best represents the technical innovation of the period: a faltering of a purely public will to change the landscape, and the creation of a financial map in which the desires for privatization and the imposition of extractive priorities can be seen to mix with the technical harbor structures that had previously been in the government realm.

fig 3

The physics of the project—manipulating tidal and riparian energy to do work and shape the landscape—was an ancient technique. The technology is essentially that of the ancient millrace: make a large volume of fluid flow through a relatively narrower passage, and you observe an increase in the velocity of that fluid. Daniel Bernoulli theorized this phenomenon in the eighteenth century, describing the form of the vessel and the necessity of an "incompressible" fluid as forming a zone of low pressure on the outer side of the escape valve, and hence an increase in velocity and subsequently force outside of that form. This principle was understood well, if intuitively, for centuries before Bernoulli—and later, Giovanni Battista Venturi—came to attach their names to it; the Bishop of Ely, for example, used this idea in the English fens to straighten and increase the power of the River Nene in the mid-fifteenth century.[14] If it was tacitly understood, it remained obscure and difficult to measure and predict. Describing hydrodynamics in open channel situations (like canals or Galveston Bay) occupied a significant amount of the time of the mathematical luminaries like Antoine de Chézy, Claude-Louis Navier, and Gaspard de Prony, whose work forms the foundation of modern

[11] "Argument of Capt. James B. Eads before the Committee on Commerce of the Senate and the Committee on Rivers and Harbors of the House of Representatives, May 21 and 22, 1884, in support of Senate Bill 1632 and a Like Bill in the House, to Provide for the Improvement of the Channel between Galveston Harbor and the Gulf of Mexico" (Washington, DC: Rufus H. Darby, 1884), Box 255, NA77-71.

[12] Martin V. Melosi and Joseph A. Pratt, "The Energy Capital of the World? Oil-Led Development in Twentieth-Century Houston," in *Energy Capitals: Local Impact, Global Influence* (Pittsburgh, PA: University of Pittsburgh Press, 2014), 43–51.

[13] Mary Jo O'Rear, *Storm over the Bay: The People of Corpus Christi and Their Port* (College Station, TX: Texas A & M University Press, 2009), 119–21.

[14] Eric H. Ash, *The Draining of the Fens: Projectors, Popular Politics, and State Building in Early Modern England* (Baltimore, MD: Johns Hopkins University Press, 2017), 29.

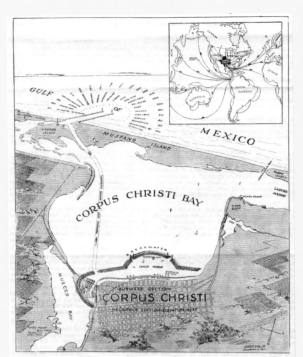

fig 3 Bird's-eye diagram of the jetty and channel construction proposed for Corpus Christi, Texas, 1920s. Corpus Christi Public Library

fig 4 Shell (*Murex brandaris*), etchin Wenceslaus Hollar, c. 1645. National Galler Washington, DC

engineering practice.[15] But bays, estuaries, and rivers are complex and contain many variables. Until the twentieth century, the Corps of Engineers had no access to the computational power needed to model hydrodynamics with a meaningful degree of accuracy. Even now, engineers still rely on mathematical shorthand and simplified formulae under continuous development and review to understand places like Galveston.[16]

However, what is persistent is the kind of intuitive grasp of volume, force, and enabling form that could, with the correct action, change land and water at a grand scale: Bernoulli's principle as a global technique. The method implied recognition that inland landscapes and large territories impinged on the function of port mechanisms, as their dimensions and the qualities of their channels were directly related to the forces produced. The watershed's potential could be seen as hydraulic, commercial, and political. Form mattered as well, primarily dimensionally and in structural substance and durability. A series of heuristic principles of form emerged in vernacular engineering, centered around rigid walls that could resist and shape the hydraulic flow. The wetland shallows' strength, control, and clear delineation was initially a technical solution but eventually became a kind of ideal aspirational form. Massively expensive to build and then maintain, the Caribbean projects started from seeds and then grew to calcify larger territories as engineers converted what capital they could get their hands on into their desire for solidity in the wetlands.

Havana's Malecón is perhaps the most famous complex, wall-like maritime construction in the region. A combination of seawall and vehicular promenade, the Malecón stretches from the old city and ancient harbor along the coast facing the Florida Straits, creating an emblematic urban social space, and regularizing the coastline. The seawall little affects the hydrodynamics of the harbor and principally serves as an echo of an important curve in the Carrera de las Indias—Spain's extractive network of maritime pathways developed some five hundred years ago. The engineer Francisco José Albear y Fernández de Lara, known for building Havana's modern water system and botanical gardens, first proposed regularizing the coral shoreline in 1874. However, construction did not begin until 1901, when occupying US military authorities started building an automobile link between the *ciudad vieja* and suburbs along the coast to the west.[17] That the people of Havana have adopted the sun-drenched Malecón as such an important place of socialization and cultural identity has obscured its origin as an infrastructure of imperial circulation. Other iconic *malecones* dot the Caribbean, where esplanades in Campeche, Veracruz, and Cartagena have taken on both the name and urban function.

fig 4

The term "malecón" is mainly associated with Spanish-speaking Latin America and did not always connote the twentieth-century auto promenade. The word's origins are uncertain, but etymologists point to its emergence in the print record during the Enlightenment when malecón was used to indicate a particular type of river engineering project meant to reinforce

[15] See Frederick B. Artz, *The Development of Technical Education in France, 1500–1850* (Cambridge, MA: MIT Press, 1966).

[16] See, for example, Bernard B. Hsieh, "System Simulation of Tidal Hydrodynamic Phenomena in Galveston Bay, Texas," Technical (US Army Corps of Engineers Waterways Experiment Station, 1996).

[17] Mario Gonzalez, *Sobre los planos, esquemas y planes directores de la ciudad de La Habana* (Havana: Grupo para el Desarrollo Integral de la Capital, 1995), 11–13; Roberto Segre, Mario Coyula, and Joseph L. Scarpaci, Havana: *Two Faces of the Antillean Metropolis* (Hoboken: John Wiley & Sons, 1997), 43–44.

[18] J. Corominas, *Diccionario crítico etimológico de la lengua castellana* 3, (Bern: Editorial Francke, 1954), 204–5.

[19] Michiel de Vaan, *Etymological Dictionary of Latin and the Other Italic Languages* (Leiden: Brill, 2008), 396.

a stream's banks to direct the flow of water. It lacked any association with human occupation or leisure as a specific bit of technical jargon. Instead, scholars have argued that malecón entered Spanish from the seafaring dialects of Corsica and Sardinia, themselves springing from Vulgar Latin and remaining largely unaffected by the influence of Arabic in the region. Interestingly, *muriconem*, malecón's progenitor in medieval Latin, is derived not from the Latin word *murus*, for wall, but rather from the term "murex," borrowed from Greek and describing a specific genus of sea snail.[18] Aristotle included the two species of murex found in the Mediterranean in his *Historia animalium*, likely because of their fame for being the source of Tyrian purple dye. Perhaps even more intriguing is the formal origin of murex, which is also closely related to where the English words mussel and muscle are derived. Murex primarily means shell—the hard, geometrically complex whorl produced by the animal for defense. Etymologically, scholars believe these words are all related because of the formal resemblance of the domed and tapered shell and a flexed muscle, such as the human deltoid.[19] Malecón, through its technical history, contains elements of hardening and sinuous form transmitted through seafarers' argot; its adoption indicates that, at least in the Caribbean context, it has some linguistic ability to capture notions of structure and force in a tidal environment.

Since the time of Cortés's landing, the inhabitants of Veracruz have relied on engineering to create a safe harbor in their tidal environment. Located on Mexico's gulf coast and its most ancient and vital port, Veracruz's first European-built fortifications included a *muro de las argollas*, a heavy masonry structure with embedded iron rings strong enough to tie vessels to. By the 1870s, the city's engineers understood the commercial impediments of exposing wharfage and looked to create a more secure harbor artificially. They drew plans for an encircling, crab-like structure that spanned from the old citadel on the Playa Norte to the Isla de la Gallega, encompassing the ancient Castillo de San Juan de Ulúa and forming a narrow entrance with the twin pincer that they planned to construct from the spit of land known as Los Hornos. Armed with their plans, the city officials traveled to Mexico City to lobby the central government for funding, only to find that James Eads had already secured contracts for all maritime engineering in the entire country. The Veracruz engineers were sent back with instructions to provide Eads with plans and hydraulic data, which they dutifully delivered. After a few months, the *yanqui* engineer sent a sheaf of drawings and a lieutenant to work with Villaseñor, the local government engineer supervising data collection, drafting, and construction. Having never visited the site himself, Eads collected his design fee, and the port, described as "la palanca mas poderosa para levantar á una nación," opened to much fanfare, bunting, and speechifying in 1882.[20]

[20] Leonardo Pasquel, ed., *Obras Del Puerto de Veracruz En 1882* (Veracruz: Editorial Citlaltepetl, 1968), 122 and passim.

[21] Michael D. Coe and Richard A. Diehl, *In the Land of the Olmec*, vol. 2 (Austin, TX: University of Texas Press, 1980), 12.

The Nahuatl term for the people of the Coatzacoalcos River basin was *ayahualoco*, meaning "surrounded by water."[21] South of Veracruz and located on the northern shore of the Isthmus of Tehuantepec, the Coatzacoalcos's estuary has been the site of intense interest and multiple explorations by those who dreamed of cutting a canal through the narrowest portion of

Mexico and connecting the Gulf to the Pacific. In 1852 and again in 1870, US engineers surveyed the barrier beach, estuary, and vast inland wetlands with the hope of designing a competing canal to rival Ferdinand de Lesseps's project in Panama. The American naval officer in charge of the expedition in 1870 found a landscape of sugar plantations and malarial jungle but stated confidently that there were "no natural obstacles to the construction of the canal which engineering, science, and liberal capital cannot overcome."[22] Labor was more difficult to come by, but the Americans believed the problem could be solved by blithely suggesting they import freedmen and women from the Reconstruction-era US South to work the project.[23] The engineer attached to the project, a civilian and Spanish national from Puerto Rico named Estevan Fuertes, concluded too that the river was amenable to improvement as it appeared to be naturally deepening itself and had begun preparing plans to build structures that would alter its currents to manipulate silt deposition to more favorable points.[24]

The authoritarian regime of Porfirio Díaz came to power in a coup in 1876, making the construction of an infrastructural connection across Tehuantepec a priority. Mexican officials eventually settled for a railroad linking the northern and southern shores as the canal project presented too many unresolved financial and technical difficulties. President Díaz and his circle of *científicos* (scientific advisors) granted a series of American-based companies land concessions and contracts to build the cross-isthmus railway, all of them failing. After years of frustration at the slow pace of construction, Díaz finally met with James Eads in 1880. Eads proposed a truly wild solution: building three parallel railroad tracks on which three high-powered locomotives would literally drag steamships across Tehuantepec. Díaz, impressed with the American, promptly fired the contractor and awarded the project to Eads. Soon after hearing of the massive change order, American and European investors and banks quickly pulled their funding for the project, indicating a wariness with Eads and the widespread judgment that the project was becoming a boondoggle.[25] His funding evaporated, Díaz eventually relented and fired Eads and placed the railroad entirely under government control. The project was ultimately completed and in operation by 1894, built by a consortium of English and American capitalists and contractors. Not long after completion, the project engineer gave a lecture before the National Geographic Society in Washington, DC, describing the project's success as illustrated by the 120,000 acres of coffee plantations that US nationals had developed since the project began. The engineer described further plans for jetties and harbor expansions on both coasts and revealed that he had been one of Eads's lieutenants in Louisiana twenty years prior. He lamented the passing of his old boss in 1887, stating that even in his deathbed, Eads had been energetically working on drawings of the mechanism for loading steamships onto locomotives.[26]

From the moment of the US invasion and occupation of Haiti in 1915, American officials and military officers used a rhetoric of destitution to portray the country and justify their control over the republic's public works

[22] Robert W. Shufeldt, "Reports of Explorations and Surveys to Ascertain the Practicability of a Ship-Canal between the Atlantic and Pacific Oceans by Way of the Isthmus of Tehuantepec" (Washington, DC: Government Printing Office, 1872), 16; see also J. J. Williams, *The Isthmus of Tehuantepec: Being the Results of a Survey for a Railroad to Connect the Atlantic and Pacific Oceans, Made by the Scientific Commission Under the Direction of Major J. G. Barnard, U. S. Engineers* (New York, NY: D. Appleton and Company, 1852).

[23] Shufeldt, "Practicability of a Ship-Canal," 18.

[24] Shufeldt, "Practicability of a Ship-Canal," 15, 34.

[25] Enrique Sodi Alvarez, *Istmo de Tehuantepec* (Mexico: Puertos Libres Mexicanos, 1967), 123–26.

[26] "Lecture before the National Geographic Society at Washington, DC, November 22, 1895, by Mr. Elmer L. Corthell, D. SC., Civil Engineer," 54th Congress, 1st session, no. 34 (1895).

27 *The Conquest of Haiti: Articles and Documents* (Haiti: The Nation, Inc., 1920), 20–21.

28 Landon Yarrington, "The Paved and the Unpaved: Toward a Political Economy of Infrastructure, Mobility, and Urbanization in Haiti," *Economic Anthropology* 2, no. 1 (January 2015): 195–98, https://doi.org/10.1002/sea2.12024.

29 "Report of the American High Commissioner at Port-au-Prince, Haiti: 1923" (Washington, DC: Government Printing Office, 1924), 9; "Second Annual Report of the American High Commissioner at Port-au-Prince, Haiti: 1923" (Washington, DC: Government Printing Office, 1924), 3.

30 "Sixth Annual Report of the American High Commissioner at Port-au-Prince, Haiti: 1927" (Washington, DC: Government Printing Office, 1928), 13–35.

31 Myrna I. Santiago, *The Ecology of Oil: Environment, Labor, and the Mexican Revolution, 1900–1938* (Cambridge: Cambridge University Press, 2006), 9.

and engineering departments. The first order of business was to construct a passable road connecting the capital of Port-au-Prince to the northern port at Cap-Haitien. To do this, the US commanders revived the road *corvée* system with gusto, compelling peasants to build highways under the watchful eyes of rifle-armed marines.[27] Infrastructural projects, such as roads, railroads, and port facilities, soon followed as the US commissioners undid several decades of underdevelopment that the Haitian elite had perpetrated to sustain their plantation economy.[28] After devastating floods in the Artibonite River valley in 1924 due to rampant deforestation inland, the Americans turned their attention to hydraulic control and agricultural development. The Artibonite, Haiti's longest river, flows westward from its origins at the border with the Dominican Republic, through a broad floodplain before discharging just south of the city of Gonaïves at a place called Grande-Saline. The Americans built dikes and cleared obstructions after the flood, somewhat regularizing the meandering stream. John Russell, the US high commissioner in charge of "build[ing] up [Haiti's] internal revenue receipts" so that the tiny republic could pay off the mountains of US and French debt it had been saddled with, saw an opportunity in the Artibonite's landscape of mangroves and salt evaporation pits. Russell's agricultural engineers calculated that the valley's 100,000 acres could be developed into lucrative coffee and cotton plantations.[29] Haiti lacked the funds to control the river and build an attractive irrigation system. Instead, he proposed that the Artibonite valley be opened to foreign capital investment since the United States had insisted on striking the section of Haiti's constitution that barred foreign land ownership. In 1927, two foreign development corporations signed contracts for long-term leases on vast swaths of Haiti's most productive farmlands, effectively reverting the landscape to a plantation oligarchy.[30] It was almost as if capital came flooding in alongside the American dikes, swamping the fields and wiping out any chance of small-scale Haitian coffee growers accumulating wealth and security through land tenure.

A similar shift in the finances and main actors can be detected in the massive restructuring of the landscape around the port of Tampico, Mexico. Tampico's region was largely considered desolate, if tropical, wasteland before the "Spindletop" discovery of oil in nearby Texas and the explosion of oilfield exploitation and its attendant infrastructure that flooded the Gulf of Mexico and Caribbean soon afterward. According to the historian Myrna Santiago, in transforming sleepy Tampico, the technocratic armies of lawyers and engineers employed by the oil companies were able to accomplish what the elites had dreamed of but never fully managed to do.[31] In rapidly creating a massive and intensive extractive and refining system, replete with its own high-efficiency "valves" in the form of ports and hardened canals, the oil companies realized the first full instance of a landscape of complete technical capitalization. Again, in the critical middle years of the 1910s, a wave of high-impact engineering churned the landscape. The oil companies diverted and dredged the Pánuco River, constructing the now familiar parallel jetties well into the gulf and regularizing the shoreline inland. Workers dug canals from the river through the nearby wetlands and into the Tamiahua lagoon, filling behind the new shorelines and making land for fields of oil pits and steel tanks. Webs of pipelines ran from the extraction fields to terminals in Tampico city, where the mangroves were bulldozed to make way for refineries and housing.[32] Where the oil companies had a congealing effect on the landscape on one plane, their omnipresence shattered the territory's ecological and political communities. Royal Dutch Shell's efforts to break troublesome strikes at the El Aguila refinery on the east side of Tampico led to corporate pressure to cordon off and separate the refinery and working-class neighborhoods into its own municipality, effectively ghettoizing elements problematic to the system.[33]

At Coatzacoalcos, Royal Dutch Shell again emerged as the new central player in these landscapes, displacing the last remnants of a public or government-sponsored agenda for the port and basin landscape. The story of S. Pearson and Son, which transformed from a civil engineering and construction firm into a Royal Dutch Shell subsidiary, describes the transmutation of technical actors and priorities in this landscape precisely. In 1894, S. Pearson had become the Díaz regime's primary engineering services contractor. The English firm began by cleaning up and thoroughly rebuilding several James Eads's (and various protegés') messes. The firm started by rebuilding the Veracruz port terminals. Then they entirely reconstructed the Tehuantepec railroad and modernized the ports at Salina Cruz and Coatzacoalcos before branching out into financing and electricity generation.[34] The firm's transformational diversification occurred in 1901, after Weetman Pearson, the firm's founder, missed a train in Laredo, Texas, and beheld the frenzy of speculative activity occurring after the Spindletop oil discovery. Wiring his agent in Mexico City, Pearson plowed all available capital into purchasing vast swaths of potential oil fields along the Veracruz coast. In a few short years, Pearson's El Aguila Oil Company had rendered the shorelines at Tampico, Coatzacoalcos, and a large portion of the state of Veracruz unrecognizable. Shell outmaneuvered Rockefeller's Standard Oil in 1919 to acquire a controlling interest in El Aguila and folded the operation into its burgeoning empire.[35]

Royal Dutch Shell is and was a dizzyingly complex, global technical entity. Scholars, however, have identified two "quirks" in the conglomerate's history, which have underscored our understanding of its success and longevity. The first is Shell's relative emphasis on in-house technical development that extends throughout its corporate structure. Shell's executive leadership is primarily drawn from its technical corps, which has led to what Tyler Priest has termed beneficial "workable interfaces between research and operations" and an embrace of a "geotechnical" vision for the corporation.[36] The second is perhaps more recondite but still illustrative of a certain kind of aspirational technical imaginary. "Shell" got its name from the inventor of the modern oil tanker ship, Marcus Samuel, who founded and named the conglomerate's corporate progenitor. Samuel, son of merchants who dealt in rare and beautiful seashells, named his bulk petroleum transport company

[32] Myrna Santiago, "Tampico, Mexico: The Rise and Decline of an Energy Metropolis," in *Energy Capitals: Local Impact, Global Influence*, eds., Joseph A. Pratt, Martin Melosi, and Kathleen A. Brosnahan (Pittsburgh, PA: University of Pittsburgh Press, 2014), 151; Santiago, *The Ecology of Oil*, 116–47.

[33] Santiago, "Tampico, Mexico," 155.

[34] Priscilla Connolly, "Pearson and Public Works Construction in Mexico, 1890–1910," *Business History* 41, no. 4 (October 1999): 48–71.

[35] Lisa Bud-Frierman, Andrew Godley, and Judith Wale, "Weetman Pearson in Mexico and the Emergence of a British Oil Major, 1901–1919," *Business History Review* 84, no. 2 (2010): 275–300, https://doi.org/10.1017/S0007680500002610.

[36] Tyler Priest, *The Offshore Imperative: Shell Oil's Search for Petroleum in Postwar America* (College Station, TX: Texas A & M University Press, 2007), 6.

after the family trade. The first ship to travel through Suez in 1898 was one of Samuel's, aptly named the SS *Murex*. Samuel appreciated the animal's container-like quality. Subsequent authors have been more critical of this zoological fascination, wryly pointing to the murex sea snail's qualities as "voracious predators" or that the famed purple dye comes from a neurotoxin the murex uses to immobilize its target.[37]

A late nineteenth-century visitor to Willemstad, the central port city on the island of Curaçao, remarked on how much the colony resembled Amsterdam. Aside from the neat houses and paved streets, the system of canals that led from the lagoon into the city and the fleet of scull-boats moving through the city were most redolent of the old city. The Dutch colony had reconfigured its economic output after abolition around sugar cane, oranges, and above all, phosphate mining.[38] Curaçao's industrial base, harbor, political affinity, and proximity to the Venezuelan oil fields made it attractive to Royal Dutch Shell, which dispatched a secret agent in 1914 to scout the island's potential for development. Several factors prompted this sudden attention. The war in Europe (1914–1918) was the first to consume gasoline on a mass scale. US-based interests owned concessions, but Congress had passed laws barring American capital investment in Venezuela, which the Dutch were allowed. Finally, and perhaps most importantly, sand and shallow water forced a geographic solution. Venezuela's most productive oilfields were in and around Lake Maracaibo, whose sandbar and regional political instability made investors skittish.

Shell solved the problem by using shallow-draft light boats to transport crude the short distance to its refineries in colonially administered Curaçao before oceanic transshipment to Europe. By 1924, the subsidiary Shell Curaçao had filled the entirety of the former Asiento and Valentijn plantations with gasworks, storage tanks, and wharves. Two years later, the traffic in the port, in both tonnage and ship numbers, had outstripped Amsterdam. Workers flocked from Europe, Venezuela, and the rest of the Antilles, and housing for both gasworks and workers quickly reshaped the harbor and solidified much of the delicate archipelago and canals of Willemstad into a solid industrial platform.[39]

Parting and distancing refining from the extraction operation did little in the long term to shield Lake Maracaibo from voracious development. The lake is 2,000 square miles and shallow, with one outlet to the sea. It is the site of the apocryphal naming of the nation of Venezuela, as early European explorers remarked on how it resembled the Venetian lagoon. Indigenous communities who lived in floating and stilted settlements occupied the shorelines until the various subsidiaries and combines of the Shell, Standard, and Gulf Oil companies descended en masse in the 1920s.[40] In the decade after 1922, when crude exports began to be measured in earnest, the big three built the first floating oil platforms, and various wildcat operations fanned inland from the shallows. The oil companies built extensive infrastructure along Maracaibo's eastern shore, much of it expressly to support the extraction and with no benefits to the populace. The Venezuelan public

[37] John Lanchester, "Gargantuanization," *London Review of Books*, April 22, 2021, https://www.lrb.co.uk/the-paper/v43/n08/john-lanchester/gargantuanisation; George E. Radwin and Anthony D'Attilio, *Murex Shells of the World: An Illustrated Guide to the Muricidae* (Stanford, CA: Stanford University Press, 1976), 1–12.

[38] Ira Nelson Morris, *With the Trade-Winds: A Jaunt in Venezuela and the West Indies* (New York, NY: G. P. Putnam's Sons, 1897), 85–89.

[39] Johannes Hartog, *Curaçao: From Colonial Dependence to Autonomy* (Aruba: De Wit, Inc., 1968), 307–14.

[40] Morris, *Trade-Winds*, 140–41; Edwin Lieuwen, *Petroleum in Venezuela: A History* (Berkeley, CA: University of California Press, 1954), 38–43.

was barred from using the asphalt roads Shell and others constructed. To control the mosquito population, the companies sprayed the region's fields with a coat of crude oil.[41] The *extranjeros* generally flouted all rules of civic and environmental order. Enormous fires consumed entire towns along the shore; the oil companies on multiple occasions used the devastation as a reason to relocate the affected population and drill in the aftermath.[42]

Terrible working conditions on the drilling rigs, frequent explosions, and the six inches of oil sludge on the lake's surface prompted Venezuelan officials to attempt reform in 1935.[43] By then, significant damage to the landscape had already occurred. The oil companies established a "leveling network" in 1929 to ascertain precisely how much subsidence was happening in the land east of Lake Maracaibo due to the extraction of volumes of oil under the surface. They also built dikes and drainage ditches, polderizing the oil fields and sensitive technical structures in a massive project encompassing 1,300 square kilometers. This system, however, has been left to the Venezuelan state and is deteriorating rapidly. Venezuelan engineers have noted that some areas have subsided 5.5 meters and were continuing to sink at a rate of 20 centimeters a year. There isn't enough pumping capacity to polder the entire lake edge, and the resultant anti-flooding system is a series of triage decisions. Over 150,000 Venezuelans live in the subsidence zone.[44]

This litany is intended to describe harbor production and littoral engineering as a long-term and accumulative process. To be sure, individual site conditions, economic circumstances, and human personalities shape the narratives of these technical projects. But in aggregate, they describe a design and construction process that takes place over generations. Design reads less like a heroic process and more akin to a fumbling search for successive handholds on a dark cliff face. The appearance of predatory shellfish at multiple points in the story too questions the appropriateness of understanding high modernist engineering as a bloodlessly rational technical process. Instead, the interest in shells, valves, fluid velocity, and expulsion illuminates a kind of technical totemism. As Veronica Davidov has described in her recent work on biomimicry, it is more productive to see an interest in natural systems not as a map to solve a particular problem but rather to see nature as an "infinitely renewable and generative mega-resource and meta-resource."[45] Nature can be inspirational when solving a specific design problem, but it also serves a key role in forming ambitions. Using the example of the "bio-envy" that inspired the design of sonar, Davidov argues that other species have left "impressions" on engineers that indirectly have left "structural, behavioral, and textural traces" on their work.[46]

It is worth considering how the isolation and amplification of biophysical processes reflect a kind of modernist totemism in the technical landscape. As anthropologists have described, totems identify an admirable quality in a nonhuman species—speed, strength, flight—and make some association between that animal and the human group.[47] Engineered landscapes are the product of the engineer's means of perceiving the world at that time and place and exist as the field in which the "multilevel praxis" of design, as

[41] Lieuwen, *Petroleum in Venezuela*, 46–49.

[42] B. S. McBeth, *Juan Vicente Gómez and the Oil Companies in Venezuela, 1908–1935* (Cambridge: Cambridge University Press, 1983), 154–55.

[43] Lieuwen, *Petroleum in Venezuela*, 74–75.

[44] A. Irazábal et al., "Drainage Problems in Areas Subject to Subsidence Due to Oil Production," *Hydraulic Design in Water Resources Engineering* (Land Drainage: Proceedings of the 2nd International Conference, Southampton University, UK, 1986), 545–54; J. Murria, J. Leal, and L. Jaeger, "Monitoring and Modeling of Groundsubsidence in Western Venezuela Oilfields: An Update," *Proceedings of the 6th International Fig-Symposium on Deformation Measurements* (Hannover, 1996), 545–56.

[45] Veronica Davidov, "Biomimicry as a Meta-Resource and Megaproject: A Literature Review," *Environment and Society* 10 (2019): 29, https://doi.org/10.3167/ares.2019.100103.

[46] Davidov, 35.

[47] See Claude Lévi-Strauss, *Totemism*, trans., Rodney Needham (London: Merlin Press, 1962), 72–91, 89: "We can understand, too, that natural species are chosen not because they are 'good to eat' but because they are 'good to think.'"

Davidov has noted, moves between site conditions and the project's aspirations for shaping the natural forces present for "use." And what is engineering, if not the isolation and differentiation of a pure force, divorced from contextual noise and free from whatever networks of complexity it exists in within an unmodernized landscape? Technical ambitions are a search for processes. We may laugh at the totemic branding exercise of a petroleum transport company, but in the deep language, there is animism acting as a metonym. How many technologies have been created and deployed, standing in for physical, biological processes like breathing, expelling, consuming, assuming territory at wildly diverging scales? In many ways, the applied sciences "in the field" largely manage to camouflage themselves in the natural world to evade definitions of "modernism" and speak to an older or more elemental desire to perform actions in a landscape.

By now, it is mainly unsurprising to hear of the unintended ecological consequences of isolating these forces and the appearance of volatile and unforeseen fissures in the landscapes' overall stability. At the highest level, engineers in all these places tried to concentrate force in an area. Design was an exercise in eliminating gradients and homogeneity over a surface, eventually implicating entire watersheds and oceanic basins as the reserve territory from which force could be recruited. As tidal and hydrological forces distilled, petrochemical, labor, and political potency settled around these edge structures. The multigenerational desire for differentiation—teasing out of the "useful" features of the landscape—produces the now-familiar idea of concentration leading to volatility. Hence the mushroom cloud over the Texas wetlands or fires raging along the banks of the Pánuco. The engineers' "use" shatters homogeneity and evenness wherever it's found. All technical landscapes become sets of capacities and tasks. In places where territories overlap, "uses" mesh and solidify. Form and consequence travel a long way from their patterns of origin, be they reputedly rational (the Marshall Plan) or less so (a childhood nostalgia for seashells). Yet the shoreline of Lake Maracaibo still sinks under the amassing of technical processes that inescapably accumulate at the landscape's edge.

The
Landscapes
of Logistics

Jay Cephas

For well over two decades, the Nueva Esperanza informal settlement has occupied a narrow stretch along a creek on the east side of Tijuana, Mexico. Irregular structures line the neighborhood's compacted dirt roads, leaning this way and that, some appearing to be as tall as three stories and seemingly cobbled together out of scrap wood, cardboard, tarpaulins, and sheet metal. The neighborhood is home to migrants from other parts of Mexico who travel to Tijuana searching for jobs. However, in Nueva Esperanza, they also find the challenges of poverty, crime, and addiction typical of urban informal settlements. Starting in August 2021, these migrants also encounter a 32,000-square-meter Amazon fulfillment center on the southeastern boundary of the settlement. This warehouse is situated in Nueva Esperanza to expand the company's delivery system within Mexico. The grey warehouse block, coded TIJ1 by the company, has the corporation's familiar "a to z" logo emblazoned at each corner and stands in sharp contrast to the surrounding informal dwellings. This juxtaposition highlights not only the vast differences in the size, scale, materiality, and quality of the structures but also the profound social inequalities pervasive in capitalist production.

TIJ1 is but the latest installation in Amazon's vast global logistics network, an array of fulfillment and sortation centers, airport hubs, and delivery stations connected by shipping ports, interstate highways, and regional airfields, and supported by a massive reserve of delivery drivers who traverse the last mile of the fulfillment system to bring packages to customers' doorsteps. This logistics system builds upon the "just in time" mode of production that replaced earlier Fordist models by extending the techniques of production beyond the warehouse. However, effectively minimizing the literal and figurative grounds between the inventory and the consumer, from warehouse to doorstep, requires even more infrastructure to simplify the process further, making the logistics network its own technical production. Remote, delimited, highly secured, and opaque, these landscapes of logistics are at once hidden and in full view. A decentralized network of buildings, roads, flights paths, and service vans, these technical lands do more than service the fulfillment of Amazon's e-commerce orders; these nodes and networks are technologically productive landscapes that also serve an ideological purpose.

The ideology underscoring logistical landscapes removes its infrastructures and networks from the collective urban imaginary and, in so doing, renders invisible the technical subjectivities required for these systems to function. Abstracting the physical work done by the hundreds of thousands of employees moving and sorting Amazon packages each day removes this labor from the public eye, a technique that is achieved using metaphors that dematerialize landscape and technology, rendering them as immaterial as the "cloud" structuring Amazon's computing network. Abstracting labor to remove evidence of physical work from the psychosocial realm thus fulfills the dream whereby all can reap the benefits of a capitalist system without labor.

The deterritorialization of technical lands relies on two ideological techniques: a visual regime of invisibility and an abstraction of production

1 "Sortation center" is the term used by the Amazon corporation, by Amazon employees, and by logistics consultants to describe the warehouses where Amazon packages are sorted in preparation for delivery. While other large logistics operations, such as the United States Postal Service, refer to the same type of logistical outpost as a "sorting center," the use of "sortation" to describe Amazon's system of classifying and distributing packages is fairly consistent across the literature. The term "sortation" is used here to maintain that consistency.

2 See Leo Marx, *Machine in the Garden: Technology and the Pastoral Ideal in America* (Oxford: Oxford University Press, 2000); and Stephen Daniels, *Fields of Vision: Landscape Imagery and National Identity in England and the United States* (Princeton, NJ: Princeton University Press, 1993).

3 Denis Cosgrove, *Social Formation and Symbolic Landscape* (Madison, WI: University of Wisconsin Press, 1998); Dianne Harris and D. Fairchild Ruggles, eds., *Sites Unseen: Landscape and Vision* (Pittsburgh, PA: University of Pittsburgh Press, 2007).

4 Dianne Harris, *The Nature of Authority: Villa Culture, Landscape, and Representation in Eighteenth-Century Lombardy* (University Park, PA: Pennsylvania State University Press, 2003); Suren Lalvani, *Photography, Vision and the Production of Modern Bodies* (Albany, NY: State University of New York Press, 1996); and Erwin Panofsky, *Perspective as Symbolic Form* (New York, NY: Zone Books, 1997).

5 Jonathan Crary, *Techniques of the Observer: On Vision and Modernity in the Nineteenth Century* (Cambridge, MA: MIT Press, 1990); see also, Walter Benjamin, "The Work of Art in the Age of Mechanical Reproduction," *Illuminations: Essays and Reflections* (New York, NY: Schocken Books, 1969); Renzo Dubbini, *Geography of the Gaze: Urban*

and its labors through the dematerialization of technology. Together these two techniques converge in the emergence of a new territorial reality that positions the spatial outcomes of these constructed conditions as a "second nature," an effect of a natural order. The aim here is twofold: first, to theorize the ideological function of the technical lands of logistics; second, to engage in a detailed verbal and aesthetic visualization of the territories and forms of labor rendered invisible by these technical lands. This foregrounding of landscape ideology and the visualization of its territories is one possible avenue towards reclaiming and recovering technical lands from the regimes of invisibility that envelop them.

Visibility and the Ideological Work of Landscape

Amazon was founded in July 1994 and three years later built the first two fulfillment centers in its distribution network: a 93,000-square-foot facility in Seattle, Washington, and a 202,000-square-foot facility in New Castle, Delaware. In 1999, the company expanded by adding five new fulfillment centers in Fernley, Nevada; Coffeyville, Kansas; McDonough, Georgia; Campbellsville, Kentucky; and Lexington, Kentucky. It also started its European operations with fulfillment centers in Regensburg, Germany, Bad Hersfeld, Germany, and Marston Gate, UK. These and other subsequent fulfillment centers, "sortation" centers, air hubs, and delivery stations comprise the bulk of Amazon's physical presence in cities and suburbs.[1] From receiving stations at main ports of entry to neighborhood delivery stations in urban centers, the locations of these logistical hubs were determined by a combination of favorable tax laws and proximity to local, regional, or national transportation networks. As of 2021, Amazon employed 1.3 million people globally (almost one million in the United States alone) and operated 938 active facilities in the United States with an additional 441 planned or under construction, in addition to its nearly 1,000 facilities outside of the United States.

Landscape is not just a thing or a place but a constitutive discourse structuring the relationships between and among social groups. That is, landscape is ideological, and as such, through both techniques and technologies, landscape mediates relationships between cultural production and material practices.[2] Like all ideologies, landscape serves to impart legibility to otherwise chaotic or irrational conditions to sustain a particular social order. Historically, landscape legibility has been explained in terms of visuality.[3] Landscape as an ideology is figured through ways of seeing and these modes of visuality have been primarily examined through forms of visual representation—namely, perspective drawings, photographs, and landscape paintings.[4] Such modes of visuality extend to a variety of landscapes, including urban landscapes and cultural landscapes, and contribute to entire visual regimes.[5] These visual regimes rely on explicit techniques of representation that are prescriptive and aim to communicate a perceived objective condition while at the same time constructing the conditions that form the subject of analysis.

From the ideological work of landscape emerges two correlations between social formations and the geographies of place—first, that landscape figures as a framework that shapes the social order by visually (and thus prescriptively) representing it; second, that landscape shapes territories by inventing new categories for classification. For instance, during the emergence of the landscape idea in the nineteenth century, the category of "nature" was constructed to contain a particular rendering of landscape. Ideas about nature informed visualization (in painting and perspective drawing) while also rendering legibility (by naturalizing environments). By the mid-nineteenth century, landscape and nature became virtually interchangeable categories, even as landscape was highly rationalized.[6]

While this relationship between the visualization of landscape and the construction of categories addresses how we might see and understand the territories before us, it does not contend with what we don't see. What is or isn't rendered visible is determined in large part by who is allowed to partake in what is common to the community and who gets to decide on that participation.[7] That is, the lack of visibility plays as much of an ideological role in configuring landscape as prescriptive visual representations. Landscapes removed from the public eye take with them the forms of labor required for creating and maintaining those landscapes, as well as the forms of labor necessary for any productive processes located within those landscapes. The public display of work has historically been used as an ideological measure of control that builds mass compliance through repeated visual exposure.[8] However, the invisibility of labor, rendered by the invisibility of its landscapes, does equally profound ideological work. The material flows and displacements accompanying territorial transformations, the fluctuations of contingent labor, and their associated narratives achieve legibility through both visuality and invisibility.[9]

Technical lands bring legibility to the range of processes occurring under their aegis in part by rendering invisible aspects of those very practices. This ideology of absence creates room in the collective imaginary for new forms of sociability. It builds upon the separation between the productive landscape and the social landscape that forms the center of the landscape idea. This separation holds in tension two opposing notions of landscape (productive and social) in relation to two opposing subjectivities (participant and observer). Purging the productive landscape from this dichotomy leaves the social landscape to fill (and fulfill) idealized social aspirations. This objectification of landscape is deployed to promote an image of landscape as entirely subjective and experiential.

The ideology of landscape that informs technical lands purges signs of labor from the landscape. Landscape then becomes a form of experience, entirely subjective and idealized, an encounter with territories in which subjects are merely passive observers of the conditions around them. Heritage preservation, green tourism, and the experience economy are a few recent examples of how this alienation between the (now absent) productive landscape and the idealized social landscape is achieved not through a

and Rural Vision in Early Modern Europe (Chicago, IL: University of Chicago Press, 2002); Hal Foster, *Vision and Visuality* (New York, NY: The New Press, 1988); Martin Jay, *Downcast Eyes: The Denigration of Vision in Twentieth-Century French Thought* (Berkeley, CA: University of California Press, 1993); and Paul Virilio, *The Vision Machine* (Bloomington, IN: Indiana University Press, 1994).

[6] Cosgrove, *Social Formation and Symbolic Landscape.*

[7] Jacques Ranciére, *The Politics of Aesthetics* (New York, NY: Continuum, 2004).

[8] J. Cephas, "Picturing Modernity: Race, Labor, and Landscape Production in the Old South," *Landscript 5,* ed. Jane Hutton (Berlin: Jovis Verlag, 2017).

[9] See Matthew Gandy, *Concrete and Clay: Reworking Nature in New York City* (Cambridge, MA: MIT Press, 2003); and Jane Hutton, *Reciprocal Landscapes: Stories of Material Movements* (New York, NY; London: Routledge, 2020).

[10] See Nezar Al Sayyad, *Consuming Tradition, Manufacturing Heritage: Global Norms and Urban Forms in the Age of Tourism* (New York, NY: Routledge, 2001); Dean MacCannell, *The Tourist: A New Theory of the Leisure Class* (New York, NY: Schocken Books, 1976).

[11] Katherine McKittrick, *Demonic Grounds: Black Women and the Cartographies of Struggle* (Minneapolis, MN: University of Minnesota Press, 2006).

formal representation but via dissolution.[10] The absence of the productive landscape in the collective imaginary does not leave a gap. Instead, its omission is precisely the means through which the social landscape is foregrounded—the (in)visibility of the productive landscape renders legible the social landscape.

Such legibility of (in)visibility renders entire populations "ungeographic," that is, literally without place.[11] The subjectivities that otherwise would occupy the productive landscape are contained within the technical lands. At the same time, the erosion of evidence of physical work from daily life inscribes a new kind of place into the collective imaginary. In this place, one can reap the myriad benefits of global capitalism without engaging in the hard work of physical labor.

This ideological landscape, devoid of the evidence of physical labor, reflects a further cleft within class divisions such that the only subjects who continue to witness physical labor are the ones engaging in physical labor. Remnants of a regime of visualization that cast the American landscape as bountiful without work, these subjects exist in the new regime of (in)visibility as a myth of a previous era. Production without labor, products without workers, and bodies without place—the (in)visibility regime disembodies labor, a move signaling yet another tactic of biopolitics.

The First Mile: From Grid to Cloud

The Amazon distribution logistics network begins at the inbound crossdock facility (IXD). Typically located near major ports of entry, the IXD receives inventory from overseas vendors and local distributors, storing it until needed at a regional fulfillment center. When inventory gets low at a fulfillment center, pallets are transported via truck from the IXD, making the facility's location near major highways necessary for the efficiency of the distribution network. At the fulfillment centers (FC), orders are processed and goods are packaged for delivery to customers. The FCs are the busiest of all the logistics network sites as they work around the clock to fulfill orders rapidly. Some of the FCs are also cold-storage distribution centers for groceries and other perishable goods. The FCs are typically located in suburban and rural industrial parks with immediate access to highways; however, high-demand items are stored in smaller distribution buildings located in cities, ensuring rapid delivery (two days or less) for Amazon Prime members. In 2021, Amazon operated 22 IXD centers and 376 fulfillment centers in the United States.

In "Postscript on the Societies of Control," Gilles Deleuze articulates a difference between the spatial conditions of disciplinary societies, which relied on spatial enclosures for maximum surveillance, and the spatiality of societies of control, which had abandoned spatial enclosures in favor of deploying numerical codes to surveil the populace.[12] In the disciplinary schema, the site of labor—whether the plantation, the prison, or the factory—enacted social order through visuality. Physical enclosures—whether architectural or landscape—set subjects in relation to one another with

[12] Gilles Deleuze, "Postscript on Societies of Control," *Rethinking Architecture: A Reader in Cultural Theory* (New York, NY: Routledge, 1997).

clear lines of sight, rational systems of organization, and rigid physical and social structures that all served to contain, restrict, and delimit. Architecture and landscape permitted seeing and being seen, collapsing visuality and spatiality into a single disciplinary system. Distinct spaces retained analogical relationships between them. The overlap of this physical order with visual order resulted in a gridded spatial diagram, whether the radial grid of the panopticon or the rectilinear grid of the agricultural field.

Whereas such disciplinary tactics sought to mold subjects by replicating them in the image of the disciplinary power, tactics of control depended on modulations—continuous and perpetual transmutations that slowly but persistently deformed the subject towards new social ends. These control mechanisms depended less on the relations between distinct spaces and more on modulated variations of continuous spaces. In lieu of walls and gates, or perhaps despite them, control relied on networks that contained through proximity and association rather than enclosure. For Deleuze, the network amorphism of societies of control enabled the deterritorialization of production and its labors—that is, the literal and figurative deconstruction of the systems structuring the social relations between commodity production and the lands making that commodity production possible.[13] This deterritorialization relied on network amorphism to position change as continuous, fluid, and thus "natural" while dematerializing the means of commodity production by positioning those means as amorphous as the territories being deconstructed. Deleuze describes deterritorialization as a smoothing out of the striated aggregation of social forms, a process that reduces and simplifies social complexities to create a seeming tabula rasa out of otherwise contingent conditions. This process of smoothing, reducing, and simplifying the inherent messiness of social life extends, in the amorphous network, to all that the network touches—including forms of production, technical practices, and laboring subjects—ultimately stripping modes of production of their materiality and contingency.

Aspects of this ideology of a dematerialized production can be gleaned from the changing modes of representation used to describe and analyze networks in the early twentieth century. In 1922, engineers sought a new simplified depiction of the multiple lines of transmission emanating from the primary nodes within telegraph networks. Rather than attempting to represent the multitude of individual telegraph wires emerging from each network node, engineers instead drew the node as a series of arcs joined in a loose oval to form a cloud-like shape. Shifting away from earlier practices of diagramming networks as simplified grids, these engineers turned to the schematic of the cloud as a simple, if not simplistic, representational symbol. Initially, this symbol served to simplify the drawing of network diagrams. However, it would eventually function as a metaphor for the growing technical networks these schematic drawings sought to document and explain. In the 1970s, telecommunications engineers used similar clouds to depict and describe communication networks. By the 1980s, computer engineers began using clouds to represent the increasingly vast, complex,

[13] Gilles Deleuze and Felix Guattari, *A Thousand Plateaus: Capitalism and Schizophrenia* (Minneapolis, MN: University of Minnesota Press, 1987).

14 Tung-Hui Hu, *A Prehistory of the Cloud* (Cambridge, MA: MIT Press, 2015).

and decentralized network connections that would serve as the basis for the Internet. The cloud as a diagram represented what these engineers already knew—that lots of connections, increasingly redundant and decentralized, lay between the many different technical nodes that made up the network.[14]

A technique that for computer engineers simplified the complexity of computer networks purely for representational purposes had by the early 2000s become a marketing ploy with the express intent of selling physical and enduring services as a form of ephemera. Promoted by Google CEO Eric Schmidt in 2006 at that year's Search Engine Strategies Conference to describe a new model for computing and data services, the notion of "the cloud" left the realm of technical representation to morph into an ideological schema for articulating a new (in)visibility.[15] Simply referring to the hosting of memory, storage, and processing power on servers in remote, rather than local, data centers, the reframing of computer networking as cloud comput-

15 Eric Schmidt, interview by Danny Sullivan, *Search Engine Strategies Conference*, August 9, 2006.

ing helped explain complex networks to the public and communicate the benefits of an even more decentralized Internet. By 2010, the term entered the mainstream as multiple tech companies explicitly referred to connections to the cloud as a selling point for their products.[16]

16 Antonio Regalado, "Who Coined 'Cloud Computing'?" *MIT Technology Review* (October 31, 2011).

The concept of the cloud increasingly replaced the material technicity of computation, the human labor supporting that technology, and the spaces within which they resided with workable magic. Two key elements underscoring cloud technology shape what Tung-Hui Hu refers to as "cloud thinking" and informs the ability of such cloud logic to deterritorialize production by dematerializing technology.[17] First, cloud technology assumes that information—or whatever one wishes to retrieve through the network—is located in a position remote from the potential user. Second, the technology makes as its core selling point the ability to retrieve that remote information on demand. The relationship between remote information and on-demand retrieval forms the core of cloud logic, which resolves the demand by collapsing the time-distance for retrieval so effectively that information appears immediately, seemingly with little if any labor involved. This relationship between remote storage and on-demand retrieval, and the reduction of the time-distance between the two, underscores how the cloud metaphor dematerializes technology, dissolving the vast networks at play into the atmosphere. In dematerializing the physicality of technical networks, the cloud metaphor by extension dematerializes the technical lands and labor that make those networks possible.

17 Hu, *A Prehistory of the Cloud*.

The Middle Mile: Recovering Territories from "Second Nature"

Middle-mile sortation centers manage the outbound transport of packages within the distribution network. Packages are sorted by ZIP code and then transferred to an air hub (for transportation out of the region) or to the United States Postal Service or an Amazon Delivery Station (for packages to be delivered within the region). Packages to be shipped privately by UPS are picked up by UPS directly at the fulfillment center and thus do not enter the sortation center. Sortation centers are typically, but not always, stand-alone buildings in suburban locations just outside of major metropolitan areas. Sortation centers close to airports function as air gateways that fly packages on Amazon Prime Air flights to other regions. Packages destined for locations outside the region are loaded onto cargo planes at night. These planes fly from their regional airport to the main sortation center near the country's geographical center, ensuring a minimal flight path for all flights. The centroid sortation center for the United States is in Hebron, KY. Packages are re-sorted in the centroid sortation center, and the planes are then reloaded with packages destined for their region. This national spoke-and-hub system—where the centroid is the main hub, and the regional sortation centers close to airports are the spokes—is the crucial logistical arrangement that allows rapid delivery across the entire country, even without using rapid carriers like UPS and FedEx. In 2021, Amazon operated ninety-one regional sortation centers (including the centroid center in Hebron, KY) and seventeen airport hubs in the United States.

A new territorial reality emerges when sites of production are transformed into (in)visibility. The social landscape rendered visible by the (in)visibility of production functions as a site of pure leisure, an effect of the visual absence of labor. Privileging the observer over the participant, these sites of leisure foreground the subject "in search of experience" and reward the commodification of leisure.[18] Such touristic landscapes must either be devoid of productive labor or transform labor into a performance that can be consumed for the experience. This reduction of landscape to experience naturalizes the dematerialization of technology by creating a "second nature"—an arena of highly constructed and domesticated landscape conditions that nevertheless carry a "first nature" ideology that figures the constructed landscape as both "original" and "pure."[19]

The Last Mile: Rematerializing Labor and Landscape

Delivery stations receive packages from the regional sortation centers for service delivery within a forty-five-mile radius. These small, localized stations were initiated in 2013 and expanded in 2017 to introduce additional dedicated delivery stations for bulky and heavy packages. Multiple delivery stations are located within a given metro area, with most stations occupying existing buildings in central urban locations. Packages are prepared for the last mile of the fulfillment system at the delivery stations, which rely heavily on Amazon Sprinter vans and independent Amazon Flex drivers to take the packages to their final destinations. Driver routes are short and highly specific, with the metro areas being effectively covered by a high number of drivers, each attending to a relatively small area. Amazon's logistics system has been mainly focused on gaining absolute control of this last mile, which had been complicated when online commerce shifted the endpoint of consumer retail from the brick-and-mortar store to the consumer's home. The last mile has historically been the costliest portion of the fulfillment system, accounting for up to one-third of total shipping costs.[20] While some packages are delivered by local couriers or transferred to USPS, the

[18] MacCannell, *The Tourist.*

[19] William Cronon, *Nature's Metropolis: Chicago and the Great West* (New York, NY: W.W. Norton Company, 1991).

[20] Jake Alimahomed-Wilson, "The Amazonification of Logistics: E-Commerce, Labor, and Exploitation in the Last Mile," *The Cost of Free Shipping: Amazon in the Global Economy*, eds. Jake Alimahomed-Wilson and Ellen Reese (London: Pluto Press, 2020).

efficiency of the last mile, and thus of Amazon's entire logistics system, has laid in the mass reserve of contingent delivery drivers, whose numbers allow for same-day delivery and Sunday delivery. In 2021, Amazon operated 454 delivery stations in the United States.

Reclaiming and recovering territory and labor from dematerialization and abstraction occurs in part by returning to place. In Nueva Esperanza, the stark inequality revealed by the material differences between the informal settlement and TIJ1 brings aspects of these technical lands into visibility. The informal settlement is decentralized and ephemeral, occupying and creating landscapes that undermine disciplinary spatial practices. It presents an entirely different rendering of the same processes and practices that shape TIJ1. The aesthetic and social clash between TIJ1 and Nueva Esperanza reveals and replicates the invisible struggles obscured by the logistics landscapes—the gendered and racialized division of labor, the exploitation of contingent and underpaid workers, and the submission of the collective good to the interests of capital.[21] If not the power to subvert, recovery can at least expose the endless social segmentation—that is, the reduction of ourselves to what Deleuze refers to as "dividuals"—that makes possible the vast social inequalities apparent at Nueva Esperanza.[22]

Recovery then can counter both material and social investment in the cloud cultures that dematerialized, deterritorialized, and dismissed the stark realities obscured by technical lands. It means foregrounding labor, rematerializing technical processes, and spatially locating production and distribution sites, all in the service of countering invisible systems of legibility. Mechanisms of recovery might include critical mapping as a technique to reclaim the invisible. Yet recovery is not about a return to some primordial nature (which never existed) or idealized modes of production. Instead, it requires exposing the constructed relationship between first and second nature and, by extension, reworking notions of the natural and the cultural.[23] It means recognizing that the messy details obscured by the cloud schema are precisely where the work is done, thus necessitating bringing that middle realm of relevance to the foreground.

[21] Ellen Reese, "Gender, Race, and Amazon Warehouse Labor in the United States," *The Cost of Free Shipping: Amazon in the Global Economy*, eds. Jake Alimahomed-Wilson and Ellen Reese (London: Pluto Press, 2020).

[22] Deleuze, "Postscript on Societies of Control," 311.

[23] Gandy, *Concrete and Clay: Reworking Nature in New York City*.

Always Already Obsolete

Fueling Zones as Technical Lands

Florian Hertweck & Marija Marić

Tank Up and Shop at Discount Prices. Save by Tanking. Save by Shopping. Discount Tank Station. Tankomat. Tanking 24/7. Quality Fuel at Discount Prices. Shell. Gulf. Esso. Luxoil. Aral. Total. Eurosuper 95. V-Power 98. Diesel.[1] Just next to the border with Germany, along with Route du Luxembourg and a couple of hundreds of meters away from the A1 highway, cars and trucks are slowing down looking for the best offer and a place to park, tank up their reservoirs, and leave.

Technical lands are inaccessible, regulated, remote, and monofunctional spaces that are usually associated with controlled environments run by complex technologies that function under special legal regimes. From airports, freeports, and spaceports to data centers, bitcoin-mining farms, and sites of industrial extraction, they appear as backstage, invisible infrastructures that embody the logic of exception—a particular set of rules and laws that apply only to those territories and spaces.

As such, technical lands could be seen as part of what Keller Easterling theorized as "global infrastructure space," referring to the "spatial products" functioning as "repeatable formulas that generate most of the space in the world."[2] From free trade zones to ISO standards and broadband networks, these "spatial products" represent a genuine outcome of the global circulation of capital. They are also a medium of what Easterling termed *extrastatecraft*, which she defines as "a portmanteau describing the often undisclosed activities outside of, in addition to, and sometimes even in partnership with statecraft," thereby often legitimizing or disguising state power.[3] In modeling exceptionality, such as the no-tax policy in the case of free trade zones, or the normativity of ISO standards, to give just some examples, global infrastructure space is made precisely in the replicability of these models, as well as their capacity to defy the constraints of the locality and instead position themselves as nodes in the supranational space of global capitalism. These "spatial products" do not appear as remote and isolated technical lands. Instead, they are embedded into everyday life and urban space, at times taking the shape of the city themselves.

Oil is everywhere—on billboards, in slogans, in the air, on the ground, in the reservoirs under the ground. If it wouldn't be sealed, the soil would also taste like oil. Endless concrete surfaces are there to operate this oil urbanism, helping easier movement of vehicles and allowing for a better management of oil spillage, both from the active motors waiting in line and from the tanking stations. Here, at Wasserbillig, it looks like only two things are certain: the flow of cars and the flow of oil.

One such example of technical lands is the fueling zones concentrated along Luxembourg's border with its neighboring countries—Germany, France, and Belgium. A genuine product of Luxembourg's low-tax economy, these fueling zones could be seen as technical lands for the global oil trade. With the policy that sets the tax on motor fuels to only 6 percent,

[1] Adveriesements for gas stations and shops in Wasserbillig, Luxembourg. This and the following text inserts describe the traveling through the Wasserbillig strip.

[2] Keller Easterling, *Extrastatecraft: The Power of Infrastructure Space*, Kindle Edition (London and New York: Verso, 2014).

[3] Easterling, *Extrastatecraft*.

Luxembourg's fueling zones, and the "tank tourism" they promote organized around cheap gas, coffee, tobacco, and alcohol, emerged as an essential node in the global and regional oil network. They are a regular destination for both haulage companies, which have redirected their European transport routes towards Luxembourg to be able to fill up the 500-liter tanks of their trucks with two pumps simultaneously, as well as residents of neighboring countries who drive up to 100 kilometers to replenish their reservoirs and stocks of cigarettes, alcohol, and coffee.[4]

Fueling zones, however, do not only fuel reservoirs but also represent a critical contribution to Luxembourg's economy. Providing approximately 10 percent of total state revenues, while positioning Luxembourg as a European country with the highest carbon footprint, fueling zones represent a triumph of collaboration between the state and global petrol businesses.[5] Their pre-history could be traced back to the postwar industrialization of the country and its subsequent transformation into what might be called a "relational state," referring to the cities and states "whose niche-economic strategies focus on intermediary services" and who represent "a product of flows and relationships mediated vis-a-vis somewhere else."[6] Initially, this transformation involved an influx of foreign banks engaged in building highly secured money bunkers with anonymized safe deposit boxes in Luxembourg's territory, and more recently—tech industry and investment funds, concentrated in the proximity of Luxembourg's internationally busy airport.

The low-tax policy has, thus, helped define Luxembourg as an important node in an international flow of capital, people, and goods, operated through infrastructures and corporate networks such as Cargolux, one of the global players in logistics and cargo transport, as well as its highly secured Freeport—a controversial duty-free space for storing wine, art pieces and diamonds. Similarly, Luxembourg's business model has been geared for decades to attract big oil companies through low taxes on minerals, petrol, tobacco, coffee, and alcohol, resulting in the emergence of distinctive geography of fueling zones along its borders that appear as supermarkets, specialized for these few commodities. In fact, next to its economic performativity, Luxembourg petrol also has a distinct social value. Historically, in the context of the country's postwar reconstruction, it has been a subject of price equalization next to other essential goods such as medicine and potatoes, remaining the only such commodity with a regulated price today.

Like free trade zones, fueling zones in Luxembourg also appear as replicable models of exception, low-tax geographies that serve as technical lands for continuous circulation of vehicles, fuel, and other commodities. The exceptionality of fueling zones, and technical lands more broadly, could also be seen as a mechanism of their replicability across the territory, placing them in line with Giorgio Agamben's idea of the "state of exception" as a practice suspending "the dominant paradigm of government in contemporary politics."[7] Seen from the point of view of a late capitalist society, defined by the seamless blurring of boundaries between physical and digital worlds,

[4] "Fuel Tourism in Luxembourg," *Canvas*, accessed July 15, 2021, https://canvas.disabroad.org/courses/4391/pages/fuel-tourism-in-luxembourg.

[5] "Fuel Tourism."

[6] Luxembourg occupies fourth place in the world GDP in terms of its share of international trade flows, investment, and cross-border revenue. See Catherine Wong, Markus Hesse, and Thomas J. Sigler, "City-States in Relational Urbanization: The Case of Luxembourg and Singapore," *Urban Geography*, (2021), https://doi.org/10.1080/02723638.2021.1878331.

[7] Giorgio Agamben, *State of Exception: Homo Sacer II* (Chicago, IL: University of Chicago Press, 2005).

fueling zones appear as "analog" and even nostalgic territorial "objects." They remind us that the remoteness of technical lands is not necessarily physical—although often imposed by the expensive land and real estate prices in and around cities—it is also symbolic, at times defined through their functional segregation and rendered invisibility. One could thus argue that their remoteness depends both on the position one is looking from, and the scales and distances inscribed into the territory itself.

But gas stations here are more than mere stops for tanking up. Surrounded by vast parking areas, all kinds of car wash, care and repair services—they are the ultimate car-comfort zones. Their lightweight prefabricated structures are made in a way to keep the car happy and allow all sorts of maximums—maximum number of cars, maximum surface for advertisements of discounts, oil companies logos and products, maximum storage space for cigarettes, alcohol and coffee. Assembled closely to each other, they constitute a boulevard-like shopping street; a drive-in that exceeds the limits of one building and instead spreads across the territory.

Are fueling zones of Luxembourg architectural objects, urban spaces, infrastructures, or landscapes? Assembled around the main street and appearing as strips flanked by small, decorated sheds with extended roofs, fueling zones are comparable to the familiar imagery and morphology of the Las Vegas Strip. Going beyond mere aesthetic fascination with the architectural typology of the gas station, the question here becomes: what can we learn from gas station strips fifty years after *Learning from Las Vegas*? What are the new and the old lessons of the built environment produced under the paradigm of consumption and subsumed by our persistent dependency on cars?

The pragmatic architectures and urbanisms of fueling zones could be seen as a spatial manifestation of circulation of oil and money because they are essentially organizational spaces simplified to optimally accommodate their one dominant function—consumption. Far from shiny glass walls of central business districts and high-tech infrastructures of smart cities, fueling zones are an example of what Manuel Castells described as the "architecture of global networks," appearing as modest spaces of logistics, or rather as technical lands of global capitalism.[8] As such, they still produce their own distinct aesthetics and politics.

Fueling zones also manifest a distinct way of occupying the land in its cultural, political, and economic complexity. They are characterized by their relationship with the land as a territory—with more than 60 percent of gas stations in Luxembourg located at the borders with its neighboring countries, and more than 80 percent of the transport fuel used in Luxembourg being purchased by foreign car and truck owners—the border condition of different tax regimes sits at the very core of fueling zones as an economic phenomenon.[9] This constellation positions fueling zones as a symbolic economic

[8] Manuel Castells, *The Rise of the Network Society*, 2nd edition (Malden, MA: Wiley-Blackwell, 2010), 15.

[9] "Fuel Tourism."

border in the context of a border-free Schengen Zone. Even when accessible, as technical lands, fueling zones nevertheless produce boundaries.

Additionally, their relationship to the land as a construction surface with economic value sheds light on the highly speculative real estate and land market in Luxembourg, which is characterized by high levels of scarcity and inequality. This condition set the base for a continuous transformation of agricultural fields into construction land.[10] Here, the process of land acquisition through which new gas stations are being built in the fueling zones, which includes concessions of the land by the municipality or the state, became part of this speculative practice, that, nevertheless, represents another significant revenue for the state budget.[11] Fueling zones could thus be seen as genuine products of the public-private partnership in the context of a neoliberal state, testifying at the same time to the competitiveness of global corporations for their stake in these border zones. As such, the technical lands of fueling zones remind us of their exploitative relationship to the land in terms of the extraction of value.

Finally, their relationship to the land as soil points out the aggressive and unsustainable character of fueling zones as economic and social practices of Luxembourg's car-dependency. Here, the soil could be seen as an archive of a global movement of oil and its devastating effects on the local environment and its ecosystems. Describing soil as "the container of evidence" of the "remains that didn't resist to dissolution," Maria Puig de la Bellacasa outlined a productive methodology which could be used to understanding Luxembourg's fueling zones soil as a container of evidence of the widespread effects of the fossil fuel culture—a model that paradoxically contributes 10 percent to the country's carbon footprint.[12] Here, one could argue that the technical understanding of the notion of land in the case of the fueling zones, is suggestive of its treatment as a wasteland—a container emptied of its environmental complexity, such as its ecosystems, and instead positioned as a site of storage and disposal.

In his essay titled "The Politics and Poetics of Infrastructure," Brian Larkin describes infrastructures as a "matter that enable the movement of other matter," pointing out that "what distinguishes infrastructures from technologies is that they are objects that create the grounds on which other objects operate, and when they do so, they operate as systems."[13] As infrastructures, fueling zones could be nodes in the global network of the flow of oil; architectures of circulation that shape landscapes of movement and pollution. Writing on the project of the Trans-Arabian Pipeline, Rania Ghosn observed how the movement of oil to the forefront of international trade, both in terms of its trade quantity and value, "was only made possible by the infrastructure that delivered it from its points of extraction to world markets."[14] She further observed how, in this context, the overcoming of distance becomes a matter of primary concern, leading to the new spatio-temporal experiences of spatial compression and acceleration of time.[15] Similarly, gas station strips are places where planetary, regional, and local scales collide and where temporalities of fast global circulation usually associated with high-

[10] The unequal distribution of land in Luxembourg is visible because the public sector owns only 10 percent of developable land. In comparison, one percent of the population owns one-quarter of all land in the country. From Florian Hertweck, "The Question of Land Reloaded," *Architecture on Common Ground. The Question of Land: Positions and Models*, ed. Florian Hertweck (Zurich: Lars Müller Publishers, 2020), 9.

[11] The land for gas stations on the highways has been a concession by the state for thirty years.

[12] María Puigde la Bellacasa, "Encountering Bioinfrastructure: Ecological Struggles and the Sciences of Soil," *Social Epistemology* 28, no. 1 (2014): 29.

[13] Brian Larkin, "The Politics and Poetics of Infrastructure," *Annual Review of Anthropology* 42 (2013): 329.

[14] Rania Ghosn, "Territories of Oil: The Trans-Arabian Pipeline," *The Arab City: Architecture and Representation*, eds. Amale Andraos and Nora Akawi (New York, NY: Columbia University Press, 2016)2016), 165.

[15] Ghosn, "Territories of Oil," 165.

speed travel meet the slow movement of freight trucks and car commuters that equally participate in this global flow.

Here, people are in a permanent state of transition—truck drivers on long routes through Europe, daily commuters from the cross-border region, even most of the workers at the gas stations power up their cars at the end of the day and leave. The landscape of fueling zones is made of stops, shops, drive-ins; its culture is organized around tanking and choosing the best deals. Although open 24/7, still, this place feels like a ticking clock; its future is uncertain. What will come to replace fuel one day in the fueling zones? Who will stop, or stay, here?

Fueling zones could also be seen as a paradigm of Luxembourg's growth-based economy. However, in contrast to other pillars of Luxembourg's economic relationality, fueling zones seem to be the most vulnerable to the challenges of contemporary society, opening up a broader question—how do we think planned obsolescence beyond an (architectural) object, and in terms of entire territories? Positioning novelty as a core feature of capitalist production, Daniel M. Abramson observed that "obsolescence, as a process, is almost by definition fundamental to capitalism ... the old, must give way to the new, or the process of accumulation fatally seizes up."[16] Here, one could ask—what are the futures of these always-already-obsolete objects that already now exist as ruins of capitalism?

Standing as monuments not only to the fossil era but to the environmental, political, economic, and social unsustainability closely tied to it, fueling zones could be seen as productive entry points in understanding how capitalist production adapts to cultural pressures, but also as a potential to navigate these processes of transformation differently. Daniel M. Abramson effectively pointed out: "The architectural history of obsolescence illustrates the flexibility of capitalism, its capacity to absorb critique and evolve from its contradictions, to exploit the built environment one way and then the other: obsolescence, then sustainability."[17] Looking back at fueling zones from the perspectives of contemporary debates on climate change and environmental degradation, the question becomes: How could we imagine these spaces going beyond technical lands of consumption when they are enabled by unsustainable low-tax policies and promises of growth? What are the possibilities of repair, both in terms of their architecture and landscapes into which they are embedded? And what would this process of repair entail? Beyond mere retrofitting or depollution or greening, how could fuel zones—standing as monuments to the broken society and broken territory—become opportunities for rethinking the notion of repair across different social and spatial scales?

[16] Daniel M. Abramson, *Obsolescence: An Architectural History* (Chicago and London: The University of Chicago Press, 2016), 6.

[17] Abramson, *Obsolescence,* 6.

The Global Industrial Feedlot Matrix

A Metabolic Monstrosity

Swarnabh Ghosh, Neil Brenner, & Nikos Katsikis

1.

In a widely debated passage in Volume 3 of *Capital*, likely written in the 1870s, Marx offered a foundational observation about capitalist industrial agriculture. When the "industrial system" is "applied to agriculture," Marx argued, it not only imposes ruination upon the humans who use machines as their means of production but also depletes the soil of the nutrients required to sustain its fertility.[1] In this sense, strategies to increase agricultural productivity through the application of industrial machinery contain an inherent contradiction. They may increase commodity output by reducing the socially necessary labor time required to produce farm products, but in so doing, they destroy the material basis of agricultural production—human workers and the soil.[2]

In making this argument, Marx drew upon the work of German agricultural chemist Justus von Liebig, who decades earlier had famously documented the vampire-like processes through which early industrial agriculture in Britain had depleted the soil's nutrients, robbing it of its capacity to support productive cultivation. This led to a process of ecological imperialism where core agro-industrial regions sought to rejuvenate their soil by transferring the requisite nutrients (in forms such as human bones or guano) from other regions, whether through direct military violence, land grabbing, or other forms of economic subjection.[3]

These dynamics entail a relentless expropriation, long-distance circulation, and industrial recomposition of materials to sustain the accumulation process. However, they exacerbate rather than resolve the original contradiction. Strategies to repair the environmental plunder wrought through capitalist operations serve, quite literally, to *displace* them by transferring their environmental load to more distant regions.[4] It is the spatial separation of industrial production from its metabolic conditions of possibility that permits agro-industrial accumulation to continue. This separation is also a rearticulation of metabolic interconnections and a rescaling of their geographies. High-throughput agro-industrial production is sustained in some regions precisely by intensifying processes of environmental degradation in other zones, including the biosphere as a whole.

A contradictory dialectic is thus revealed. Agro-industrial intensification hinges upon the appropriation of material inputs (raw materials, fertilizers) from distant locations, their circulation to the zone of industry (a complex problem of logistics, energy, and labor), *and* the ecological degradation of the spaces in which those processes occur, from the local to the planetary. Indeed, it can be argued that all forms of capitalist industrial production—extraction, agriculture, manufacturing, and logistics—hinge simultaneously upon the appropriation of "cheap natures" and the relentless destruction of their environmental foundations.[5] Even if they are sited far beyond the high-throughput industrial field, mine, or factory, processes of environmental load displacement and the exhaustion of ecological surpluses are constitutive of capitalist industrial development. These dynamics are not, as mainstream economists claim, mere market failures or "externalities," but

[1] Karl Marx, *Capital, Vol. III*, (London: Penguin Classics, 1993), 637.

[2] John Bellamy Foster, "Marx's Theory of Metabolic Rift: Classical Foundations for Environmental Sociology," *American Journal of Sociology* 105, no. 2 (1999): 366–405.

[3] Brett Clark and John Bellamy Foster, "Ecological Imperialism and the Global Metabolic Rift: Unequal Exchange and the Guano/Nitrates Trade," *International Journal of Comparative Sociology* 50, no. 3–4 (June 2009): 311–34.

[4] Alf Hornborg, *Global Ecology and Unequal Exchange. Fetishism in a Zero-Sum World* (London: Routledge, 2011).

[5] Jason W. Moore, *Capitalism in the Web of Life: Ecology and the Accumulation of Capital*, 1st edition (New York, NY: Verso, 2015); John Bellamy Foster, Brett Clark, and Richard York, *The Ecological Rift: Capitalism's War on the Earth* (New York, NY: Monthly Review Press, 2010).

6 Nancy Fraser, "Behind Marx's Hidden Abode: For an Expanded Conception of Capitalism," *New Left Review*, no. 86 (2014): 55–72.

are the very conditions of possibility for capitalist operations—socioecological "hidden abodes" that directly support and sustain the accumulation process while being obscured from view.[6]

This chapter explores the implications of this proposition with reference to the hidden abodes and monstrous environmental contradictions of industrial livestock production since its origins in the late nineteenth century. We offer a metabolic genealogy of the livestock mega-factories known as Concentrated Animal Feeding Operations (CAFOs) and their conditions of possibility within broader circuits and political ecologies of capital. These spaces of hyper-rationalized, securitized, and militarized animal slaughter and processing are among the most iconic expressions of the contemporary industrial livestock regime. In world-ecological terms, however, CAFOs are nodes within a planet-encompassing metabolic circuit fueled by fossil energy, voracious land-use intensification, colossal infrastructural investment, and rampant environmental destruction.[7] Industrial livestock production is, therefore, not only premised upon the operationalization of the bounded technical lands in which CAFOs are situated. But, more importantly, it also hinges upon the construction of multiscalar *operational landscapes* that support this circuit of capital and onto which its socio-environmental contradictions are projected.

7 Tony Weis, *The Ecological Hoofprint: The Global Burden of Industrial Livestock* (London: Zed Books, 2013); Mindi Schneider, "Developing the Meat Grab," *The Journal of Peasant Studies* 41, no. 4 (2014): 613–33.

We refer to the worldwide network of such operational landscapes as the Global Industrial Feedlot Matrix (GIFM). The GIFM includes labor relations, land-use systems, industrial infrastructures, relays of fossil-based energy, logistics grids, plumes of carbon emissions, as well as technoscientifically mediated multispecies entanglements between human worker-consumers, commodity animals, and pathogens. The GIFM is the product and medium not only of corporate accumulation strategies but also of geopolitical power, state spatial strategies, and regulatory projects. As we argue below, national governments and multilateral agencies are important institutional animators of the technological, political-economic, territorial, and environmental transformations that underpin the GIFM's operations. Drawing upon a tradition of critical agrarian studies known as food regime theory, we seek to articulate the GIFM and its changing geographies to the geohistory of capitalist industrial agriculture—in particular, the "political construction of agrifood orders shaped by, and shaping, specific accumulation dynamics."[8]

8 Philip McMichael, *Food Regimes and Agrarian Questions* (Rugby: Practical Action Publishing, 2014), 8, passim.

Although some of its elements emerged during the British-centered imperial food regime of the late nineteenth century, the GIFM was consolidated with the intensification of industrial meat production in the United States Corn Belt during the postwar, US-led global food regime, where it encompassed a fossil-fueled, regional economic geography of mechanized slaughterhouses, monofunctional feed croplands, industrial fertilizer plants, storage facilities and railroads. In the post-1980s period, with the crystallization of the neoliberal food regime, the constitutive elements of the GIFM have been dramatically upscaled to form an intercontinental system that includes monocrop soy feed plantations in South America and new zones of high-throughput industrial agribusiness concentration in erstwhile "rural" zones of China. These links of the industrial livestock commodity chain are meshed together via transcontinental logistics circuits (including shipping lanes, ports, roads, and rail networks) and the global financial networks through which investments on commodity futures are speculatively channeled into land, labor, and infrastructure. This upscaled, neoliberalized formation of the GIFM involves new patterns of carbon-intensive land-use simplification, infrastructural consolidation, long-distance commodity transport, hypertrophic mega-concentration of industrial animals, and the consequent degradation and wasting of land, bodies, soil, water, and air on a planetary scale.

2.

Technologies for the large-scale production of commodity animals were pioneered in the Central Slaughterhouse of La Villette in Haussmann's Paris during the 1860s. As Sigfried Giedion noted in his mid-century exploration, even in the absence of extensive mechanical infrastructures, La Villette represented an unprecedented centralization, technical rationalization, and spatial systematization of the constituent processes of animal slaughter and processing.[9] In contrast to later, Taylorist-Fordist models of mechanized livestock production, La Villette preserved an ethos of individualized supervision of each animal, from farmyard to abattoir and butcher.

fig 1

La Villette's metabolic circuitry was relatively localized. The commodity animals it processed were drawn from proximate farming hinterlands, and its products were primarily oriented towards metropolitan consumption within Paris through newly expanded city markets. In his *Mémoires*, Haussmann characterized La Villette as "one of the most considerable works accomplished by my administration ... paralleling the great sewer constructions."[10] Much like Haussmann's more widely celebrated boulevards, squares, and gardens, La Villette became an important infrastructural prototype—in this case, for emergent approaches to commodity-animal slaughter in major nineteenth-century European metropolitan centers.[11]

Crucially, La Villette was not only an infrastructural model but a metabolic one. It was embedded within a regional agrarian system where previously fallow land had been "replaced by a N2 fixing fodder crop such as clover, alfalfa, peas or horse beans."[12] This form of land-use rotation produced "a considerable increase in livestock density and hence in manure availability and cereal yield," but without imposing "a significant change either in farm size or the structure of the landscape."[13] La Villette was a production node and infrastructural conduit embedded within this relatively "autotrophic" agrarian system. As such, it demonstrated how the slaughter and processing of commodity animals could be rationalized for local consumption while sourcing the latter through an intermeshed system of land use, labor deployment, and feed-crop production in relatively contiguous hinterland zones.

The development of large-scale industrial slaughterhouses and meatpacking plants was consolidated and significantly upscaled during the

[9] Sigfried Giedion, *Mechanization Takes Command: A Contribution to Anonymous History* (New York, NY: Oxford University Press, 1948), 209–11.

[10] Haussmann, quoted in Giedion, *Mechanization Takes Command,* 209.

[11] Giedion, *Mechanization Takes Command,* 210.

[12] Gilles Billen, Sabine Barles, Josette Garnier, Joséphine Rouillard and Paul Benoit, "The Food-Print of Paris: Long-term Reconstruction of the Nitrogen Flows Imported into the City from its Hinterland," *Regional Environmental Change* 9 (2009): 19.

[13] Gilles Billen et. al, "The Food-Print of Paris," 19.

fig 1 Pig slaughterhouse in La Villette, Paris, 1874. Tilly Smeeton, et al, woodcut illustration, Journal Universel, no. 1640, volume LXIV, August 1, 1874, Paris Musées/ Musées Carnavalet

last decades of the nineteenth century in the US Midwest. This process was initiated in Cincinnati (the original "Porkopolis") and was subsequently articulated across an intermetropolitan, pig-production network that included Chicago, Kansas City, St. Louis, Milwaukee, and Omaha. Across this emergent regional system of industrial pig production, massive mechanical infrastructures and territorial enclaves were constructed in which millions of animal-bodies were processed according to a purely calculative, profit-oriented logic, as the raw material in a complex relay of mechanized production, packaging, storage, and transport.[14] In his chapter "Mechanization and Organic Substance," Giedion surveys the chief elements of the high-throughput "disassembly line" that was set into motion in the metropolitan industrial stockyards of the Midwest. Its elaborate technical infrastructure included equipment for such gruesomely specialized tasks as hog-cleaning, pig-scraping, spine-cleaving, and mechanical skinning.[15] The horrific spectacle of mass animal death was normalized, Giedion posits, through the construction of elaborate technical spaces in which industrial machinery could process the organic substance of animal bodies with maximal precision and speed to enhance material throughput and, by consequence, commodity outputs. The tightly choreographed assemblage of technology, infrastructure, and spatial organization in the Chicago stockyards forecast the subsequent generalization of mass production systems across other leading sectors in the emergent, US-centric accumulation regime of the twentieth century.[16] Henry Ford modeled the automobile assembly line of his fabled Highland Park car factory on "moving lines [of animals] that had been operating at least since the 1850s in the vertical abattoirs of Cincinnati and Chicago, with deadly efficiency and to deadly effect."[17]

Despite its extensive deployment of industrial equipment, the slaughterhouses of Cincinnati were mainly supplied with cattle and pork that were herded into the city from the proximate agricultural region. With the advent of the railroad in the second half of the nineteenth century, Chicago's livestock supply zone expanded from contiguous prairie regions outwards to the Great Plains, stretching from Texas to the Canadian border, where Indigenous lands had been enclosed through the genocidal violence of settler colonialism, and where pasturelands now replaced the once plentiful herds of bison.[18] For Giedion, the colossal infrastructural equipment of Chicago's Union Stockyards was directly connected to the "free tracts of grassland" on the Great Plains, where livestock herds could be raised and shipped by rail to centralized hubs for slaughter and packaging.[19] The popular mythology of the free and open range, perpetuated uncritically by Giedion, was belied by the brutal slaughter of Native American peoples through which the Great Plains pasturelands had been established, and by the accretion of landscape interventions through which the supposed "free tracts" of open range had been engineered. Moreover, their primary nonhuman inhabitants—the rapidly expanding cattle herds—were likewise direct products of settler colonialism; they had been imported to the Americas by the Spanish, and subsequently by the English, creating a "bovine melting pot."[20]

[14] William Cronon, *Nature's Metropolis: Chicago and the Great West* (New York, NY: Norton, 1992), 207–62.

[15] Giedion, *Mechanization Takes Command*, 228–40.

[16] Cronon, *Nature's Metropolis*, 229.

[17] Nicole Shukin, *Animal Capital: Rendering Life in Biopolitical Times*, Posthumanities 6 (Minneapolis, MN: University of Minnesota Press, 2009), 87.

[18] Giedion, *Mechanization Takes Command*, 218–19; Cronon, *Nature's Metropolis*, 207–30.

[19] Giedion, *Mechanization Takes Command*, 211–14.

[20] Chris Otter, *Diet for a Large Planet: Industrial Britain, Food Systems, and World Ecology* (Chicago, IL: The University of Chicago Press, 2021), 27.

[21] Cronon, *Nature's Metropolis*, 218–24.

[22] Cronon, *Nature's Metropolis*, 247.

[23] Cronon, *Nature's Metropolis*, 221; Otter, *Diet for a Large Planet*, 27–28.

[24] Cronon, *Nature's Metropolis*, 223.

[25] Cronon, *Nature's Metropolis*, 248, 221–22.

With the consolidation of the industrial meat system, the plains themselves underwent a further round of large-scale landscape transformation.[21] Especially in closer proximity to Chicago, pastureland grasses were superseded by industrially produced corn as the main feed for livestock, along with "tame" hay as feed for hogs.[22] The subsequent parcelization of the plains through railroads, barbed-wire fencing, feedlots, and other rangeland-management techniques contributed to new patterns of intensive grazing and livestock concentration. These practices led, in turn, to a biological transformation of cattle into more docile animals suitable for industrial processing.[23] The conversion of grassland to pasture and then cropland and feedlot, and the concomitant replacement of bison with industrial animals, drastically reconfigured the "substrate" of inherited webs of life.[24] The result of these "sweeping environmental manipulations" of the Great Plains landscape and the commodity animals it produced was, as William Cronon argues, not only the accelerated industrial development of Chicago but the consolidation of an "integrated system of meat production that reached from the Rockies across the tallgrass prairies of Iowa and Illinois all the way to Chicago and beyond."[25]

The incipient industrial production of livestock during this period was thus inextricably linked to broader transformations in the metabolism of capitalist agriculture and its geographies. For much of the nineteenth century, the dominant agricultural model in the US Midwest had involved a mixed farming system based on the rotation between corn, which was used for animal feed; wheat, which was used for household consumption and, to a lesser extent, as a cash crop sold to local mills; and oats, which were used to feed draft animals such as horses. Livestock were fed in open feedlots, while animal waste was used as manure to fertilize proximate fields. Much like in the regional hinterland of Haussmann's Paris, feed for livestock and food for household consumption were largely produced on the same land parcel and through a set of locally managed metabolic circuits. Commodified relationships were, to a significant degree, restricted to the buying and selling of livestock, grains, tools, and land itself.

With the consolidation of the first global food regime under British imperial hegemony in the late nineteenth century, this agrarian system was severely destabilized and eventually superseded. The introduction of fossil energy—in the spheres of circulation (through the railways) and production (through coal-powered industrial slaughterhouses)—contributed not only to the concentration of meat production in major cities, but to a dramatic expansion, upscaling, and subsequent specialization of primary production areas across the Midwestern region. These shifts also entailed the development of extensive agrarian zones oriented exclusively towards the production of animal feed monocrops. The cash nexus was increasingly generalized as commodity outputs were reoriented towards extraregional markets, from the US East Coast to Britain and, to a lesser extent, Europe. The lineaments of a grain-livestock "complex" were thus established in which concentrated industrial livestock production and monoculture feed landscapes were at once functionally and spatially intermeshed.[26] The contemporary commodity chains and political ecologies associated with the GIFM are an outgrowth of this mid-century intermeshing in the US Midwest.

The emergent metabolic circuitry of the GIFM was also subject to relatively circumscribed, yet consequential versions of the environmental contradictions that would, during the subsequent century, cascade across the planet. First, whereas the expansion of the US industrial livestock system had been fueled in significant measure due to the exhaustion of meat and grain landscapes in imperial Britain, the problem of declining ecological surplus soon began to afflict the settler-colonial territories as well, including the US Midwest. This burgeoning soil-fertility crisis led to a massive intensification of capitalization processes during the post-1930s period, primarily through the extensive deployment of machinery and industrial fertilizer. Second, the intensification of industrial livestock production involved the unchecked discharge of fetid waste directly into adjacent urban environments—soil, air, and water. The Union Stockyards of Chicago are a notorious example of such toxic industrial externalizations, which were pervasive in mechanized slaughterhouses across Midwestern cities during the latter half of the nineteenth century.[27] Its sewage, consisting of manure, offal, blood, and wastewater, was channeled directly into the South Fork of the Chicago River, creating a noxious stench that pervaded surrounding neighborhoods.[28]

fig 2

A series of colossal infrastructural investments—the construction of the Illinois and Michigan Canal (the 1860s) and the Sanitary and Ship Canal (1900)—enabled the reversal of the Chicago River's flow direction. Although these emergent strategies of industrial landscape remediation channeled the effluence of industrial waste from the stockyards further downstream, they severely exacerbated the problems they were meant to resolve, both in the stockyard district and in downstream locations, including some as distant as Louisiana.[29] During the following century, the further consolidation of industrial livestock as a leading global agricultural commodity would at once intensify and upscale this toxic ecological "hoofprint," with devastating consequences for landscapes and their myriad forms of life, both human and nonhuman, across the planet.[30]

3.

The post-1930s period witnessed the emergence of a new formation of industrial animal slaughter and processing—the vertically integrated broiler chicken industry. Between 1934 and 1994, the number of broiler chickens produced annually in the United States increased from 34 million to over 7 billion, and annual per capita consumption increased from around 0.7 pounds to nearly 70 pounds.[31] This unprecedented explosion in chicken production and consumption was propelled in part by a series of technological innovations designed to subsume the entire life cycle of chickens—from their genetic material and breeding to their feeding, fattening, and eventual slaughter—to the dictates of industrial commodity production. William

[26] Harriet Friedmann, "Distance and Durability: Shaky Foundations of the World Food Economy," *Third World Quarterly* 13, no. 2 (1992): 371–83.

[27] Sylvia Hood Washington, *Packing Them In: An Archeology of Environmental Racism in Chicago, 1865–1954* (Bloomington: Lexington Books, 2004).

[28] Michael Chieffalo, *Dung, Death and Disease: Livestock and Capitalist Urbanization in the United States from the Early Nineteenth Century to the Present*, PhD thesis, Graduate School of Design, Harvard University (Cambridge, MA: Harvard University, 2021).

[29] Chieffalo, *Dung, Death and Disease*, 122.

[30] Weis, *The Ecological Hoofprint*.

[31] William Boyd and Michael Watts, "Agro-Industrial Just-in-Time: The Chicken Industry and Postwar American Capitalism," *Globalising Food: Agrarian Questions and Global Restructuring*, eds., David Goodman and Michael Watts, 139–65 (Oxford: Routledge, 1997), 140.

fig 2   Union Stockyards, Chicago, USA, 1878.
Charles Raschler, color lithograph, published by Walsh & Co,
c. 1878, Chicago, Library of Congress

Boyd aptly describes this transformation as a form of "biological intensification."[32] It included extensive state-supported experimentation in the use of antibiotics (such as penicillin and tetracycline) and monoculture-derived feed, as well as the selective breeding of industrial chickens—metabolically "efficient," fast-growing poultry whose life cycles were engineered to increase throughput, reduce costs, and maximize profits.

An iconic example of the latter was the hybrid "meat-type" broiler chicken, an outcome of the "Chicken of Tomorrow" breeding contests promoted by the poultry firm A&P and the US Department of Agriculture between 1948 and 1951.[33] By the late 1950s, these and related efforts had transformed the backyard chicken into a "highly efficient machine for converting feed grains into cheap animal-flesh protein."[34] These strategies also enabled the systematic confinement of chicken populations within fossil energy-guzzling industrial processing facilities throughout their entire life cycle. The technology of intensive confinement was fundamental to the upscaling of poultry production and the temporal rescaling of the chicken life cycle. In her pioneering *Animal Machines*, Ruth Harrison offered a powerful description of intensive confinement:

> The day-old chicks are installed, eight or ten thousand at a time ... in long, windowless houses punctuated only with extractor fans in serried rows along the ridge of the roofs, and air intake vents along the side walls. In a big establishment, these sheds will be ranked side by side each with its giant feed storage hopper standing as if on guard at one end, the whole array looking like an incongruous factory, sprouting, for no apparent reason, in the middle of some remote field.[35]

Since the 1960s, the "incongruous factories" in which chickens are raised, slaughtered, and processed have grown to unimaginably gigantic proportions. In April 2021, Tyson Foods, one of the world's largest producers of broiler chickens, inaugurated a new "poultry complex" in Humboldt, Tennessee. With a cost of nearly half a billion dollars, this production facility is spread over 370,000 square feet, contains a hatchery, feed mill, and processing plant, and has the capacity to produce more than 1.2 million chickens per week.[36] The transformation of poultry production during the post-World War II period was thus inextricably linked to the bio-industrial and genetic transformation of the chicken itself: "[T]he amount of time required to turn a day-old chicken into a full-grown broiler decreased by about 20 percent between 1947 and 1951 alone."[37] By the late twentieth century, broiler chickens matured to marketable weights in just six to seven weeks, nearly three times faster than in the 1940s.[38] In the same period, feed requirements were reduced by more than one half per chicken. Through an elaborate system of industrial engineering, more commodity chickens were being produced more rapidly based on lower caloric inputs.

The rapid industrialization of chicken production in the postwar period was inextricably linked to the consolidation of a "distinctively American,

[32] William Boyd, "Making Meat: Science, Technology, and American Poultry Production," *Technology and Culture* 42, no. 4 (2001): 652.

[33] H. L. Shrader, "The Chicken-of-Tomorrow Program: Its Influence on 'Meat-Type' Poultry Production," *Poultry Science* 31, no. 1 (1952): 3–10.

[34] Boyd, "Making Meat," 638.

[35] Ruth Harrison, *Animal Machines: The New Factory Farming Industry* (London: Vincent Stuart, 1964), 43.

[36] Tyson Foods, "Tyson Foods Invests $425 Million in New Tennessee Poultry Complex."

[37] Steve Striffler, *Chicken: The Dangerous Transformation of America's Favorite Food* (New Haven, CT: Yale University Press, 2005), 16.

[38] H. D. Griffin and C. Goddard, "Rapidly Growing Broiler (Meat-Type) Chickens: Their Origin and Use for Comparative Studies of the Regulation of Growth," *International Journal of Biochemistry* 26, no. 1 (1994): 20.

39 Boyd and Watts, "Agro-Industrial Just-in-Time," 145–46.

40 Michael J. Watts, "Are Hogs like Chickens? Enclosure and Mechanization in Two 'White Meat' Filières," *Geographies of Commodity Chains*, eds., Alex Hughes and Suzanne Reimer (London: Routledge, 2004), 39–62; Pew Commission on Industrial Farm Animal Production, "Putting Meat on the Table: Industrial Farm Animal Production in America" (United States: Pew Commission on Industrial Farm Animal Production, 2008); J. L. Anderson, *Capitalist Pigs: Pigs, Pork, and Power in America* (Morgantown, WV: West Virginia University Press, 2019).

41 On the "Livestock Revolution" see Christopher Delgado et al., "Livestock to 2020: The Revolution Continues," International Agricultural Trade Research Consortium, International Trade in Livestock Products Symposium, Auckland, New Zealand, January 18–19, 2001.

42 Harriet Friedmann and Philip McMichael, "Agriculture and the State System: The Rise and Decline of National Agricultures, 1870 to the Present" *Sociologia Ruralis* 29, no. 2 (1989): 107.

43 Boyd and Watts, "Agro-Industrial Just-in-Time," 148.

44 Friedmann, "Distance and Durability," 376.

flexible, just-in-time production system," dominated by large agribusiness corporations like Tyson, Perdue, and Holly Farms.[39] These "regional integrators" pursued the vertical integration of various stages of chicken production, including feed manufacturing, under a unified corporate structure. This presaged the broader reorganization of livestock production into vertically integrated agribusiness commodity chains in the late twentieth century, a process that further increased the quantity of material throughput in production and ratcheted up the environmental devastation unleashed through its metabolic relays.[40]

The proximate origins of the much-discussed contemporary "Livestock Revolution" are to be found in the upscaling of industrial poultry production in the postwar United States.[41] The integration of poultry production chains by large agro-industrial capital was constitutive of the broader restructuring of the US and, by extension, the transnational agrifood system in the 1950s and 1960s. As Harriet Friedmann and Phillip McMichael note in their classic study of global food regimes, the vertical integration of production led to "a new specialization at farm and regional levels between livestock production on one side and on the other, the components of manufactured composite feeds."[42] The broiler chicken industry, for instance, first emerged in the Delmarva Peninsula on the eastern seaboard of the United States in the 1920s and was subsequently consolidated in the American South, where it was intensively concentrated within specialized agro-industrial districts in northwestern Arkansas, northern Alabama, and northern Georgia. By the late 1960s, this "southern production complex" had expanded to incorporate subregions in Mississippi and North Carolina.[43]

The organizational and spatial recomposition of poultry production also drove a concomitant restructuring of commodity agriculture in the United States and beyond, in significant measure due to the sector's overarching dependence upon industrially sourced feed crops such as soybean and maize. According to Friedmann, feed crop production zones "were as important to the emergence of the livestock complex as factory production of poultry and pork, and the growth of cattle feedlots."[44] The restructuring of feed crop agriculture across the United States coincided with a shift from low-input agricultural *expansion* to high-input agricultural *intensification*. The former was characterized by relatively small increases in crop yields based mainly on the territorial expansion of farmland, a process that was exhausted by the early twentieth century. By contrast, high-input agro-industrial intensification was premised upon strategies to increase productivity through the generalized application of inorganic, synthetic (nitrogen) fertilizers and herbicides, and through the introduction of hybrid (genetically modified) plants. Together with continuing mechanization, these developments allowed the concentration and densification of processing facilities in conjunction with an aggregate explosion of feed crop yields.

These intertwined processes of operational intensification and spatial centralization were, in turn, premised upon a similarly dramatic increase in the use of fertilizer, from less than 3 million pounds in the 1950s to more than 10 million in the late 1970s, and an even more immense increase in the use of herbicides and pesticides.[45] The growth of corn yields was accomplished through an intensification of production rather than through an expansion of territorial acreage (some of which was, in any case, being shifted to soybean production during this period). Soybeans also replaced other feed crops previously cultivated to support draft animals, whose function was now largely obsolete due to mechanization. After World War II until the 1970s, soybean acreage steadily expanded, and this plentiful supply of cheap feed crops underwrote a massive increase in poultry and livestock production.[46] Much of the new soybean production occurred in specialized agrarian regions, notably in the Corn Belt, where it was planted in rotation with corn, resulting in a composite "Corn and Soy Belt." Soy crop yields more than tripled between the 1950s and the late 1970s, and industrial inputs into the latter increased even more rapidly: fertilizer application grew tenfold; herbicide application increased by a factor of thirty.[47]

fig 3 fig 4

The United States was, therefore, the originary site of the Livestock Revolution, and as such, it was also the world's first "Soybean Republic."[48] The mutual upscaling of livestock and feed crop production and the consolidation of a transnational "livestock complex" were distinctive features of the postwar agrifood system.[49] While the industrial livestock sector remained nationally circumscribed in the United States and Western Europe, the feed sector assumed increasingly transnational dimensions during the postwar period. As Friedmann explains, "once crops and livestock producers were linked by corporations, inputs could in principle come from anywhere."[50] Until the 1970s, a series of favorable regulatory arrangements provided US soybean producers privileged access to European markets. Subsequently, however, North Atlantic agribusiness firms began to source feed components, including oilseeds and feed grains, from Third World regions. Following the 1972–73 food price spike, when United States soybean exports were drastically curtailed by the national government, several Latin American countries—notably Brazil and Argentina—entered the global soybean trade, increasing their soybean acreage at an unprecedented pace. As we will see below, this set the stage for a major recomposition in the global political economy of export-driven commodity agriculture during the closing decades of the twentieth century.

The postwar consolidation of industrial poultry in the United States reflected a broader transformation of the metabolic organization of capitalist livestock production and its compounding biophysical contradictions. Just as the broiler industry was emblematic of the technological innovations central to large-scale industrial livestock production, so did it offer an early illustration of its devastating environmental consequences. Industrialized poultry production generates vast amounts of organic and chemical waste—blood, feathers, bones, feces, offal, unhatched eggs, carcasses, and so forth—whose "disposal" exerts immense pressure on local, regional, and, ultimately, planetary ecosystems. Citing the early example of Gainesville,

[45] Biing-Hwan Lin, Merritt Padgitt, Len Bull, Herman Delvo, David Shank, Harold Taylor, "Pesticide and Fertilizer Use and Trends in US Agriculture," *Agricultural Economic Report*, no. 717 (Washington, DC: USDA Economic Research Service, 1995).

[46] Jean-Pierre Berlan, Jean-Pierre Bertrand, and Laurence Lebas, "The Growth of the American 'Soybean Complex'," *European Review of Agricultural Economics* 4, no. 4 (1977): 395–416; Matthew Roth, *Magic Bean: The Rise of Soy in America* (Lawrence, KS: University Press of Kansas, 2018).

[47] James M. MacDonald and William D. McBride, "The Transformation of U.S. LiveStock Agriculture: Scale, Efficiency, and Risks," *Economic Information Bulletin No. 43* (Washington, DC: USDA Economic Research Service, 2009); Lin et al., "Pesticide and Fertilizer Use."

[48] Turzi, "The Soybean Republic."

[49] Friedmann, "Distance and Durability."

[50] Friedmann, "Distance and Durability," 377.

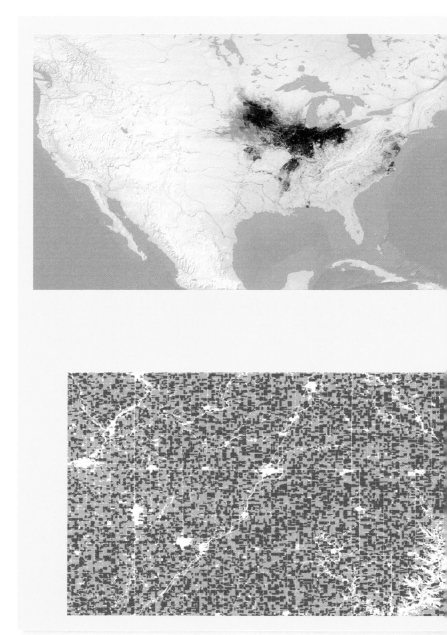

fig 3   The corn and soy belt, 1950. National one-kilometer rasters of selected Census of Agriculture statistics allocated to land use for the time period 1950 to 2012, released in 2016. US Census and USGS

fig 4   Corn and soybean cultivation terns in northwest Iowa, 2018. National Ag Statistics Service Cropland Data Layer, USGS a USDA

Georgia, Paul Josephson documents how the upscaling of poultry production in the late 1940s and 1950s generated a profusion of waste byproducts that overwhelmed the regional sewerage system.[51] The streams, wetlands, and waterways of its natural drainage area rapidly deteriorated, filling up with "muck, guts, blood, feathers, and wastewater."[52] Subsequent efforts to manage this deluge of waste, including the construction of a sewage treatment plant, proved ineffective as the sheer volume of waste quickly overwhelmed the treatment plant "with grit and feather, and with suspended and precipitating solids."[53] The Delmarva Peninsula, where industrial poultry production first emerged in the 1920s, still produces more than 600 million chickens annually. Here, the "regional environment must contend with some 1.5 billion pounds (680,000 metric tons) of manure every year—*more chicken shit than the waste load from a city of 4 million people*."[54]

In the second half of the twentieth century, strategies to manage unusable biowaste involved the construction of new infrastructural spaces—including, perhaps most prominently, the "slurry lagoon." These "lagoons" are containment and storage structures where "slurry," a mixture of biowaste and water produced by spraying immense quantities of freshwater in animal enclosures, is gathered and treated with bacteria. However, slurry lagoons have proven utterly ineffective at "containing" their toxic contents—a combination of fecal matter, bodily fluids, pathogens, antibiotics, and trace elements of metals and salts. An NRDC report documents a litany of cases in which slurry lagoons owned and operated by some of the largest livestock corporations in the world have catastrophically failed, releasing millions of gallons of contaminated biowaste into aquifers, waterways, coastal wetlands, agricultural fields, and water supply systems.[55]

The systemic ecological instabilities generated by industrial livestock production extend far beyond the factory farm and its proximate surroundings. As radical geographer Toni Weis succinctly notes, "the biophysical overrides used in factory farms and feedlots cannot contain all of the problems they create, and over time new and greater risks are established."[56] The intensification of feed production in the second half of the twentieth century has further exacerbated the progressive exhaustion of soil fertility that Justus von Liebig had investigated in the mid-nineteenth century. Attempts to overcome soil exhaustion through the application of increasing quantities of synthetic nitrogen fertilizers have not only locked in the reliance of feed production on fossil energy, specifically natural gas, but also contributed to the generalized disruption of the nitrogen cycle and the concomitant degradation of regional ecosystems, with nitrogen and phosphorous discharge from croplands poisoning aquifers and waterways across the United States national territory.

4.

One of the most consequential transformations in the global agrifood system since the late 1970s has been the multiplication, upscaling, and reterritorialization of industrialized meat production and consumption. This "new" Livestock Revolution has entailed the expansion of the US model

[51] Paul R. Josephson, *Chicken: A History from Farmyard to Factory* (Cambridge; Medford, MA: Polity, 2020).

[52] Josephson, *Chicken: A History*, 131.

[53] Josephson, *Chicken: A History*, 131.

[54] Josephson, *Chicken: A History*, 132; emphasis added.

[55] Robin Marks, "Cesspools of Shame: How Factory Farm Lagoons and Sprayfields Threaten Environmental and Public Health" (National Resources Defense Council and the Clean Water Network, 2001).

[56] Weis, *Ecological Hoofprint*, 138.

[57] In China and Brazil, for instance, per capita meat consumption between 1977 and 2017 increased ninefold and threefold, respectively; see Hannah Ritchie and Max Roser, "Meat and Dairy Production," *Our World in Data* (August 2017), https://ourworldindata.org/meat-production.

[58] Guanghong Zhou, Wangang Zhang, and Xinglian Xu, "China's Meat Industry Revolution: Challenges and Opportunities for the Future," *Meat Science* 92, no. 3 (2012): 188–96.

[59] Mindi Schneider, "Wasting the Rural: Meat, Manure, and the Politics of Agro-Industrialization in Contemporary China," *Geoforum* 78 (January 2017): 89; see also Zhaohai Bai et al., "China's Livestock Transition: Driving Forces, Impacts, and Consequences," *Science Advances* 4, no. 7 (2018), https://doi.org/10.1126/sciadv.aar8534.

[60] Weis, *The Ecological Hoofprint*, 8.

[61] Bai et al., "China's Livestock Transition," 7; Pierre Gerber et al., "Geographical Determinants and Environmental Implications of Livestock Production Intensification in Asia," *Bioresource Technology* 96, no. 2 (2005): 263–76; Hanxi Wang et al., "Study on the Pollution Status and Control Measures for the Livestock and Poultry Breeding Industry in Northeastern China," *Environmental Science and Pollution Research* 25, no. 5 (2018): 4435–45; FAO, "Guidelines to Control Water Pollution from Agriculture in China," FAO Water Reports (Rome: Food and Agriculture Organization of the United Nations, 2013).

[62] Schneider, "Wasting the Rural," 62.

[63] Ministry of Ecology and Environment, People's Republic of China, "Regulations on Prevention and Control of Pollution by Scaled Livestock and Poultry Breeding Industry Officially Enforced" (2013), http://english.mee.gov.cn/News_service/infocus/201401/t20140115_266435.shtml.

of intensive livestock production across the industrializing global South, a shift that has had devastating environmental consequences on a planetary scale.[57] Perhaps the most iconic expression of this process has been the industrialization and upscaling of livestock production in China, which overtook the United States as the world's leading meat-producing country in the early 1990s. While the liberalization of the Chinese livestock sector commenced in the early years of the reform era, the 1990s witnessed the rapid transformation of livestock production, propelled by state and private investments in industrial technology, advanced production facilities, and large-scale transport and utilities infrastructure.[58] Consequently, over the past three decades, traditional smallholder and backyard forms of commodity-animal production have been widely superseded by heavily capitalized, vertically integrated, high-throughput systems of industrial livestock processing. These sectoral realignments have produced what Mindi Schneider has characterized as a "party-state led and agribusiness-operated industrial meat regime."[59]

The development of China's industrial meat regime represents a world-historically significant upscaling of the "industrial grain-oilseed-livestock complex"—the "dominant system of agriculture across the temperate world" whose planetary landscape, in Tony Weis's vivid imagery, resembles "islands of concentrated livestock within seas of grain and oilseed monocultures, with soaring populations of a few livestock species reared in high densities, disarticulated from surrounding fields."[60] In China, the proliferation of these "disarticulated islands" of livestock production has contributed to a cascade of interrelated socioecological crises, including (a) the drastic increase in environmental pollution resulting from greenhouse gas and ammonia emissions; (b) the degradation, contamination, and eutrophication of aquifers, rivers, lakes, and coastal waters due to the discharge of reactive nitrogen, phosphorous, heavy metals, feed additives, and animal excrement; and (c) the chronic recurrence of infectious disease outbreaks and epidemics.[61] Despite these proliferating crises, the Chinese state continues to promote industrialized meat production as a central basis of food security for its domestic bourgeoisie and, thus, a major component of national industrial development strategy. As Schneider argues, "the development of industrial meat and the meatification of Chinese diets is a political and economic objective for creating and sustaining urban middle and upper classes, and for economic growth and capital accumulation for domestic state and private agribusiness firms."[62]

In recent years, the Chinese state has instituted regulations to mitigate environmental pollution from CAFOs and other large-scale livestock operations.[63] In addition to stipulating procedures for waste disposal, the so-called CAFO Law of 2014 prohibits the construction of such facilities near "urban residents, areas of cultural, educational, or scientific research, or near a population intensive area."[64] This regulation appears to signal growing official disquiet regarding the environmental dangers of industrial livestock production, and to promote a new economic geography of this sector in erstwhile "rural" zones of smallholder agriculture, fragmented wilderness areas, and other putatively "remote" landscapes. The state-mediated dispersal of large-scale livestock operations from urban and peri-urban regions into "rural" or extrametropolitan territories is significantly intensifying the processes of smallholder and agrarian dispossession that have underpinned the development of the industrial livestock sector in China since the late 1990s, while also reterritorializing its wide-ranging environmental impacts.[65]

The infrastructural and spatial expressions of these ongoing transformations are starkly illustrated in major recent investments by large Chinese agribusiness firms to create new sites of high-throughput livestock production, at some remove from human population centers. Currently, the "world's largest pig farm" is under construction by Muyuan Foods in a relatively remote location in the southwestern region of Henan province.

fig 5

This "mega-farm" is reported to be "roughly ten times the size of a typical breeding facility in the United States" and aims to produce over 2 million pigs annually.[66] To achieve this startling production turnover, the mega-farm will mobilize a complex network of monitoring devices and processing equipment, including "'intelligent' feeding systems, manure-cleaning robots, and infrared cameras to detect when pigs have a fever."[67] Meanwhile, in Yaji Mountain Forest Park, located in the Guangxi region of southern China, Guangxi Yangxiang Co Ltd is constructing the "tallest pig farm in the world," a mega-structure that is eerily reminiscent of the speculative proposal for "Pig City" advanced two decades ago by Dutch design office MVRDV.[68]

fig 6

This eleven-hectare facility is configured as a massive complex of multistory production units, a kind of "vertical" CAFO, with the capacity to produce 840,000 pigs annually. One news report dryly notes that the pigs in this facility "are restricted to one floor for their whole lives to avoid mixing animals." In addition to dedicated ventilation systems, each "housing" unit is being equipped with "elevators for transporting animals and a specific pipeline to direct dead piglets to internal incineration areas."[69]

Although they are embodied in extreme technospatial forms that evoke scenes from science fiction dystopias, these and similar agribusiness strategies represent the simultaneous generalization and continuation of livestock production techniques that were pioneered by US agribusiness firms under the postwar, US-led, global food regime. The relentless drive to achieve economies of scale through the hyper densification of animal populations and the hyper-rationalization of production serves to amplify—and further disperse—the myriad socio-environmental risks associated with the industrial meat regime. For example, as radical epidemiologist Rob Wallace has demonstrated with reference to emergent infectious diseases such as avian flu (H5N1), SARS, and COVID-19, agribusiness strategies of "biosecurity" and "biocontainment" are devastatingly ineffective at containing the unruly viral ecologies that are incubated within CAFOs. Pathogens

[64] Rebecca Smith and Xiao Mingxin, "CAFOs in the US and China: A Comparison on the Laws That Protect Water Quality from Factory Farming" (USAID Asia and Vermont Law School, 2014), 21.

[65] Schneider, "Developing the Meat Grab."

[66] Dominique Patton, "Flush with Cash, Chinese Hog Producer Builds World's Largest Pig Farm," Reuters, December 7, 2020, https://www.reuters.com/article/us-china-swinefever-muyuanfoods-change-s-idUSKBN28H0MU.

[67] Patton, "World's Largest Pig Farm."

[68] MVRDV, *Pig City*, Design Proposal for Stroom Den Haag, Centre for Visual Arts, The Hague (2001).

[69] Michael Standaert and Francesco De Augustinis, "A 12-Storey Pig Farm: Has China Found the Way to Tackle Animal Disease?", *The Guardian*, September 18, 2020, https://www.theguardian.com/environment/2020/sep/18/a-12-storey-pig-farm-has-china-found-a-way-to-stop-future-pandemics-.

fig 5 "World's largest pig farm" in Henan province, China, before and during construction, 2018–2020. Google Earth, accessed on January 14, 2022

MVRDV's 2001 proposal for "Pig City"
e "tallest pig farm in the world" currently
construction in Yaji Mountain Forest Park,
xi, China. MVRDV, 2022; Reuters, 2018

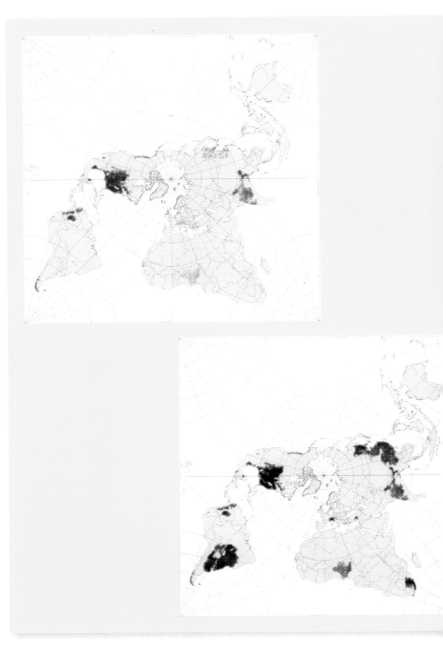

fig 7   The planetary expansion of soybean
production areas, 1980-2016. Toshichika Iizumi, Global
Dataset of Historical Yields v1.2 and v1.3, 2019

that emerge from such facilities are frequently projected into surrounding populations and ecosystems, both human and nonhuman, where they may engender severe public health risks.[70]

In this sense, the sprawling pig city on the fields of Henan and the massive pig skyscrapers on the forested mountaintops of Guangxi are not merely bizarre architectural spectacles that have appeared in otherwise pristine, "rural" landscapes. Both sites must be understood as contextually specific infrastructural assemblages enmeshed within the broader operational landscapes, metabolic circuits, and political ecologies of the GIFM, whose spatial parameters have now been extended to a transcontinental scale. Rather than protecting the populations of dense metropolitan areas from the environmental dangers of CAFOs, the new economic geography of industrial livestock production in China may serve to destabilize the general conditions of production and reproduction far beyond these facilities, creating new political ecologies of degradation, danger, and disease that are not likely to be contained effectively within the "wasted" rural zones in which they are situated.[71]

Industrialized livestock production in China is systemically reliant upon the import of massive quantities of animal feed from other parts of the world, notably North and South America. Despite recent attempts by the Chinese state to increase domestic feed production, the demand for feed crops vastly outstrips national production capacity. One study estimates that in 2010, "feed import was equivalent to 16 million hectares of arable land, which is equal to 45% of China's arable land used for feed production."[72] In this sense, the technical appellation "landless production system," often used as a corporate shorthand for CAFO-based production systems, is an ideological obfuscation. These disarticulated islands of concentrated livestock must be situated within a world-ecological context that now centrally includes the South American "seas of grain and oilseed monocultures" that directly support their high-throughput industrial metabolism.[73]

Since the 1990s, the growing demand for animal feed has led to the formation of what Philip McMichael has characterized as an "East Asian import complex."[74] This transcontinental political-economic and metabolic matrix is grounded upon new North-South and South-South interregional commercial relations in which feed crops and flex crops such as soybeans, corn, and palm oil are produced, circulated, and channeled into industrial operations. In tandem with the construction of these new transnational circuits of agricultural commodity trade, state-aided Chinese agribusiness firms have begun to compete more directly with Euro-American agribusiness corporations for access to resource frontiers in South America, Central Asia, and Africa.[75] The upscaling of industrial livestock production in East Asia has thus been a leading driver of global commodity frontier expansion and new infrastructural investments across Latin America, especially in the feed crop sector.[76]

The soybean commodity chain is among the leading edges of livestock-induced agro-industrial restructuring and landscape simplification in Latin

[70] Robert G. Wallace, *Big Farms Make Big Flu: Dispatches on Infectious Disease, Agribusiness, and the Nature of Science* (New York, NY: Monthly Review Press, 2016). For further elaboration on the link between the GIFM and emergent infectious disease, see Neil Brenner and Swarnabh Ghosh, "Between the Colossal and the Catastrophic: Planetary Urbanization and the Political Ecologies of Emergent Infectious Disease," *Environment and Planning A: Economy and Space* (2022), https://doi.org/10.1177/0308518X221084313.

[71] Tony Weis, "The Accelerating Biophysical Contradictions of Industrial Capitalist Agriculture: The Contradictions of Industrial Capitalist Agriculture," *Journal of Agrarian Change* 10, no. 3 (2010): 315–41; Schneider, "Wasting the Rural."

[72] Bai et al., "China's Livestock Transition," 6.

[73] Weis, "The Accelerating Biophysical Contradictions."

[74] Philip McMichael, "A Global Interpretation of the Rise of the East Asian Food Import Complex," *World Development* 28, no. 3 (2000): 409–24; see also Jostein Jakobsen and Arve Hansen, "Geographies of Meatification: An Emerging Asian Meat Complex," *Globalizations* 17, no. 1 (2020): 93–109.

[75] Gustavo Oliveira and Mindi Schneider, "The Politics of Flexing Soybeans: China, Brazil and Global Agroindustrial Restructuring," *The Journal of Peasant Studies* 43, no. 1 (2016): 167–94; Philip McMichael, "Does China's 'Going Out' Strategy Prefigure a New Food Regime?" *The Journal of Peasant Studies* 47, no. 1 (2020): 116–54.

[76] On commodity frontiers see Moore, *Capitalism in the Web of Life*; see also Sven Beckert et al., "Commodity Frontiers and the Transformation of the Global Countryside: A Research Agenda," *Journal of Global History* 16, no. 3 (2021): 435–50.

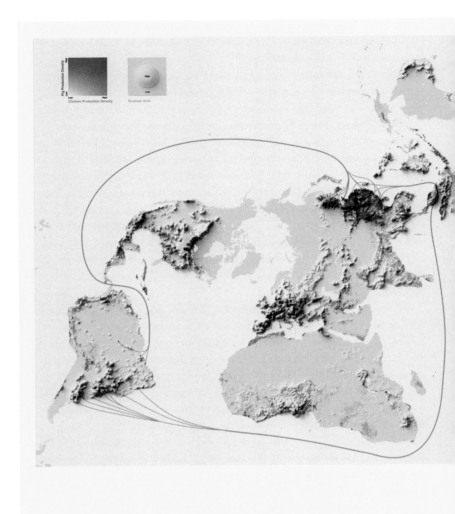

fig 8 Elements of the Global Industrial Feed-lot Matrix with populations of industrial chickens shown in blue and pigs shown in red. Grga Basic and Nikos Katsikis

America. Since 1990, global soybean acreage and output have increased by over 118 percent and 220 percent, respectively. In 2018, global soybean production exceeded 380 million tons, around three-fourths of which were used for livestock feed.[77] In South America, where about half of the world's soy is produced, one of the most consequential geographical transformations in recent decades has been the dramatic expansion of soybean production across vast cropland zones of Brazil, Argentina, Bolivia, and Paraguay. Much of this expansion was led by US and Western European agribusiness corporations whose involvement in soy production significantly intensified during the 1990s, a period of neoliberal regulatory reform in which major Latin American states sought to revolutionize agrarian economies by facilitating foreign direct investment and reorienting production towards cash-crop exports. As a result, transnational agribusiness conglomerates such as ADM, Cargill, and Bunge acquired regional firms and made large-scale investments in land, equipment and spatial infrastructure to support the expansion of export-oriented soy production.[78] During the last decade, as North American and Western European corporations further consolidated their position as leading exporters of soybean from South America, Chinese "dragon head"—companies aligned with or partly owned by regional governments such as COFCO, Beidahuang, and the Chongqing Grain Group—have likewise begun to play an increasingly important role in organizing several key export-oriented feed-crop commodity chains.[79]

fig 7

The agribusiness-led expansion of soybean production has hinged upon large-scale land grabs, enclosure, and expropriation facilitated by neoliberalizing South American national governments. This has meant, on the one hand, a significant intensification and acceleration of depeasantization processes, as smallholders are dislodged from inherited forms of agrarian life and often displaced to metropolitan centers in search of waged or informalized subsistence labor. Equally constitutive of this transformation is a new wave of large-scale infrastructural investment—much of it financed by multilateral institutions and development banks—to support mono-crop soy production; the procurement and distribution of fertilizer; the processing and storage of soy; and its long-distance circulation as freight via roads, rivers, and rail lines to ports and transcontinental systems of container shipping.[80] For instance, several projects recently initiated as part of Brazil's Investment Partnership Program (Programa de Parcerias de Investimentos) are principally oriented toward expanding and upgrading rail and road connections from its agribusiness regions to both the southern and "Northern Arc" ports. These projects include the Norte-Sul Railroad, the East-West Integration Railroad, and the BR-163 highway, which connects the soy-producing regions of northern Mato Grosso to Miritituba Port on the Tapajós river.[81] In this sense, the spatial configurations of the GIFM today stretch from the mega-fields, "soybean cities," processing facilities, agrochemical laboratories, distribution warehouses, and logistics systems of Latin America to the variegated industrial meat production infrastructures

[77] Hannah Ritchie and Max Roser, "Forests and Deforestation," Our World in Data, 2021, https://ourworldindata.org/soy.

[78] Gustavo Oliveira and Susanna Hecht, "Sacred Groves, Sacrifice Zones and Soy Production: Globalization, Intensification, and Neo-Nature in South America," The Journal of Peasant Studies 43, no. 2 (2016): 251–85; Oliveira and Schneider, "The Politics of Flexing Soybeans"; Gastón Gordillo, "The Metropolis: The Infrastructure of the Anthropocene," in Infrastructure, Environment, and Life in the Anthropocene, ed. Kregg Hetherington (Durham NC: Duke University, 2019), 66–96.

[79] Schneider, "Dragon Head Enterprises and the State of Agribusiness in China," 16–17.

[80] Peter Richards and Leah VanWey, "Where Deforestation Leads to Urbanization: How Resource Extraction Is Leading to Urban Growth in the Brazilian Amazon," Annals of the Association of American Geographers 105, no. 4 (2015): 806–23; Gordillo, "The Metropolis."

[81] Delmy L. Salin, "Soybean Transportation Guide: Brazil 2020," USDA Agricultural Marketing Service (2021).

of China, from container shipping ports and multimodal logistics hubs in coastal cities to CAFOs and associated packaging, storage, and distribution systems across the Chinese metropolitan system, now stretching deep into erstwhile "rural" zones where new strategies of agro-industrial intensification are being mobilized.

fig 8

The political ecologies of the GIFM extend still more broadly: they encompass the wide-ranging environmental impacts of industrial livestock production at each step of this planet-encompassing, fossil-fueled commodity chain. These include, for example, intensified deforestation, forest and land degradation, habitat fragmentation, and biodiversity loss in the Brazilian Amazon, the Argentinian Gran Chaco, and other zones of monocrop expansion in South America; the greenhouse gas emissions associated with the production and circulation of feed crops and processed meat across vast swathes of the world economy; and wide-ranging flows of toxic waste—from fertilizer, wastewater and manure to offal and carbon—that is accreted and discharged but never truly externalized, through the operations of the industrial meat regime, whether in the monoculture landscapes of Mato Grosso, the mega-ports of the Pearl River Delta, the CAFO landscapes of Henan, or the pig skyscrapers of Guangxi.[82] Further still, the political ecologies of the GIFM encompass the flows of unpaid work/energy that are appropriated from animal and human bodies, fossilized biomass, and organic matter and then channeled into the circuit of capital, leaving behind vectors of world-ecological devastation that are rendered invisible in the growth-centric ideologies of mainstream economics.[83] Thus, as Weis notes, while "the inequality associated with cycling grains and oilseeds through livestock might appear less conspicuous than with cycling them through cars," it is in practice a multiscalar cascade of intermeshed forms of appropriation, plunder, and destruction.[84] The economies of scale pursued through the GIFM "hinge on many unaccounted, non-renewable and actively destructive fixes" and, in this sense, rest upon a dangerous fantasy of endless, fossil-fueled agro-industrial growth.[85]

From this perspective, the post-1980s upscaling of China's industrial livestock sector, the acceleration of agribusiness-led landscape standardization in Latin America, and the consolidation of new, transcontinental logistics circuits connecting Brazilian, Argentinian and Chinese ports are interconnected elements of a worldwide system of productivity and plunder that produces myriad "sacrifice zones" of toxic waste, heightened ecological risk, and severely degraded public health conditions. At each link within this variegated commodity chain, elaborate (and increasingly costly) technoscientific strategies are rolled out to secure "biophysical overrides"—that is, to externalize (spatially) and displace (temporally) the environmental dislocations induced by this process, and thus to enhance economic growth and profitability.[86] Throughout the *longue durée* of the GIFM tracked in this essay, such strategies have served mainly to canalize the brutality of the industrial meat regime onto nonhuman animals, devalued workers, racial-

[82] N.I. Gasparri, H.R. Grau, and J. Gutiérrez Angonese, "Linkages between Soybean and Neotropical Deforestation: Coupling and Transient Decoupling Dynamics in a Multi-Decadal Analysis," *Global Environmental Change* 23, no. 6 (2013): 1605–14; Elizabeth Barona et al., "The Role of Pasture and Soybean in Deforestation of the Brazilian Amazon," *Environmental Research Letters* 5, no. 2 (2010): 024002; Henning Steinfeld et al., "Livestock's Long Shadow: Environmental Issues and Options" (Rome: Food and Agriculture Organization of the United Nations, 2006), Weis, "The Accelerating Biophysical Contradictions," passim.

[83] Moore, *Capitalism in the Web of Life*; Fraser, "Behind Marx's Hidden Abode."

[84] Weis, "The Accelerating Biophysical Contradictions," 329.

[85] Weis, "The Accelerating Biophysical Contradictions," 321.

[86] Weis, "The Accelerating Biophysical Contradictions," passim.

ized Others, and both proximate and distant ecosystems. And while they inflict devastating violence upon human populations, nonhuman species, the earth, and the biosphere, such attempted externalizations recurrently fail. Strategies to territorialize the biophysical contradictions of capital prove futile, whether within slurry lagoons, "biosecure" CAFOs, or other biocontainment enclaves. In an interconnected web of planetary life, the socioenvironmental destruction induced by the GIFM further proliferates and intensifies, eroding the general conditions of production, and indeed of life itself, from the field and the factory-farm to the biosphere as a whole.

The "cheapness" of industrial meat is thus revealed not only as costly but, in world-ecological terms, as *deadly*. As Weis explains, the stakes of this "costly cheapness" could not be more grave:

> Yet however capitalist agriculture might be reconstituted beyond fossil energy—in a world in which roughly one in seven are already malnour-ished, the class-based competition for grains and oilseeds is intensify-ing, rising food costs and climate change impacts loom portentously and unevenly, and world population continues to grow towards 9 billion—there is much reason to believe that any such reconstitution will only speed the world towards capitalism's ultimate precipice: revo-lution or barbarism.[87]

[87] Weis, "The Accelerating Biophysical Contradictions," 333–34.

The GIFM is a metabolic *monstrosity* in precisely this sense. Behind the veneer of its colossal infrastructural equipment, its complex systems of landscape engineering, its massive capacity to extract, process, and circulate materials, and its finely tuned, intercontinental choreography lurks a wretched, brutalized world—of degraded life, colonized territories, poisoned environments, and foreclosed futures. It is only through the radical politicization of such technical systems—by revealing the systemic violence through which they are reproduced—that we can begin to envision and to construct alternative frameworks of socioecological coexistence that prior-itize solidarity, comradeship, care, and mutual aid (human and nonhuman alike) over the capitalist imperative of endless growth.

Vertical Imperialism

The Technical Lands of Mining Extraction

Stephen Graham

Extraction sustains our society .... [However], as the world population becomes more urban and more spatially removed from the landscapes that supply its raw materials and energy needs ... our reliance on remotely extracted natural resources only continues to increase, while our relationship to the landscapes of extraction recedes ever further from daily view.[1]

Introduction: The Deep Frontier

Critical discussions of colonialism and imperialism have traditionally maintained an overwhelmingly horizontal frame. Books and atlases of exploration have long used a bird's-eye view to mark colonial conquests as sequences of colored shapes on flat cartography. In turn, maps of the resulting horizontal extent of empires are clichés of imperial propaganda and school geography.

By startling contrast, the subsurface resources that have so often driven imperial-colonial campaigns are rarely mapped for widespread attention. Beyond the professional worlds of geologists or mining engineers, vertical sections or diagrams of imperial efforts to reach deep-lying minerals and fossil fuels are remarkably unusual. Meanwhile, the broader extractive economy remains neglected in many political and ecological debates. These, too, often display what has been called a "surface bias" stemming from the dominant use of flat cartography as fundamental means of illustration, visualization, and imagination.[2]

In particular, such a "flat" bias has long existed in debates about the politics of geography. As US geographers Jody Emel, Matthew Huber, and Madoshi Makene emphasize, "Geographical engagements with the relations between power and space have consistently focused on 'surface imaginaries' of horizontal space at the expense of 'vertical' inquiries into power over subterranean matter .... Given the role of mining in the history of colonialism, this is a substantial oversight."[3]

As geographers try and connect mining and extraction to the cities that depend on them, within a context of planetary urbanization, scholars and activists are now working hard to rectify this neglect by analyzing the history, politics, and contemporary manifestations of the colonial or post-colonial underground.[4] This is important because, as our planet urbanizes, the extraction of commodities is inevitably becoming more central to global capitalism.[5] Corporate investment in the technical lands of mining is proliferating with the boom and bust of the end of the twentieth and the start of the twenty-first centuries shaped heavily by planetary resource grabs for nonrenewable commodities. In 1995, the uranium-, diamond-, and metal-mining industries were worth $80 billion globally; by 2008, they were worth $463 billion.[6]

Canadian sociologist Henry Veltmeyer has described this rapid growth as being based on a new model of extractive imperialism—a form of primitive capital accumulation that has stark similarities to the "old" styles of colonial extractivism organized by the European empires in the nineteenth century.[7]

[1] Stephanie Carlisle and Nicholas Pevzner, "Introduction: Extraction," *Scenario Journal* 05 (Fall 2015), http://scenariojournal.com/article/introduction-extraction/.

[2] Edward Said called this Western colonialism's "cartographic impulse," its tendency to use cartographic surveying techniques to fuel imperial control and domination. Edward Said, *Culture and Imperialism* (London: Vintage, 1994), 272; see Anthony Bebbington and Jeffrey Bury, *Subterranean Struggles: New Dynamics of Mining, Oil, and Gas in Latin America* (Austin, TX: University of Texas Press, 2013), 1.

[3] Jody Emel, Matthew Huber, and Madoshi Makene, "Extracting Sovereignty: Capital, Territory, and Gold Mining in Tanzania," *Political Geography* 30, no. 2, (February 2011): 70–79, 72.

[4] The "colonial or post-colonial underground" comes from Heidi Scott, "Colonialism, Landscape, and the Subterranean," *Geography Compass* 2, no. 6 (2008): 1853–1869. See Martín Arboleda, "Spaces of Extraction, Metropolitan Explosions: Planetary Urbanization, and the Commodity Boom in Latin America," *International Journal of Urban and Regional Research* 40, no. 1 (January 2016): 96–112.

[5] See Philip John Usher, *Exterranean: Extraction in the Humanist Anthropocene* (New York, NY: Fordham University Press, 2019).

[6] Björn Surborg, *The Production of the World City: Extractive Industries in a Global Urban Economy*, PhD thesis (Vancouver: University of British Colombia, 2012), 89, https://open.library.ubc.ca/handle/2429/40719.

[7] It should be remembered that in the past two decades, many populist governments in Latin America sought to renationalize mining and minerals to benefit more from their exploitation and reduce negative environmental and social impacts. Figures are cited

in Henry Veltmeyer, "The Political Economy of Natural Resource Extraction: A New Model or Extractive Imperialism?" *Canadian Journal of Development Studies/ Revue Canadienne d'études du Développement* 34, no. 1 (2013): 79–95.

[8] Samarendra Das and Miriam Rose, "Prosperity or Plunder?: The Real Story Behind the Global Mining Industry," *Foil Vedanta*, (August 12, 2015), http://www.foilvedanta.org/articles/prosperity-or-plunder-the-real-story-behind-the-global-mining-industry/.

[9] Figures from George Monbiot, "So You Need that Smart Cuckoo Clock for Christmas, Do You?" *The Guardian*, November 25, 2013; Arboleda, "Spaces of Extraction," 2.

[10] Björn Wallsten, "The Norrköping Iron and Copper Mine," Linköping University, (2013), https://www.iei.liu.se/envtech/aktuellt/1.520116?l=en.

[11] Arboleda, "Spaces of Extraction," 5.

[12] Andrew Curley and Majerle Lister, "Already Existing Dystopias: Tribal Sovereignty, Extraction, and Decolonizing the Anthropocene," *Handbook on the Changing Geographies of the State* (London: Edward Elgar Publishing, 2020).

[13] Figures cited in Arboleda, "Spaces of Extraction," 6.

[14] See Saskia Sassen, "A Savage Sorting of Winners and Losers: Contemporary Versions of Primitive Accumulation," *Globalizations* 7, no. 1–2 (2010): 23–50.

[15] Maristella Svampa, "Commodities Consensus: Neoextractivism and Enclosure of the Commons in Latin America," *South Atlantic Quarterly* 114, no.1 (2015): 65–82.

As mining activists Samarendra Das and Miriam Rose write, "The modern notion of 'development,' backed by the World Bank, IMF, and UN, suggests that the evolution of the human race is directly linked to their consumption of mined resources."[8]

The figures here are startling. Production of mined cobalt grew by 165 percent between 2003 and 2013 while iron ore exploitation rose by 180 percent, with a 50 percent increase in nonferrous-metals exploration between 2010 and 2011. Within only ten years, from 1995 to 2005, world-wide production of iron increased by 50 percent, aluminum increased by 64 percent, and copper increased by 42 percent.[9] All such production increases involve deepening the vertical reach of mining which consists in digging further and further down, whether in open or shaft pits, to reach remaining, and increasingly scarce, reserves. (It is estimated that humans have already mined more copper than is left in the surface layers of Earth's crust.[10])

In Latin America and Africa—the two largest concentrations of the mining frenzy—this shift has been called the "reprimarization" of global capitalism. Remarkably, it means that exports of extracted and mined resources are becoming *more* valuable to the broader economic fortunes of such places (not less than all traditional models of development would have it). From a figure of 7 percent of overall GDP in 1970, commodity exports in Latin America rose to a figure of 10 percent by 2010.[11] Such a transformation focuses on a renewed form of primitive accumulation, this time refocused on massive growths in foreign corporate investment centered on extracting mined commodities and raw materials. More and more of the subsurface domains within and beyond the borders of Latin American states have been handed to overseas extraction corporations as concessions to exploit.[12] The undergrounds of countries and continents are thus remade as volumes of postcolonial sovereignty as legal agreements parcel them out to global mining firms often under the control of armed state security or private, para-military forces, or both.

To take just two powerful examples. Between 2004 and 2008, the area of the national territory of Peru given over to exploration and exploitation by oil corporations grew from 14 to 72 percent. Between 2002 and 2009, the area of Colombia allocated to mining companies went up over 450 percent, from 1.05 million hectares to 4.77 million hectares.[13] Such imperial resource grabs are pivotal but neglected elements within a neoliberal version of capitalism that produces an increasingly savage sorting of a small cabal of über-wealthy winners centered on the finance and corporate districts focused on a few global cities and a mass of losers.[14] Fully 76 percent of Latin America's exports in 2011 were made up of agricultural, mineral, and commodity raw materials (compared to only 34 percent of the world as a whole).[15]

Looking Up, Looking Down: Skyscrapers as "Inverted Minescapes"

One effect of the flatness of current discussions about exploration, colonialism, and empire is the assumption that the technical lands sustaining transport, infrastructure, and mobilities rest entirely on or above Earth's surface. And yet, just as shipping, railways, roads, telecommunications, and aircraft have been the basis for extending empires horizontally beyond current frontiers, colonial penetrations deep below Earth's surface rely on their own transport system. The technological key to mining downwards is the very thing that enabled buildings to extend upwards: the lift or elevator. However, the two systems are rarely discussed together because mining elevators have typically had a different moniker: the "cage."

Even more rarely discussed than the politics of above-surface elevators are the politics of subterranean elevator travel. Subsumed within the crucial but usually invisible worlds of mining, these political inclinations are even more startling than those above ground. It is also rarely realized that technologies building massive vertical mining structures deep into the ground have fundamentally coevolved with tech that enabled skyscrapers to reach high into the sky.

Located at the cores of the world's global cities, including those aspiring to become global, clusters of corporate skyscrapers house executives, stock markets, and super-rich financiers that draw vast wealth from the deep, neocolonial excavation of scarce and valuable metals and ores in the world's peripheries. The latter provides some critical materials used to construct vertical urban towers. And yet it remains rare indeed for popular graphs showing the rising heights of skyscrapers—and their accelerating and lengthening elevators—over the last century to also show the parallel, but much more extraordinary and dangerous, excavations using mining "cages" as the means of vertical transportation.

One rare example of such a diagram accompanied architect Rem Koolhaas' exploration of architectural fundamentals at the 2014 Architecture Biennale in Venice.[16] Such a perspective reveals that mining cages have been plummeting miners over a kilometer vertically down into the Earth for nearly a hundred and fifty years (since 1875). It also shows that the world's deepest mines currently are over four kilometers deep—at least four times deeper than the other, much more familiar icon of modernity, the super-tall skyscraper.

In his pioneering work on the imperial resource grabs that sustained the rapid growth of San Francisco in the nineteenth century, Berkeley geographer Gray Brechin explored the deep but neglected historical connections between mining and skyscrapers in unprecedented detail.[17] He shows how many crucial technologies creating corporate towers in North American downtowns emerged in nineteenth-century mines. For example, the deepening gold mines of the Californian Gold Rush in the 1850s necessitated ventilators, multilevel telephones, early electric lighting, and high-speed safety-cage elevators that would later be pivotal to constructing the first downtown skyscrapers. "All were demanded and paid for by the prodigious output and prospects of the gold mines of California," he writes. In addition, the use of square supports, initially in wood, to build large, multistory structures within mines to provide support as mined material was removed later provided the basis for the famous steel girder structures of the first

[16] Rem Koolhaas, "Elevator," *Fundamentals: 14th International Architecture Exhibition*, ed. Rem Koolhaas, La Biennale di Venezia: (Venice: Marsilio, 2014).

[17] Gray Brechin, *Imperial San Francisco: Urban Power, Earthly Ruin* (Berkeley, CA: University of California Press, 2003).

fig 1 Contemporary illustration of the complex technologies necessary to sustain a silver mine at Comstock Lode in Nevada, 1870s. Wikipedia, Library of Congress, public domain

corporate towers. The parallel processes of using these suites of technologies to dig down, to provide the raw materials to construct raised-up skyscrapers were not lost on contemporary commentators. "Imagine [the mine] hoisted out of the ground and left standing on the surface," reporter Dan De Quille wrote in 1877. Now imagine the viewer

would then see before him [*sic*] an immense structure, four or five times as large as the biggest hotel in America, about twice or three times as wide and over two thousand feet high. In a grand hotel, communication between these floors would be by means of an elevator; in the mine would be in use the same contrivances, but instead of an elevator, it would be called a "cage."[18]

[18] Brechin, *Imperial San Francisco*, 67.

fig 1

Brechin draws on the legendary urban critic Lewis Mumford's (1895–1990) use of the term "mega-machine" to indicate where financial industries constitute an economic "apex" based on the exploitative and dangerous "base," involving processes of mining, especially gold and silver.[19] Brechin stresses that Dan De Quille's vision is even more evident in the contemporary context of super-tall one-kilometer towers, three-to-four-kilometer-deep mines, and super-deep pits and quarries. He even suggests that the clusters of finance towers that have signified global cities for a century and a half should be seen as little more than "inverted minescapes."[20]

[19] From base to apex, Lewis Mumford's "pyramid of mining" centers on mining, metallurgy, mechanization, militarism, and finance. See Lewis Mumford, *Technics and Civilization* (Berkeley, CA: University of California, 2010), 193.

Such an idea forces us to consider how skyscrapers reach upward from the staked territorial claims of expensive real estate at the hearts of global cities: the tiny pieces of land at the heart of a small sample of metropolises from which global capitalism is directed.[21] Brechin addresses the unusual question of how such towers are ultimately reliant on a wide range of mined materials for their construction and on speculative and commodified wealth that is also heavily dependent on mining.

[20] See Gavin Bridge, "The Hole World: Scales and Spaces of Extraction," *Scenario Journal* (Fall 2015), http://scenariojournal.com/article/the-hole-world/.

[21] Brechin, *Imperial San Francisco*, 70.

It is worth looking in detail at contemporary but neglected examples of the profound connections between deep mining and tall buildings. Doing this helps illustrate the enormous contemporary power of Brechin's critical but often overlooked ideas. It is particularly revealing to trace the extractive resources necessary to build and sustain today's mushrooming "super-tall" skyscrapers. Dubai's Burj Khalifa ultra-thin pinnacle—still the world's tallest skyscraper at 830 meters—is especially instructive here. A crucial starting point for such a task is to realize, as sociologist Mimi Sheller has put it, "The ... skyscrapers that serve today as the cathedrals of late modernity are grounded in the heavy (and dirty) industries of power generation, mining, refining, and smelting."[22] In understanding the Burj Khalifa's particular connections with extraction and mining, three related and overlapping processes need to be understood in parallel.

[22] Mimi Sheller, *Aluminium Dreams: The Making of Light Modernity* (Cambridge, MA: MIT Press, 2014), 25.

Extractive Footprints

First, the considerable effort needed to provide the material for the tower needs to be addressed. To construct the Burj Khalifa in Dubai, 55,000 tons of steel, 250,000 tons (or 330,000 cubic meters) of high-performance concrete, 700 tons of aluminum, and 85,000 square meters of glass were necessary. Such headline figures translate to a remarkable 79 tons of steel, 357 tons of concrete, a ton of aluminum, and 121 square meters of glass for each of the 700 apartments in the building.[23]

Many other materials—Egyptian marble and Indian granite for flooring and upscale worktops and tables—were also necessary in smaller quantities to fit out the interior of the Burj with the required luxury aesthetic.[24] Deeply mined gold, platinum, diamonds, and other precious stones and metals filled the shelves of the entire indoor souk. Specialized gold was used in the construction of the enormous Dubai Mall, which acts like an "anchor" at the base of the tower. Even when such headline figures are considered, it is rarely emphasized that producing such extraordinary volumes of construction materials must, in turn, involve the mining, extraction, and processing of countless tons of limestone, gypsum, bauxite (from India and Guinea), iron ore (from Australia and Brazil),[25] coal (to produce the steel and aluminum), and a wide range of other minerals, ores, aggregates and fuels across many locations to extract and refine the raw materials to the extent required for final use in construction and building.

Crucially, the mining, manufacture, and transport of most materials are also very energy-intensive, requiring enormous amounts of scarce water resources and greenhouse gas emissions. "In most projects in the UAE, however, materials are evaluated and selected based on aesthetics and cost and not on their energy and environmental performance."[26] Dubai, moreover, has so exhausted its own marine sand deposits through extensive dredging to construct artificial islands that—bizarrely for a desert nation—it had to import the sand required to produce the concrete for the Burj from Australia.[27]

Added to dependencies on coal, iron, aluminum, sand, and aggregates are the vital roles of other "base" metals such as copper, nickel, zinc,[28] and the rarer earth metals such as tantalum, tin, tungsten, and gold (collectively, 3TG), in skyscraper construction and operation. The 3TG are often labeled "conflict minerals" because they can lead to resource wars surrounding their extraction in some key conflict zones, notably Rwanda and the Democratic Republic of Congo.[29] These materials are crucial in furnishing buildings like the Burj and global cities like Dubai.

In the pivotal iron-and-steel sector, global demand for iron ore, partly caused by the worldwide proliferation of vertical architectural projects, has forced prices to rise dramatically. In 2008, iron ore prices rose between 50 and 60 percent. Even with more recent price reductions due to the global economic slump, the three dominant iron ore companies, including Brazil's Vale, Rio Tinto, and BHP Billiton, are increasing investments and expanding production. (Qatar is rapidly building up an iron ore business in Brazil to provide for its meteoric urban growth.)

[23] It must be remembered, of course, that the Burj Khalifa houses hotels, offices, and restaurants, as well as apartments. Apartments take up the bulk of the tower. However, the fact that fully 29 percent (244 meters) of the tower is unoccupiable "vanity height," added purely to increase the tower's height, clearly makes a huge environmental footprint even worse. If this "vanity spire" were a free-standing building, it would be the eleventh tallest in Europe.

[24] Remarkably, for such a tiny nation, the UAE is the third-largest marble importer in the world.

[25] For each ton of steel produced, about 1400 kg of iron ore and 800 kg of coal are required. To make 1000 kg of iron ore in a surface mine, between 2000 kg and 8000 kg of material needs to be extracted. This process creates significant air, land, and water pollution.

[26] Hassan Radhi, "On the Effect of Global Warming and the UAE Built Environment," *Global Warming*, ed. Stuart Arthur Harris, (Vienna: Sciyo, 2010), 98.

[27] Desert sand is unsuitable for construction because of its high salt content and because its grains are very smooth and so do not adhere together. In 2012, nearby Qatar was the world's largest importer of sand and gravel, importing $6.5 billion worth of the material. With each ton of cement needing around 7 tons of sand and gravel, approximately 1.15 million tons were required to build the Burj tower alone. The United Nations noted that "the world's use of aggregates for concrete can be estimated at 25.9 billion to 29.6 billion tons a year for 2012 alone. This represents enough concrete to build a wall 27 m high by 27 m wide around the equator," Pascal Peduzzi, "Sand, Rarer Than One Thinks," *Environmental Development* 11, (2014): 208.

David Robertson, a business correspondent for *The Times*, suggests that the spectacular growth of steel-hungry skyscrapers, as well as the construction of enormous factory landscapes in China, are so dependent on vast supplies of iron ore (as well as other metallic ores), "It seems inevitable that we will soon be talking about the strategic importance of these metals in the same way that we talk about oil." Consequently, he argues that the epicenter of the global economy may no longer focus on the financial cores of London and Wall Street or even upstart global cities like Dubai. Instead, the focus shifts to the technical lands of resource extraction that dot the world's peripheries. Instead, the iron-ore producing peripheries of rural China, western Australia, northern Brazil, and elsewhere are "vast expanse[s] of red earth in the middle of nowhere"[30]

Architects Liam Young and Kate Davies further emphasize this point in their writing about exploring the pit and shaft mines that sustain the world's cities. "Here lies the shadow of those cities," they write as they venture to the bottom of deep iron ore pits in the desert interiors of Western Australia. Here they find what they call "[t]he silent twin: the void where a landform once was. These are the dislocated resource sites that support the world that we know."[31]

The environmental and social impacts of each stage of the mining, transportation, processing, and construction associated with all these sectors, need to be considered. All are controlled by a few giant and often esoteric multinationals; use vast amounts of scarce water and energy; are huge polluters; and are run and owned by tiny cabals of super-rich elites of financiers and predatory speculators, often through corrupt alliances with states at various scales backed by local security forces or their own violent militia.

Evidence of violations of human rights, labor rights, and ideas of environmental justice by transnational mining companies is abundant.[32] Such companies often leave catastrophic social and environmental devastation in their wake. Indigenous and local people in the Global South are often displaced by the mine companies' violent "security" forces.[33]

Trade unionists and community activists working against mining corporations are often targeted and killed. Toxic and polluted air, water, and landscapes contribute disproportionately to global climate crises and often leave poverty and sickness for generations after the mining corporations extracted, exhausted, and abandoned their technical lands.[34] With crucial soil removed, dumped, and heavily polluted, agriculture and foraging are impossible long after the mining corporations have left. For this reason, activists call disused mining areas "sacrifice zones."[35] The US Environmental Protection Agency ranks metal mining as the most toxic of all industries, even in the relatively well-regulated context of the United States.[36]

Cambridge criminologist Laura Gutiérrez Gómez studied abuses by gold mining corporations in Colombia. She characterizes their actions as criminal behavior, claiming mining corporations are a form of accumulation by dispossession and organized through systematic state-led corporate harm against the health, welfare, and prosperity of local communities.[37]

[28] The use of the word "base," as in "base metal," to describe relatively common, non-precious, and nonferrous metals is telling. It stems from the old fourteenth-century French word *bas* (depth); the critical meaning here, reflecting the metals' pivotal roles in modern industrial economies, is "bottom, foundation, pedestal."

[29] Peter Eichstaedt, *Consuming the Congo: War and Conflict Minerals in the World's Deadliest Place* (Chicago, IL: Chicago Review Press, 2011).

[30] David Robertson, "From Oil to Strategic Red Earth," *Emirates 24/7*, February 4, 2008, http://www.emirates247.com/eb247/opinion/analysis/from-oil-to-strategic-red-earth-2008-02-04-1.216241.

[31] Liam Young and Kate Davies, "Unknown Fields," *Volume* 31, (Spring 2012): 6–14.

[32] The best sources of this are the websites of NGO mining advocacy networks. See, for example, http://english.jatam.org/content/view/4/4/; http://miningwg.com; http://londonmining-network.org.

[33] This is the so-called resource curse: an initial stimulation of growth based on mining and commodity exports, reduced wealth, and deepening social, environmental, and health problems caused by the primitive accumulation of mining corporations and the hemorrhaging of profits to financiers in distant global cities. See Kenneth Hermele and Karin Gregow, *From Curse to Blessing? Africa and the Raw Materials Race* (Stockholm: Forum Syd, 2011).

[34] Meredith J. DeBoom, "Climate Necropolitics: Ecological Civilization and the Distributive Geographies of Extractive Violence in the Anthropocene," *Annals of the American Association of Geographers* 111, no. 3 (2020): 900–12.

35 See Lindsay Shade, "Sustainable Development or Sacrifice Zone? Politics Below the Surface in Post-Neoliberal Ecuador," *The Extractive Industries and Society* 2, no. 4 (2015): 775–84.

36 Brian Owens, "Extreme Prospects," *Nature*, (March 20, 2003): S4–S7.

37 Laura Gutiérrez Gómez, *Accumulation by Dispossession Through State-Corporate Harm: The Case of Anglo-gold Ashanti in Colombia* (Utrecht: Wolf Legal Publishers, 2013).

38 James Wilson, "UAE to Invest $5bn in Guinea Bauxite Project," *Financial Times*, November 25, 2013, http://www.ft.com/cms/s/0/5a069168-55e8-11e3-96f5-00144feabdc0.html#axzz3TWFWwf9t.

39 Simeon Kerr, "Emaar Founder Eyes Africa's Commodity Riches," *Financial Times*, March 4, 2011, http://www.ft.com/cms/s/0/bd7a1002-7662-11e0-b4f7-00144feabdc0.html#axzz3prGQE7yO.

40 Anil Bhoyrul, "Emaar Chairman Alabbar Plots $10bn Mining Empire," *Arabian Business*, May 4, 2011, http://m.arabianbusiness.com/emaar-chairman-alabbar-plots-10bn-mining-empire-397880.html.

41 Moscow, Rio, Sydney, Mexico City, and Hong Kong are also important. See Surborg, *The Production of the World City*, 74.

Political Economies of Extractive Control and Financing

A second process linking the Burj with mining involves the growing effort by UAE elites to shift their substantial surplus capital away from oil towards mining and extraction. The mass engineering of skyscrapers, infrastructure projects, and huge islands has pushed Dubai and the UAE to finance and control global mining, metal refining, quarrying, and aggregate extraction industries. Increasing efforts are being made to control the geographically spread minerals, mining, and extraction industries "upstream" of the construction process in the UAE and Gulf through ownership or joint ventures.

Dubai companies are diversifying rapidly to deal with the inevitable future of reduced oil wealth. They recently gained "downstream" control of new bauxite mines in Guinea in West Africa. This is a central factor given the importance of aluminum in skyscraper and infrastructure construction.[38] But refined aluminum is also Dubai's most important industrial export. In fact, the state-owned company Emirates Global Aluminum (EGA) is one of the biggest aluminum producers in the world. "Dubai is the New York for Africans now," Mohamed Ali Alabbar, CEO of the Dubai real estate giant Emaar, said in 2011, "I really see that the link between Dubai, UAE, and Africa is getting stronger and stronger."[39]

As well as gold, bauxite, and iron ore in Guinea-Conakry, Emaar is taking control of significant stakes in oil and gas concessions in Uganda, bauxite in Malaysia, oil and gas in Gabon, uranium and hydrocarbon interests in Niger, copper in the Democratic Republic of Congo, gold and coal deposits in Madagascar, phosphate concessions in Mauritania. "The Burj was over," Alabbar said on another occasion, reflecting on the mineral strategies. "I was thinking where to go, what to do next?"[40]

The rapid diversification in cities like Dubai into the control and financing of transnational extraction hints at the broader role that a small group of global cities plays in the geopolitical economics of global mining. For the small group of these cities where the world's major mining corporations have their headquarters—especially cities like Toronto, New York, Santiago, London, Los Angeles, and Johannesburg,[41] where the world's major mining corporations have their headquarters—directly derive much of their the wealth and power that drives their increasingly vertiginous skylines through the profits, wealth and speculation linked to mining.

Few people realize that the mushrooming cluster of towers that comprise Toronto's finance district and stock exchange (TSX) now constitute the mining industry's most important global hub. Following a recent period of aggressive expansion by the Canadian mining industry through acquisitions of smaller companies in Latin and Central America and Africa, 75 percent of global mining companies are now headquartered in Toronto. About 60 percent are listed on TSX. And in 2012, 70 percent of the equity capital raised for mining globally was raised in Toronto.

Canadian mining corporations—supported by generous national and local governments—are now especially powerful in mining gold and other precious and strategically scarce metals.[42] Local lobbying and donations from Toronto's wealthy mining sector means that everything from hospitals, businesses, schools, and university chairs to art centers and museums now receive direct sponsorship from mining within Toronto and Ontario. Such "philanthropy" has even allowed mining companies to influence primary education in the city's schools so that any social or environmental criticism of its impacts on the extraction zones of the global south are removed from books and other teaching content.[43]

To explore the heart of this power, in 2013, local activist Niko Block went to the Prospectors and Developers Association of Canada (PDAC) conference. By far the biggest conference in global mining, with 30,000 delegates from 100 countries, this huge and pivotal gathering is held annually in downtown Toronto. This reflects the vital importance of the city, and Canada more generally, to contemporary global mining. The conference, in effect, is a giant event through which the detailed shaping of the world's technical lands of mining and quarrying takes place.

Wandering the free bars around the convention center at the 2013 event, Block noted US Geological Survey stands showing off surveys detailing Afghanistan's deposits of gemstones, iron, magnesite, chromite, copper, and lithium (an increasingly vital resource given the massive growth of battery-powered appliances, machines, and vehicles relying on lithium-ion batteries). He also attended dozens of technical discussions on valuing the latest super-deep reserves and the challenges of using the latest 3D visualization and radar systems to help improve prospecting for remaining deeply buried metals and minerals.[44] Late at night, Block saw echelons of chubby mining executives returning from nights of the town arm in arm with local sex workers.

Meanwhile, across town, a startlingly different conference was taking place: a small-scale congress of global NGOs discussing efforts to resist the violent eviction of Indigenous communities living around the technical lands of mining and extraction in the remote, peripheral regions of Guatemala, the Congo, and Mexico. Here, the agenda was somewhat different. It focused on the burning of villages, on environmental and health crises, om the murder of activists and trade unionists by private paramilitaries,[45] and of intimidation of women in mining areas by mass rape—sometimes by proxy militia employed by the very same mining corporations whose executives were living it up across town.

"We are exploiting people and places that are otherwise made invisible to us," Block wrote. "Mining is the business that built the skyscrapers at Bay [Street] and King [Street in the financial district of central Toronto], which absorbs the money as it cascades into the city, as though from out of the clear, blue sky before rippling outward through downtown and toward [the neighborhoods of] Ajax, Markham, Brampton, Burlington."[46]

[42] See Veltmayer, "Extractive Imperialism."

[43] See Stuart Tannock, "Mining Capital and the Corporatization of Public Education in Toronto: Building a Global City or Building a Globally Ignorant City?' *Burning Billboard*, September 2009, http://burningbillboard.org/wp-content/2009/08/Mining-and-Education-in-Toronto-2009-Report.pdf.

[44] "Corporate and state power in the natural resource sector is commonly constituted through volumetric practices, as those who live alongside resource extraction will know all too well. I mean this not in the simple sense that mining is about moving quantities of earth, but in the sense … that the exercise of power involves technologies of calculation, visualization, and manipulation around volume," Gavin Bridge, "Territory, now in 3D!" *Political Geography* 34, (2013): 56.

[45] See Tess Lea, "Indigenous Social Policy, Settler-Colonial Dependencies, and Toxic Lingering: Living Through Mining and Militarism in the Anthropocene," *Shifting States: New Perspectives on Security, Infrastructure, and Political Affect*, ed. Alison Dundon and Richard Vokes, (London: Routledge, 2020), 97–111.

[46] Figures and discussion from Niko Block, "On the Roots of Our Skyscrapers: The Cynicism and Depravity of Toronto's Extractive Economy," *Critical Utopias*, July 23, 2013, http://criticalutopias.net/2013/07/23/on-the-roots-of-our-skyscrapers-the-cynicism-and-depravity-of-torontos-extractive-economy/.

Oil and Skyscrapers

Penultimately, we must attend to the extractive sources of the wealth required to build the Burj and other Gulf towers in the first place. Here we must address the most crucial commodity chain of all, which underlies the spectacular vertical architectural constructions in the Gulf: the reliance on the speculative profits of oil extraction to fund the construction of mega-structures like the Burj. Durham geographer Gavin Bridge explains, "Today the fantasy skylines of Houston or Dubai achieve a similar inversion" to the "inverted minescapes" of San Francisco's towers in the late nineteenth century. "Their thrusting towers and sprawling infrastructure embody the three-dimensional geographies of oil and gas fields in the Gulf of Mexico and the Middle East from which their wealth and power derive."[47]

A further connection between mining and skyscrapers like the Burj Khali-fa involves the flows of surplus capital from the extractive peripheries of the world into the burgeoning forests of the elite, super-luxury, housing towers in the cores of the world's global cities. As often corrupt extractive oligarchs search for low-tax and high-return safe-havens for their bounties of excess capital in volatile economic times, invariably, the booming real estate markets of cities like London, New York, Miami, Vancouver, and Singapore are at the tops of their lists. Many hard-to-trace shell companies buying the most expensive *überwealth* condos in the most prestigious emerging towers in New York, London, and other key global cities are fronts for mining oligarchs.[48]

The Deepest Frontier: Technical Lands of the Push for Deep Gold

Gold value is a kind of fiction, embodied by a block of material wrung like blood from a stone from vast tracts of the earth to end up in a vault, in the earth.[49]

To sustain the "inverted minescapes" of today's burgeoning global cities, the volumetric technical lands that support deep mining must reach ever further into Earth's crust. This is necessary to reach the remaining ores and metals that are scarce and have high demand and high prices now that the more accessible, shallower reserves are exhausted. The frenzy for gold is driving the most extraordinary of all these deepening descents into Earth's crust. Forty percent of the gold sector is controlled by dealers in Dubai, the "City of Gold." While no longer setting international exchange rates, this high demand is maintained because nation-states still preserve some of their financial reserves in bullion. This works because global elites and middle classes still covet gold and, most importantly, because investment demand for gold always benefits from its image as a low-risk haven in times of economic turbulence.

Global gold demands are increasingly challenging to meet, however. "New shallow deposits [of gold] aren't easily being discovered around the world," Ray Durrheim, a South African seismologist, reported in 2007.

[47] Even the oil-generated peak electricity consumption of the tower—36 mega-watts—is remarkably high, enough to power around 27,000 average Californian suburban homes. (The UAE has the largest per-capita environmental footprint on Earth). The quote is from Gavin Bridge, "The Hole World."

[48] Persistent research by the *New York Times* has identified examples here. One is min-ing magnate Anil Agarwal who is notorious for the pollution around his mines in Zambia and the violation of Indigenous land rights around proposed mines in his native India. Another is Russian oil magnate and politician Andrey Vavilov, who has long faced alle-gations of corruption. See Louise Story and Stephanie Saul, "Towers of Secrecy," *New York Times*, February 7, 2015, http://www.nytimes.com/2015/02/08/nyregion/stream-of-foreign-wealth-flows-to-time-warner-condos.html.

[49] Young and Davies, "Unknown Fields."

"The resources are at greater depths."[50] Across the world, gold miners, just like miners for other precious and non-precious metals, are digging down to unprecedented depths and exploiting resources in more politically volatile places. In South Africa—a nation which, in 140 years, has produced 40,000 metric tons of gold, a figure that is 50 percent of all gold ever mined on the planet—the push for remaining ores is overwhelmingly a push for unprecedented depth. The prolonged historical exhaustion of gold ores and the existence and mapping of super-deep ore fields means South Africa is seeing the deepest push for gold, and indeed the deepest mines anywhere, as companies and political elites seek to shore up rapidly waning production by exploiting new super-deep and challenging-to-reach reserves.

To respond to high demand and high prices,[51] in the context where resources within 2 kilometers of the surface have long been exhausted, South Africa's gold mines are drilling to unheard-of depths. The Mponeng mine—60 kilometers from Johannesburg—aling with the adjacent Tau Tona mine—currently the world's deepest. Mponeng is a poster child for "ultra-deep" gold mining. Super-long elevator descents reach over 3.5 kilometers (2.2 miles) into Earth's crust at speeds of 60 kilometers per hour. To put this into perspective, this depth is 10 percent the thickness of Earth's continental crust in South Africa. As architect Daniel Fernández Pascual puts it, "As for today, the 'deepest nation-state' in the world is South Africa."[52]

Mponeng's huge vertical, three-deck elevators take 120 miners at a time, with 4,000 miners plummeting down every day. The cages descend through the first leg of 2.5 kilometers—a distance ten times longer than the elevators to the viewing deck of the Empire State building—in only six minutes. At such depths, the temperature of the rock is slightly closer to the heat of the planet's core. This temperature is caused by radioactive decay and, leftover from the planet's formation, reaches 60 degrees Celsius. To stop the miners from literally baking alive and bring the prevailing temperature to a still stifling 28 to 30 degrees Celsius, the entire mine must be refrigerated using 6,000 tons of ice a day through special fridge shafts.

The object of such heroic and dangerous labor is a single extremely valuable gold seam, only 30 to 50 centimeters thick, laid down by ancient water flows in deltas and shallow seas some three billion years ago.[53] AngloGold Ashanti, the company that owns Mponeng, produces 5,500 tons of rock a day yet obtains only 10 grams of gold per ton. This still amounts to 55 kilograms of gold per day, worth over $2 million in September 2015.

Multilevel mines like Mponeng, whose galleries can stretch for many kilometers out from the cage shafts, are carefully designed using the latest geological sensing and visualizing technologies. (Mponeng has around 250 miles of tunnels, 36 miles longer than the entire New York subway system.) In these types of mines, rock-mechanics experts and specialist engineers undertake complex three-dimensional planning and modeling to decide which rocks can be most safely and profitably excavated while minimizing the risk of collapses, major seismic events, or fractured rock.

[50] Quoted in Nick Wadhams, "Digging for Riches in the World's Deepest Gold Mine," *Wired* (March 2011): 24.

[51] Prices per ounce of gold went from $400 in 2003 to $1,700 at the end of 2012 and dipped to $1,060 in December 2015. By November 2021, they were at $1,792 per ounce.

[52] Daniel Fernández Pascual, "The Clear-Blurry Line," *The Funambulist Papers* 20, February 2012, http://thefunambulist.net/2012/02/21/guest-writers-esssays-20-the-clear-blurry-line-by-daniel-fernandez-pascual/.

[53] All the gold on Earth was manufactured in the unimaginably ancient death-throes of stars. It is only water flows that accumulate scarce gold deposits into denser concentrations that can be profitably mined. See Sarah Zhnag, "Terrifying Facts About the World's Deepest Gold Mine," *Gizmodo*, December 16, 2013, http://gizmodo.com/terrifying-facts-about-the-worlds-deepest-gold-mine-1484301368.

54 Matthew Hart, "A Journey Into the World's Deepest Gold Mine," *Wall Street Journal*, December 13, 2013, http://online.wsj.com/news/articles/SB1000142405270230485480457923664079 3042718.

55 D. H. Diering, "Ultra-Deep Level Mining—Future Requirements," *The Journal of The South African Institute of Mining and Metallurgy*, (October 1997): 249–256.

56 Elizabeth Rebelo, "World's Deepest Single-Lift Mine Ever," *Mining Weekly*, September 29, 2003, http://www.miningweekly.com/article/worlds-deepest-singlelift-mine-ever-2003-09-29. Added to this, automated self-driving trucks are now widely used to move ore between the excavation galleries and the vertical cages.

57 Martin Creamer, "AngloGold Ashanti Moving Closer to Ultra-deep Mining Goal," *Mining Weekly*, March 2, 2013, http://www.miningweekly.com/article/anglogold-ashanti-moving-closer-to-ultra-deep-mining-goal-2013-02-05.

58 Mining accidents kill around 12,000 workers a year. See Olivia Lang, "The Dangers of Mining Around the World," *BBC News*, October 14, 2010, http://www.bbc.co.uk/news/world-latin-america-11533349.

Matthew Hart, a journalist for the *Wall Street Journal*, journeyed to the depths of the Mponeng mine in 2013. Echoing Brechin's influential idea of skyscrapers as inverted minescapes, his experience allowed him to compare the mine's cages/elevators with the super-fast, high-tech elevators sustaining the world's tallest building. Hart reflects that in the Burj Khalifa, a fleet of fifty-seven elevators move people up and down, using "sky lobbies" as staging posts between elevator journeys. On reaching the base of Mponeng's first cage run, by contrast, Hart and colleagues "had traveled five times the distance covered by the Burj Khalifa's system and had done it in a single drop." They then walked to the vast subterranean "lobby" to the "the cage that would take us deeper, to the active mining levels that lay far below. We stepped into the second cage and in two minutes dropped another mile into the furnace of the rock."[54]

To parallel their pivotal role in pushing ever-taller skyscrapers, faster and bigger elevator systems are crucial in opening deeper and deeper layers of gold, other metals, and minerals to systematic exploitation. The weight of ropes in both mine and skyscraper elevators is a pivotal constraint. Back in 1997, mining engineer D. H. Diering admitted, "If someone asked the question 'what would stop us going to 5,000 [meters] today, assuming there was an ore body worth going to and enough money to pay for it?' the simplified answer would be 'ropes!'"[55] Innovations like the carbon fiber rope being launched for skyscraper elevators are thus likely to fuel the latest in a long line of technological crossovers over the next twenty years in the parallel push upwards for skyscrapers and downward for mines.

Remarking on the need for lighter ropes in elevator lifts, *Mining Weekly* reports, "With improved winder and rope technologies, cages can now be hoisted below 3,000 meters in a single drop." To the mining industry, such a prospect offers "great economic benefit in deep-level mines as it enables personnel to reach the rockface far sooner and thus have a more productive time at the face."[56]

In 2012, Mponeng alone produced $950 million worth of gold. Tempted by such extraordinary riches, gold mining corporations are already planning even deeper shafts to reach untapped, ultra-deep resources. For example, the AngloGold Ashanti corporation reached depths of 4.5 kilometers in 2018, tempted by the estimated "100-million ounces of gold that cannot be mined conventionally," deep within South Africa's goldfields.[57]

The elevators in relatively high-tech deep mines are dangerous (although they are nowhere near as deadly as the improvised shafts and galleries that access the thousands of illegal, informal, or artisanal mines dotting these regions in Latin America, Africa, and parts of Asia).[58] In May 1995, in the most notorious deep-shaft disaster so far, the engine of an underground railcar in the Anglo-American Corporation's Vaal Reefs Mine near Orkney, South Africa, broke loose and fell down a two-kilometer (7,000 ft.) elevator shaft. Crushing a two-deck cage completely flat, it instantly killed the 105 men within it. Like all major South African mines, Mponeng also reports regular deaths and injuries during "normal" operations. In South Africa, an average of five miners die each week.[59] At least six fatalities were reported in the mine by *Mining Weekly* in March of 2012; the causes involved seismic collapses (which can reach a five on the Richter scale), heavy machinery malfunctions, and electrocution.

Annual reviews of mine performances, along with detailed data on ore extractions, remaining reserves, profits, and costs, usually incorporate platitudes about fatalities. Under the subheading "Sustainability Performance," one review states, "There were regrettably eight fatalities at the West Wits operations during 2012: three each at Mponeng and TauTona, and two at Savuka .... The board and management of AngloGold Ashanti extend their sincere condolences to the family, friends, and colleagues of the deceased."[60]

"We would not generally oppose the idea of ultra-deep mining if our people were safe," explained Lesiba Sheshoka, South Africa's National Union of Mineworkers (NUM) representative who organized a national mineworkers strike in 2012 told the *National Geographic* in 2007. "But we are opposing it on the basis that ... we have already seen a significant rise of fatalities."[61] Such resistance to ultra-deep mining fails to even address the gold industry's catastrophic record of fatalities and debilitating illness through degenerative and crippling respiratory diseases like silicosis, nor its appalling track record in legal denials for liability. South Africa's NUM, along with 3,500 ex-miners, is currently suing UK-owned gold firms in London to force recognition of the problem; there are at least 50,000 ex-gold miners in South Africa with silicosis (which is often fatal through reduced resistance to TB).

What is especially striking is that while huge investments go into deeper and deeper mines to keep miners alive while mining (and of course, to secure and protect the all-important gold), very little has been done about the air and ventilation problems that cause silicosis. "It was always possible through ventilation and proper clothing to protect people from silica dust in [gold] mines," NUM president, Senzeni Zokwana said when interviewed about the legal challenge. "But in the past, men were down [the mines] just to break rocks and make money."[62] Richard Spoor, an attorney representing some of London claimants, agrees. "It was cheaper for the gold mining industry to cripple and maim workers by exposing them to excessive levels of dust," he says, "than it was to take steps to protect their health."[63]

As in many other extractive industries, gold miners face real dangers struggling to improve wages and conditions and often face heavily armed state police working on behalf of mining and political elites. In one of the worst such stand-offs in recent times, forty-four mine workers striking for improved pay were massacred, with seventy-eight others receiving serious gun-shot wounds by South African police at the Marikana platinum mine, 20 kilometers north of Mponeng in August 2012.[64]

The technical lands sustaining gold mining also have severe social and environmental impacts beyond the risks they create to the miners themselves. Toxic acids and cyanides used in gold-ore processing can often create devastating health and environmental spills. Moreover, the physical

[59] Terry Bell, "Miners Who are Doing Dirty Work Deserve Better," *Business Report* 6, October 2000, http://www.queensu.ca/samp/sampresources/migrationdocuments/commentaries/2000/better.htm.

[60] AngloGold Ashanti, *Operation Profile: West Wits South Africa* (2012), 4, http://www.aga-reports.com/14/download/AGA-OP14-sa-westwits.pdf.

[61] Wadhams, "Digging for Riches in the World's Deepest Gold Mine," 24.

[62] Cited in Tracy McVeigh, "South Africa's Miners Take Lung Disease Fight to London," *The Observer*, April 27, 2014, http://www.theguardian.com/world/2014/apr/27/south-african-miners-lung-disease-fight-london.

[63] Cited in Jennifer Schmidt, "Gold Miners Breathe the Dust, Fall Ill: 'They Did Not Give Me Nothing,'" *NPR*, October 22, 2015, http://www.npr.org/sections/goatsandsoda/2015/10/22/450312266/gold-miners-breathe-the-dust-fall-ill-they-did-not-give-me-nothing.

[64] See Crispen Chinguno, "Marikana Massacre and Strike Violence Post-apartheid," *Global Labour Journal* 4, no. 2 (May 2013).

movement and dumping of waste mine tailings can be devastating for ecosystems that get in the way. On average, it has been estimated that 20 tons of toxic mining waste must be dredged out of the earth, processed, and disposed of to produce the gold necessary to make a single, 10-gram, 18-carat gold ring.

This essay is adapted and updated from the text in the final chapter of *Vertical: The City from Satellites to Bunkers* (Verso, 2016).

Hell on *a* Hill

U*n*/B*u*ilding the Coalfield-to-Prison Pipeline

Billy Fleming *&* A L McCullough

In Eastern Kentucky, the symbolism of new prisons built on top of former coal mines is clear. These facilities infuse local imaginaries with the promise of being the next great form of economic development. Perched atop mountains artificially flattened by industrial dynamite, penitentiaries fill both literal spatial cavities and the economic and affective voids left by coal and the extractive process known as mountaintop removal.[1]

Introduction

More than 1.5 million acres of abandoned mine lands stipple and pock the undulating landscapes of Appalachia. In its shorn mountaintops and slag-filled valleys, the specter of the region's long-declining coal industry is infused into its people and place. Human death and disease are prevalent from toxic exposure to mining and processing coal, the leachate-filled waterways and aquifers downstream from the mines, and the dwindling biodiversity accompanying mountaintop removal. Sometimes described as an internal colony, Appalachia has long been a technical site of extraction and disposal in the United States.[2] Land theft by settlers in the eighteenth century led to industrialized timber plantations in the nineteenth, some of which still operate today.[3] Throughout the twentieth century, as the timber industry shifted south and west to chase larger, deregulated commodity landscapes, the coal industry came to dominate Appalachia.[4] Rather than embark upon a national effort to remediate and otherwise invest in the toxic lands of Appalachia, domestic policymakers spent the past half-century pursuing a divest-and-depopulate agenda in the region.[5] Basically, the costs of undoing the damage wrought by the timber and coal industries were deemed too large and the people living there too unimportant.

As a result, the region remains one of the poorest in the United States, with "diseases of despair" like opioid addiction nearing the highest rates in the country.[6] In their essay on the rise of the carceral state as means of economic development, Ryerson and Schept write, "Since the 1980s, 350 new prisons have been built in rural areas … this is what we are told to expect and believe is the last hope for poor rural areas around the country, especially in Appalachia."[7] In the context of decades-long precarity and cratering local economies, "prison growth in Central Appalachia is part of a dramatic trend in rural prison siting across the United States … in communities where industrial decline and soaring poverty rates render land cheap, and residents eager for new forms of employment, detention spaces are commonly pitched as economic development projects."[8] In Appalachia, many of those detention spaces are built atop the abandoned mine lands of the now-defunct coal industry.

By sheer acreage, Appalachia's coal-to-prison pipeline is one of the country's most extensive contiguous technical lands. In keeping with the broader theme of this volume, these sites "are often geographically remote and highly (in)visible, subject to both heightened surveillance and painstaking forms of obfuscation. They maintain special legal status and—more specifically—

[1] Brett Story, *Prison Land: Mapping Carceral Power across Neoliberal America* (Minneapolis, MN: University of Minnesota Press, 2019).

[2] Sam Adler-Bell, "Appalachia vs. the Carceral State," *New Republic*, November 25, 2019, https://newrepublic.com/article/155660/appalachia-coal-mining-mountaintop-removal-prison-fight.

[3] John Gaventa, *Power and Powerlessness: Quiescence and Rebellion in an Appalachia Valley* (Chicago, IL: University of Illinois Press 1982).

[4] Karida Brown, *Gone Home: Race and Roots through Appalachia* (Chapel Hill, NC: University of North Carolina Press 2019).

[5] Tarence Ray, "Hollowed Out: Against the Sham Revitalization of Appalachia," *The Baffler*, September 2019, https://thebaffler.com/salvos/hollowed-out-ray.

[6] Christine Schalkoff et al., "The Opioid and Related Drug Epidemics in Rural Appalachia: A Systematic Review of Populations Affected, Risk Factors, and Infectious Diseases," *Substance Abuse* 41, no. 1, (August 12, 2019): 35–69.

[7] Sylvia Ryerson and Judah Schept, "Building Prisons in Appalachia," *Boston Review*, April 28, 2018, http://bostonreview.net/law-justice/sylvia-ryerson-judah-schept-building-prisons-appalachia.

[8] Story, *Prison Land*.

[9] Jeffrey S. Nesbit and Charles Waldheim, "Introduction: Reading Technical Lands," 29, in this volume.

exceptional protocols concerning the nonhuman."[9] Either the prison or the abandoned coal mine alone would easily qualify as a technical land under this definition. Together, the coalfield prisons of Appalachia represent some of the world's most technically precise and surveilled landscapes. They are also critical sites in the fights for prison abolition, energy transition, and the realization of the Green New Deal.

Three major subsidies drive prison-building on abandoned mines in Appalachia. First, the Abandoned Mine Lands (AML) Program—created through the Surface Mining Control and Remediation Act of 1977—distributes grant funds for new capital projects on abandoned mine sites across the United States. Appalachia is home to the highest concentration of these sites. The AML has become a source of pork-barrel spending for elected officials, especially those in the states that comprise Central Appalachia (Kentucky, West Virginia, and Tennessee). There, elected officials often use the program to burnish their criminal justice bona fides by spending AML funds on new prison facilities in the region. Second, the sites themselves are often ideal for new construction; they are flat (a rarity in Appalachia), connected to existing infrastructure, and extremely cheap. Finally, the land remediation requirements on AML sites are far less stringent for housing incarcerated people than they would be for almost any other residential

[10] Adler-Bell, "Appalachia vs. the Carceral State."

use.[10] Along with prairie grass plantings and indefinite abandonment, prison-building is now one of the most common forms of AML remediation in the region. It is by far the most capital intensive of the three. Yet in Central Appalachia, every economic development incentive is stacked to entice building hell on a hill.

This Appalachian noir can be understood, at least in part, by viewing the half-century-long policy of depopulation through divestment in the region and the twenty-year investment in prison-driven economic development as synonymous forces. Central Appalachia is a largely forgotten landscape, underfunded and abandoned by federal policymakers. To borrow once again from Story, that half-century depopulation program through divestment created a series of spatial, social, and economic voids in the region. These voids then created the conditions for a regional economic development program organized around the carceral system to emerge—one that promised to fill those voids literally and metaphorically with prisons facilities and jobs. Today, the region is now home to one of the largest carceral archipelagos in the world. As Story writes,

> The U.S. operates the largest archipelago of jails and penitentiaries in the world. And yet it can be hard to find the prison in today's landscape. Prisons are, after all, by design and definition, spaces of disappearance. They disappear the people inside of them. And they are themselves increasingly disappeared from the dense social spaces where many of us live and move around.[11]

[11] Story, *Prison Land*.

To view them in this way is to see an invisible region powered by a hidden industry. For Central Appalachia, this invisibility relates to the region's status as a resource hub for the rest of the world. Detention facilities have replaced the exploding mountains and buried streams of one extractive regime. Both rely on the logistics of extraction and disposal to operate. Both have long over-promised and under-delivered in Appalachia. Or, as Martín Arboleda describes, the region operates as part of "a dense network of territorial infrastructures and spatial technologies,"[12] intentionally obscured from the public and yet integral to the construction and operation of contemporary urbanism—in this case through the cheap electricity that the region's coalfields provide. Rendering incarcerated people invisible for the prisons themselves is necessary to uphold the industry itself. Prisons shifted from menacing, highly visible sites of public punishment into their contemporary forms, in part, to quell growing movements for reform and decarceration that accompanied prior eras of prison-building in the United States. Put another way—if prisons and the carceral system were made legible and visible to more people, they might once again become sites of public opposition and protest. Siting these prisons in remote locations, using nondescript forms on highly surveilled compounds, ensures their invisibility to the broader public. Framing prison-building as a recession-proof economic boom for regions like Central Appalachia and rendering the facilities and people inside invisible and thus removed from scrutiny is central to the carceral project.

[12] Martín Arboleda, *Planetary Mine: Territories of Extraction under Late Capitalism* (New York, NY: Verso, 2020).

This chapter explores the production and life of these interrelated, immiserating systems in Central Appalachia, focusing on the declining coal and fossil fuel industry, its toxic landscapes, and the ever-expanding carceral system as its economic replacement. We briefly review the histories of the AML program and its role in bolstering the prison-industrial complex across the region's mine-pocked landscapes. We then reframe these racialized landscapes as critical sites of contestation in the fights for climate justice, sustainable energy, and the realization of the Green New Deal. The chapter concludes with a brief exploration of alternative forms of economic development in Appalachia and argues for an abolitionist project of un/imagining the political and economic regimes that produce technical lands.

fig 1

Prison-Building Atop the Abandoned Mine Lands of Appalachia

Detention facilities built atop abandoned mine lands in Appalachia follow a series of technical specifications, employ surveillance and monitoring technologies, and serve as literal and metaphorical spaces of disappearance in the sociospatial and ecological landscapes of the region. The mine lands are carefully delineated and tested for criteria pollutants and other toxic effluents throughout their life cycle. When a mine is no longer productive and decommissioned by its coal operator of a state environmental protection agency, it must adhere to the "approximate original contour" (AOC) stipulation, which requires that all mine lands be returned to their pre-mountaintop removal elevation. When an abandoned mine site is converted to a prison, it comes with a requirement that any such facility contains enough

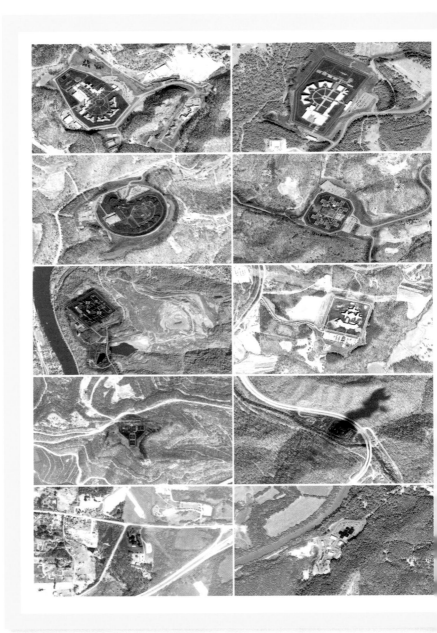

fig 1 Appalachia detention and correction facilities. World Imagery, Maxar

fig 2   Appalachia detention and correction
facilities. World Imagery, Maxar/NC CGIA/Shelby Co., AL

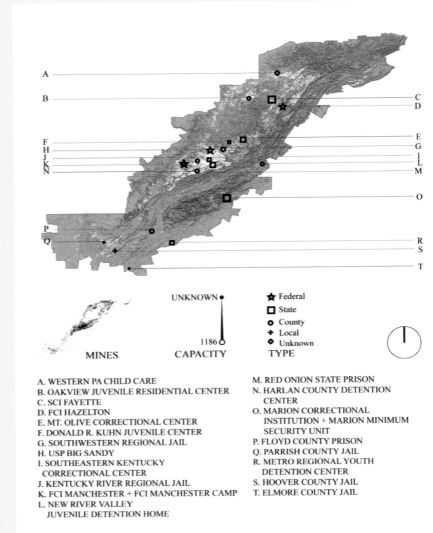

UNKNOWN •

1186 ○
CAPACITY

MINES

★ Federal
☐ State
○ County
+ Local
◇ Unknown

TYPE

A. WESTERN PA CHILD CARE
B. OAKVIEW JUVENILE RESIDENTIAL CENTER
C. SCI FAYETTE
D. FCI HAZELTON
E. MT. OLIVE CORRECTIONAL CENTER
F. DONALD R. KUHN JUVENILE CENTER
G. SOUTHWESTERN REGIONAL JAIL
H. USP BIG SANDY
I. SOUTHEASTERN KENTUCKY
   CORRECTIONAL CENTER
J. KENTUCKY RIVER REGIONAL JAIL
K. FCI MANCHESTER + FCI MANCHESTER CAMP
L. NEW RIVER VALLEY
   JUVENILE DETENTION HOME

M. RED ONION STATE PRISON
N. HARLAN COUNTY DETENTION
   CENTER
O. MARION CORRECTIONAL
   INSTITUTION + MARION MINIMUM
   SECURITY UNIT
P. FLOYD COUNTY PRISON
Q. PARRISH COUNTY JAIL
R. METRO REGIONAL YOUTH
   DETENTION CENTER
S. HOOVER COUNTY JAIL
T. ELMORE COUNTY JAIL

fig 3   Global Multi-Resolution Terrain Elevation Data 2010. USGS Earth Resources Observation & Science (EROS) Archive

on-site electricity generation and storage capacity to continue running normal operations in the event of a region-wide blackout.[13] Every aspect of the coalfield-to-prison pipeline in Central Appalachia is precisely specified, circumscribed, and managed through a blend of labor-intensive and technological instruments—from the electrons in their circuits to the biota in their landscapes, to the incarcerated people who are considered less than human once they enter the carceral system.

In keeping with the broader theme of this volume, these prison lands "are often geographically remote and highly (in)visible, subject to both heightened surveillance and painstaking forms of obfuscation. They maintain special legal status and—more specifically—exceptional protocols concerning the nonhuman."[14] As this particular case shows, technical lands have a way of accumulating and reproducing themselves in space. In Central Appalachia, the formulation of mine lands, their abandoned afterlife, and their contemporary reimagining as prison lands are varying forms of technical lands, bounded in space and extremely durable over time. These spaces of exception—rendered invisible and yet integral to the functioning of contemporary capitalist cities—become fixed sites of technical lands in the service of global and racial capitalism. Whether through convict-leasing programs or other exploitative labor practices, technology transfers and commercialization, or their status as invisible lands and facilities, the coalfield-to-prison pipeline in Central Appalachia exemplifies the notion that once a parcel becomes a technical land, it is always a technical land.

fig 2

In total, 761 carceral facilities are operating in Appalachia—46 federal facilities, including penitentiaries and detention centers; 214 state facilities; 446 county facilities; and 53 local or multi-jurisdictional facilities. This includes some 22 juveniles, medium, or maximum-security facilities housing nearly 11,000 people located on or within a quarter mile of a toxic site registered with the AML program. At least 15 of these AML prisons have been built since 1992, and approximately 2 percent of Appalachia works in one of them—some 3,200 people.[15] With nearly $5 billion in public operating support for the facilities themselves, more than $10 billion in capital expenditures on the facility construction, and billions more on the critical infrastructure necessary to serve them (for example, water treatment plants, roadways, utility corridor, and capacity expansions, etc.), these facilities represent one the most heavily subsidized economic development programs in the country.[16] Yet, they often fail to deliver on their core promise of job creation and local wealth. Most of their workers are hired from outside the community, and even if they weren't, the pay is often far lower, the construction jobs far fewer, and the broader economic impact far more negligible than prison boosters claim.[17] While on average, 80 percent of prison jobs in Appalachia go to outside candidates.[18] In McCreary County the outcome was even more dire, resulting in very little of the claimed economic benefit to the town in the form of new taxpayers:

[13] Richard Heinberg, *Blackout: Coal, Climate, and the Last Energy Crisis* (New York, NY: New Society Publishers 2009).

[14] Nesbit and Waldheim, "Introduction," 29.

[15] This figure was calculated using the "Census of Jail Facilities, 2006" dataset from the Bureau of Justice Statistics, https://www.bjs.gov/content/pub/pdf/cjf06.pdf.

[16] Alison Stine, "The Phantom Promise: How Appalachia was Sold on Prisons as an Economic Lifeline," *Yes! Magazine*, November 8, 2019, https://www.yesmagazine.org/economy/2019/11/08/kentucky-prison-big-sandy-appalachia.

[17] For more on this, see Gregory Hooks et al., "Revisiting the Impact of Prison Building on Job Growth: Education, Incarceration, and County-Level Employment, 1976–2004," *Social Science Quarterly* 91, no. 1: 228–44; and Robert Todd Perdue and Kenneth Sanchagrin, "Imprisoning Appalachia: The Socio-Economic Impacts of Prison Development," *Journal of Appalachian Studies* 22, no.2: 210–23.

[18] Macey Logan Hall, "Prison Siting in Appalachia: Carceral Expansion, Neoliberalism, and Environmental Harm," master's thesis, Eastern Kentucky University (2019).

In McCreary County, Kentucky, few residents were qualified for jobs at a local federal prison, as it was "highly recommended" that candidates have undergraduate degrees and prior experience working as correctional officers. In the end, roughly 90 percent of the prison's jobs went to transfers, who did not choose to live in, and thus provide tax support to, McCreary County.[19]

A blend of financial and regulatory subsidies, anchored by the AML program, have made prison-building atop abandoned mine lands one of Appalachia's most prevalent (and insidious) economic development strategies. Three main pillars support this prison-building regime. First, there are direct subsidies, in the form of federal grants and loans, administered through the AML program that is often paired with state and local economic development incentives, including tax credits and supplemental grants and loans that specifically target prison-building and other capital-intensive remediation strategies on the region's legacy mine sites. For instance, USP Letcher, a proposed (and ultimately abandoned) prison development project outside of Whitesburg, KY, received more than $500 million in direct subsidies for its construction—which would have made it the most expensive USP facility in the country.[20] Second, there is a bundle of regulatory subsidies that allow for less stringent remediation strategies on mines sites earmarked for prison construction *and* permit the co-location of prison facilities, landfills, and other heavy industrial facilities and technical lands at the core of the environmental justice movement. For instance, USP McCreary near Pine Knot, KY, rests beside a freight airport, coal slurry ponds, industrial pork farm and processing center, and one of the region's oldest coal-powered electricity plants—a site of mass technical land accumulation. Third, each prison-development project is accompanied by a set of local land-use subsidies, including gifted parcels, capital-intensive infrastructure improvements (for example, roads and wastewater treatment plants), and, in keeping with their status as spaces of exception, a suspension of land development regulations that might otherwise thwart prison construction in the region. For instance, USP Big Sandy, near Inez, KY, received state and local capital improvement grants to construct a new wastewater treatment plant—without which, the prison itself would not have been authorized for construction due to Clean Water Act concerns in the region.

fig 3

The AML was authorized as part of the Surface Mining Control and Remediation Act of 1977 (SMCRA). Introduced by Rep. Morris Udall (D-AZ), the SMCRA intended to "hold the entire coal industry responsible for reclaiming coal mine lands left abandoned across the country," with the majority of those lands clustered in Appalachia.[21] Though the program was slow to develop, by 2013, it was responsible for channeling more than $5.7 billion into AML remediation projects covering nearly 800,000 acres across the United States. The program has a backlog of almost 6.2 million acres left to

[19] Kate Jenkins, "How Federal Prisoners Might Become Appalachia's New 'Black Gold,'" *Scalawag*, January 27, 2017, https://scalawagmagazine.org/2017/01/how-federal-prisoners-might-become-appalachias-new-black-gold/.

[20] Story, *Prison Land*.

[21] Eric Reece, *Lost Mountain: A Year in the Vanishing Wilderness* (New York, NY: Riverhead Books 2006).

clear, clustered in Central Appalachia and the Southwest, at an estimated cost of $9.6 billion.[22]

Upon passage, the SMCRA required coal mine operators to return as much of their site to the AOC as feasible. But, as Eric Reece documents in *Lost Mountain*, state and local officials quickly devised ways to work around this provision and keep the coal industry magnates who underwrite their campaigns and political ambitions happy. He writes:

> Perhaps sensing that the AOC stipulation would be a hard sell, lawmakers allowed coal operators to obtain a variance if they could prove that the post-mined land would be put to higher or better uses. In the beginning, this meant commercial development ... often prisons and other detention facilities ... It eventually became much cheaper [for operators] to plant grass and call it a pasture or move the site into receivership and let local officials build a prison.[23]

The AML was imagined for the specific, technical purpose of channeling federal investment into the mine lands rapidly abandoned by the coal industry during a previous energy transition. It employs an exact technical specification (the delineation of abandoned mine lands), operates through a specific technical standard (the AOC), and targets a particular set of criteria (pollutants) and technical standards (set and regulated by the EPA) to cover the measurement and remediation of heavy metals, acid drainage, and other toxic elements of abandoned mine lands.[24]

Though the AML is ostensibly open to funding any project that meets the AOC specifications or the waiver qualifications of a higher and better use for the sites, the program has produced three primary outcomes since its inception: 1) the conversion of abandoned mine lands into grassland, usually led by the coal operator; 2) the indefinite abandonment of the site without any remediation work whatsoever, generally as the land moves from private to public ownership through bankruptcy proceedings; and 3) the construction of prison facilities through public agencies with public funds, as previously noted. Though hundreds of elected and appointed officials are implicated in this coalfield-to-prison pipeline, none have played a more prominent role than Representative Harold Rogers (R-KY) in restructuring Appalachia's economic development program around prison-building.[25] As Ryerson and Schept document:

> Rogers has capitalized on the rapid expansion of our nation's prison system ... making it one of his primary strategies for economic development. USP Letcher will be the fourth federal prison built in Eastern Kentucky since 1992 ... and at $510 million, it will be the most expensive federal prison ever built, surpassing USP Big Sandy just two counties north ... yet, the federal Bureau of Prisons does not think the facility is necessary.[26]

[22] Eric Dixon and Kendall Bilbrey, "Abandoned Mine Land Program: A Policy Analysis for Central Appalachia and the Nation," Report: AML Policy Priorities Group, July 8, 2015, https://legacy-assets.eenews.net/open_files/assets/2015/07/09/document_gw_01.pdf.

[23] Reece, *Lost Mountain*.

[24] United States Environmental Protection Agency, "Abandoned Mine Site Characterization and Cleanup Handbook," EPA Report: 910-B-00-001, August 2000, https://www.epa.gov/sites/default/files/2015-09/documents/2000_08_pdfs_amscch.pdf.

[25] Ryerson and Schept, "Building Prisons in Rural Appalachia."

[26] Ryerson and Schept, "Building Prisons in Rural Appalachia."

Framed as a form of economic development, Rogers and other boosters of the carceral system have successfully tapped the AML and similar state-level grants to channel billions of dollars into prison-building across Appalachia.

The Office of Surface Mining Reclamation and Enforcement (OSMRE) is responsible for coordinating and administering the permitting process on these sites. However, like environmental regulations in the United States, much of who is allowed to apply for, secure, and otherwise access these AML remediation permits is determined by individual states. In those states, regulatory capture is often rampant, with coal and fossil fuel industry leaders exerting significant, outsized influence over the permitting and development process. Also, much of the environmental regulatory state operates at less than total capacity. In 2016, before the election of Donald Trump, the EPA and its state equivalents were operating at 1987 staffing levels. This lack of a fully staffed regulatory regime contributes to ecological disasters like the BP Deepwater Horizon Spill and the unchecked methane flares of the natural gas industry within and beyond Appalachia.[27]

[27] Christopher Sellers et al., "The EPA Under Siege: Trump's Assault in History and Testimony," Environmental Data & Governance Initiative Report, June 2017, https://envirodatagov.org/publication/the-epa-under-siege/.

Though housing, schools, and other land uses that might bring people into regular, direct contact with these sites are closely scrutinized, if not altogether banned without prohibitively expensive site remediation, no such scrutiny is applied to prison development. As a result, placing incarcerated people atop highly toxic abandoned mine lands has not yet halted a single project administered by the OSMRE. The agency is not authorized to consider the human health impact on incarcerated peoples on these toxic sites because most of this nation's legal system does not treat incarcerated people as fully human. Whether through the loss of voting rights or the barriers to employment once they are released or through the suspension of labor protections for work performed while incarcerated, inmates are simultaneously imagined as political tools. Phenomena like prison gerrymandering enable localities to include prison populations in their census counts, thus driving up federal formula funding and electoral power, without allowing incarcerated or formerly incarcerated people to fully participate in civic life. Ultimately, the only considerations that have successfully halted prison construction to date have been through provisions in the Endangered Species Act—one of the few regulatory powers that the OSMRE is authorized to halt a remediation project over. OSMRE is an incredibly powerful and lucrative regulatory subsidy for the region's prison industrial complex.

The final element of the subsidy regime underpinning prison construction in Appalachia are the local land-use benefits conferred to the industry through the AML program. The flattened sites—shorn and razed by strip mining and mountaintop removal—coupled with proximity to existing infrastructure create a sort of ready-made development proposition for prison builders. Of course, these land-use subsidies would be of value to any developer in the region. Still, they're particularly of higher value to prison developers when paired with the lax environmental regulations and multiple states and federal funding sources for prison-building within the AML foot-print. The AML program (and its state equivalents) includes lax environmental regulations administered by the OSMRE. Leveled parcels, and their proximity to critical infrastructure, form the core of the coalfield-to-prison pipeline in Appalachia.

A single industry often dominates rural economic development in the United States.

When Gilmore describes prisons as partial geographic solutions to political crises, she is asking us to take seriously the spatial dimensions of the prison industrial complex as clues pointing to the actual crises, rooted in capitalism, rather than the spurious crises of so-called crime or lawlessness for which are prisons are claimed as deputized solutions. Space, it turns out, matters a great deal.[28]

[28] Story, *Prison Land*.

Corporate agriculture in the Mississippi Delta and Midwest, oil and gas in the Great Plains and Gulf South, defense contractors in the Southwest and Mid-Atlantic. Rural economic development is channeled through the prison industrial complex in Central Appalachia and so many other rural communities. In fact,

[b]etween 1990 and 1999, approximately 1/3 of all new rural prison development occurred in four of the most economically depressed regions: the West Texas plains, South Central Georgia, the Mississippi Delta, and the coalfields of Appalachia ... there, supporters argue for the prison not only as a source of crucial waged labor ... but also as a kind of Keynesian development tool, providing construction jobs, spreading gas and water infrastructure to remote areas.[29]

[29] Story, *Prison Land*.

While the sites have apparent interest and import to design politics and justice questions, we are far more interested in the structural conditions that make the carceral state possible. The precarity and multigenerational disinvestment in rural communities result from globalized racial capitalism injected into rural communities through false promises of wealth and wage creation. This deception profoundly impacts rural America's quality of life, human health, and landscapes.[30] As Story argues, "The prison is more than just a building or the numbers of people inside the building ... it is a robust and extensive industrial complex that is fully imbricated in the functioning of the contemporary capitalist economy."[31] A key challenge then—one where the built-environment professions have something to contribute—is to imagine alternative forms of rural economic development, predicated on something other than mass human trauma, that can power regions like Central Appalachia. In the final section of this chapter, we explore two such alternatives: one, linked to the decommissioning and repurposing of Appalachian prisons, is about channeling public investment into new industrial actors in the region; the second, predicated on democratizing the design

[30] Brett Story et al., *The Prison in Twelve Landscapes* (New York, NY: Grasshopper Film, 2016).

[31] Story, *Prison Land*.

process, centers on tool-building and uplifting community-led visions of alternate futures for Appalachian places.

Alternative Futures in Appalachia's Coalfield Prison Communities

When abandoned mine lands and other toxic sites enter the built environment lexicon, it is often through forms of phytoremediation and restoration ecology—largely passive, though sometimes intensive, interventions that deploy plants and other biological agents as instruments.[32] The problem with relying on these kinds of strategies in poor cities and regions like Central Appalachia is that they offer very little if any, real material benefits or economic impact. Suppose a central challenge for prison abolitionists and climate justice activists in Central Appalachia is the ability to offer an alternative jobs program to counter the hegemony and false promises of the carceral state. In that case, there is a real need for more expansive thinking about the kinds of industrial formations, labor strategies, and infrastructural investments in the region. As proponents of degrowth and austerity politics surely know, no viable political coalition exists for material deprivation. Investment in something other than coal, natural gas, and prison-building is needed alongside a program to dismantle and decommission those noxious industries.

Much of this radical reimagining has already begun through organizations like Reimagine Appalachia, 100 Days in Appalachia, Black in Appalachia, and many other racial justice and climate activists in the region. There is no shortage of vision and energy for cooperative agriculture and forestry, renewable energy manufacturing and deployment, and environmental remediation in the region. And through national frameworks like the Red, Black, and Green New Deal—a fusion of climate and racial-justice movements, centered on decarceration and public investment in frontline communities—the broader national framework for an alternative political economy is becoming legible.

The task, then, for designers in regions like Central Appalachia is to find ways to align our labor, operations, resources, and instruments with the movements already doing that work. This can include form, aesthetics, and other visual and spatial dimensions to join the broader calls for prison abolition and a just energy transition in the region. This kind of translational work can mutually reinforce goals that shorten the gap between an imagined future and our present reality. The idea is to make these movements' "radical" demands appear far more pragmatic. We do this by creating projects that restructure, rather than reproduce, racialized power dynamics in Central Appalachia. Or, as Paul Wellstone argued, to approach these questions of prison abolition, energy transition, and climate justice with humility by recognizing that "successful organizing is based on the recognition that people get organized because they, too, have a vision for the future."

Two such alternatives can be considered. The first, developed by Amber Hassanein, Ada Rustow, and A. L. McCullough, is material—a program to decommission the rural prisons of Appalachia and convert them and their

[32] They rely on the bioaccumulation of heavy metals and other criteria pollutants by certain plant species, the intensive management of those plantings (they must be removed and incinerated off-site to fully remove toxins), and other more conventional, cut-and-fill-based interventions to bring some form of ecological function to sites often stripped of all or most biotic activity. Freshkills (Staten Island, Field Operations), London Olympic Park (London, Hargreaves Associates), and Germany's Emscher Landscape Park (Ruhr Valley, Internationale Bauausstellung) are among the field's most prominent examples of such work. See Frederick Steiner, Richard Weller, Karen M'Closkey, and Billy Fleming, *Design with Nature Now* (Cambridge: The Lincoln Institute of Land Policy Press, 2019).

surrounding landscapes into rural electric co-ops. The second, developed by McCullough, is procedural—a workbook aimed at demystifying and democratizing the design process for activist groups in the region.[33]

In a manual titled "Building Microgrids on Federal Land: A Big Sandy Case Study," Hassanein, Rustow, and McCullough identify a key feature of Appalachia's carceral system to repurpose: every detention facility built after 1991 is required to have the ability to island themselves off the grid through hyper-resilient, on-site microgrids. Without adding any new generation or storage capacity to the USP Big Sandy site, they estimate that the prison's existing microgrid could power neighboring Inez, a town of around 2,000 people. This outcome generally holds across other state and federal facilities built atop the region's coalfields. Hassanein, Rustow, and McCullough also show how Big Sandy and other detention facilities built atop abandoned mines are ideal sites for new, renewable energy generation. This is partly because the sites tend to be at high elevations, relatively flat, and free of obstructions. They are essentially Appalachia's ideal locations for wind and solar power generation.

Their proposal offers a first step on the broader path to building a world without prisons. In the case of USP Big Sandy, that would require the following: the decommissioning of the facility and decarceration of its inmates; the transfer of the facility from the Bureau of Prisons to local control in the form of a rural electric co-operative; the on-site investment in renewable energy generation to create new construction jobs and cleaner energy sources in the region; and, as part of a region-wide decarceration strategy, an investment in the broader industrial capacity of Appalachia to produce the turbines and photovoltaic panels necessary to implement such a plan at any accurate scale. This is where their attention to material redistribution is particularly important.

In their proposal, the prison lands themselves become a source of democratic control and wealth-building through the framework of a rural electric co-op—institutions administered by farmers, teachers, nurses, and other rural community members rather than absentee landowners and corporate managers. Through lower electricity rates, the ability to sell excess power to the grid, and investments in site remediation and on-site clean energy generation, they also deliver material benefits directly to ratepayers and community members—transforming a site of trauma into one of regeneration. In this potential future, the prison sites themselves are decommissioned and converted into community-controlled utilities as the broader system of abandoned mine lands and remediation funds are then put to a different use—namely, the buildout of clean energy manufacturing facilities atop the 6.2 million acres of remnant coalfields. Modeled in some ways on Germany's Internationale Bauausstellung Emscher Park—a decades-long, public investment-led transformation of the nation's Ruhr Valley coalfields through their alternative form of rural economic development—their plan aims to fuse the demands of prison abolitionists and climate-justice advocates with the aims of industrial policy technocrats. The prison lands become sources of clean and democratically controlled

[33] Billy Fleming, "Frames and Fictions: Designing a Green New Deal Studio Sequence," *Journal of Architectural Education* 75, no. 2 (September 7, 2021). Both alternatives were developed in Fleming's multi-year "Designing a Green New Deal" studio sequence.

energy, the abandoned mines become nodes in a regional system of clean energy technology and manufacturing, and the cycles of extraction—from timber to coal to natural gas to incarceration—are finally broken.

In the abandoned mine lands of Appalachia, this national-scale ruralization of mass incarceration takes on one of its most perverse forms. For more than thirty years, prison-building became a central pillar of rural economic development in the United States. In the former coalfields of Appalachia, Story's analysis of prisons as spaces of disappearance is particularly useful. After all, these spaces are intentionally difficult to find and thus "disappeared," much the same way the incarcerated "disappeared" from society once they enter the criminal justice system. Norton and Schept capture this rising rate of incarceration and rural prison development, writing, "If incarceration rates were to continue to rise in Kentucky as they have since 2000, every person in the state would be behind bars in 113 years."[34] In this way, the second intervention, *A Workbook for Dreaming* by McCullough, provides working tools for the people of Appalachia to refigure futures of incarceration and environmental degradation toward community-led dreams and visions.

The workbook, inspired by Kaba and Hassan's *Fumbling Towards Repair*,[35] is an abolitionist toolkit—replete with group exercises, storytelling, and other forms of community accountability. It is organized around the premise that everyone has dreams for the future of their community—and that none of those dreams involve being incarcerated in a toxic prison. These dreams often lack spatial and aesthetic qualities, but the larger, transformative ideas are often already in place. In the workbook, readers encounter a series of activities to walk their neighbors, friends, and community members through the design process to develop their spatial visions grounded in place to compete with the ideas offered by people like Rep. Hal Rodgers. The design process generates images that augur a particular future and can produce alternatives to the rural economic development being sold to the Appalachians today. At its core, *A Workbook for Dreaming* argues that the design process can and should be shared, that it can open up alternative futures for the region's abandoned mine lands and carceral geography, and that de-emphasizing *the designer* while emphasizing *the design process* is one way to build the kinds of collective futures already being imagined in Appalachia.

From Technical Lands to Political Economies of Appalachia

This chapter centers on a story of the political economies and ecologies of the fossil fuel system—one that fundamentally reshaped the physical and socioeconomic geography of Appalachia. It does so through the technical lands framing of this volume, at least in part, to foreground the necessity of unbuilding and unmaking the region's abandoned mine lands and carceral landscapes. Existing technical lands require an ideological project—one in which certain people, landscapes, and materials are valorized, and others are disposable. In the case of the prisons atop abandoned mine lands at the

[34] Jack Norton and Judah Schept, "Keeping the Lights On Incarcerating the Bluegrass State," *Vera Institute for Justice In Our Backyards Series*, March 4, 2019, https://www.vera.org/in-our-backyards-stories/keeping-the-lights-on.

[35] Mariame Kaba and Shira Hassan, *Fumbling Towards Repair: A Workbook for Community Accountability Facilitators* (New York, NY: AK Press, 2019).

core of this chapter, the disposability of the inmates, guards, and communities surrounding the facilities is undeniably clear. Put another way, Appalachia's prison-building enterprise embodies the kinds of control, extraction, surveillance, and obfuscation that define technical lands as a system of classification.

While we are convinced of "technical lands" as a functional classification system, we are less confident of its utility in the kind of speculative work we described in Appalachia—at least beyond its ability to help us see how this system works. In Appalachia's coalfield-to-prison pipeline there is a real need to puncture that technical complexity—to demystify and otherwise unpack how this system works and how it might be unmade. Without such an intervention, these technical lands will remain inaccessible, impenetrable, and, as Story reminds us, invisible to the people whose lives and livelihoods are bound up in the carceral state's sprawling footprint. The facilities and their landscapes matter greatly to landscape architecture and the broader world. But prison abolition is not simply a matter of deleting correctional facilities from the built environment. Instead, as Ruth Wilson Gilmore writes, "Abolition is about abolishing the conditions under which prison became the solution to problems, rather than abolishing the buildings we call prisons."[36]

So, if technical lands are a valuable framework for classifying and understanding the operations of Appalachia's coalfield prisons, then an alternative framework rooted in what Kaba and Hayes describe as "a state of unrestrained imagination" is needed to move from analysis to intervention in the region's broader political economy.[37] They describe a community organizing an accountability process through which an imaginary jailbreaking can occur—one in which the inevitability of prisons is challenged, and the societal transformations that would be required to render them unnecessary are the focus (rather than the prison sites themselves). In their view, technical lands like prisons, military installations, abandoned mines, and borderlands are artifacts of hegemonic power—classifications intended to obfuscate how a particular system works and how its benefits and costs are distributed. How and where those technicalities are unwound and democratized remains to be seen. But there is no more urgent place to invest in that work than the coalfield prisons of Appalachia.

[36] Ruth Wilson Gilmore, "Ruth Wilson Gilmore on Covid-19, Decarceration, and Abolition," April 17, 2020, https://www.haymarketbooks.org/blogs/128-ruth-wilson-gilmore-on-covid-19-decarceration-and-abolition.

[37] Mariame Kaba, *We Do This 'til We Free Us: Abolitionist Organizing and Transforming Justice* (New York, NY: Haymarket Books, 2021).

Envirotechnical Lands

Science Reserves and Settler Astronomy

Caitlin Blanchfield

As we connect with the elements, what's our reciprocal relationship going to be? Maunakea we look at as the hiapo. In our genealogy, it was the firstborn to Wākea and Papa. Maunakea in its presence and how it stands, it is what captures and distributes the water, it is what gives us multiple climate zones. It's what gives us all these different wau, it's what gives us our minerals.[1]

I sit with Lanakila Manguail, a Kanaka Maoli (native Hawaiian) *kia'i* (protector) and cultural practitioner, on a hillside in Honoka'a on Hawai'i's Hamakua Coast. Behind us, the dense guinea grass is electric against the sea. In front of us, mulchy earth beds are ready for kalo seeds. Soon we will be planting. But now Manguail explains the origin of the mountain whose slopes we sit on—a mountain he and many others have fought to protect for decades. In 2014, Manguail gained attention by storming the ground-breaking ceremony for the Thirty Meter Telescope (TMT), interrupting local politicians and representatives from the TMT corporation poised to put the first spade into the sacred mountain's northern plateau.[2] A few months later, hundreds camped at the junction to the Maunakea access road, the only route up to the 13,796-foot summit where the telescope was to be built, blocking the construction equipment. Protectors successfully held off construction until December 2015 when the Hawai'i Supreme Court ruled that the Bureau of Land and Natural Resources (BLNR) had illegally issued a Conservation District Use Permit (CDUP) when they had proceeded without a contested case hearing.[3] The BLNR had to consider the permit again. The contested case hearing was granted and worked its way through the court system for over two years while cultural practitioners and environmental advocates submitted hours of testimony on behalf of the mountain. Despite overwhelming evidence of Mauna a Wākea's spiritual power, genealogical significance, and right to be protected, the court ruled the TMT could be built.

In July of 2019, thousands of Kānaka Maoli and their allies were again camped at the access road, protesting the desecration of the *mauna* and its continued development for astronomy. The camp, which attracted kia'i from across the islands and world, disbanded in December 2019. A small base camp remains. But the movement to protect Maunakea extends beyond the opposition to the TMT. It is an intergenerational struggle to oppose indus-trialization and scientific development on Kanaka lands. *Kupuna* (elders), cultural practitioners, environmental activists, and other allies have stood in opposition to the desecration of a sacred *piko* (genealogical connection, umbilicus), the industrialization of a unique and fragile ecosystem, the history of documented mismanagement and improper environmental review, and the expropriation of stolen Hawaiian land for a project many Hawaiians oppose. They oppose the processes of technical lands, including legal documents, reports, and construction projects that turn mountaintops into telescope platforms in the name of American hegemony.

fig 1

[1] Interview with Lanakila Manguail, Honoka'a, Hawai'i, April 11, 2021.

[2] Big Island Video News, "TMT Opponents Halt Ground Breaking Ceremony," October 7, 2014, https://www.bigislandvide-onews.com/2014/10/07/raw-video-tmt-oppo-nents-halt-groundbreak-ing-ceremony/.

[3] The spelling of Maunakea differs across contexts. *Maunakea* means "white mountain" in the Hawaiian language. A common spelling is Mauna Kea, but many Kānaka Maoli now recommend Maunakea as one word instead of Mauna Kea, referring to any white mountain. The mountain is also called Mauna a Wākea, or Mountain of Wākea, the father of the Hawaiian people. I will primarily use Maunakea in this essay but use Mauna Kea when used in an official title or Mauna a Wākea when the mountain is referred to as such.

fig 1 "Road Closed due to Desecration," kia'i
block the Mauna Kea Access Road. Kapulei Flores

As Jeffrey S. Nesbit describes, technical lands are "instrumentalized lands, encompassing zones of military testing, scientific experimentation, or infrastructural operation. Often, the designation of a land as 'technical' opens up legal possibilities for exclusion, enclosure, or even the suspension of certain regulations."[4] Since the 1960s, astronomers and local politicians in Hawai'i have used scientific instruments and jurisdictional documents to try to transform Maunakea into a technological landscape. And since the 1960s, Hawaiians have refused them. Technical lands can be literal battlefields, places where the soil itself is rendered technological through things like unexploded ordinance or uranium deposits left behind. Examples of such technical lands are the Nevada Nuclear Test site, the White Sands Missile Range—as discussed in the work of Peter Galison—as well as the Hawaiian island of Kaho'olawe and the Pōhakuloa Training Area at the base of Maunakea.[5] But these landscapes are also battlefields in the broader sense, sites of contestation over ownership, jurisdiction, use, and meaning. In this chapter, I examine the "science reserve"—a designation that the Department of Land and Natural Resources (DLNR) ascribed to Maunakea in 1968—as a tool intended to make the land technical, thereby opening it up for capitalist development.[6] However, while the DLNR and others sought to use the lands for the astronomy industry, kia'i organized for its protection. Unlike Western experts employing preservation paradigms, kia'i are people whose *kulena* (responsibility) is to be custodians and guardians—protection is a personal and community-based ethic.

The movement to protect Maunakea and oppose the TMT has been written about by many scholars, including many Kānaka who are deeply connected to the mauna and the movement. Learning from this rich scholarship and work, this chapter shows how colonial land policy was crafted to expropriate Hawaiian land and set the terms by which rights to land and its protection are discussed.[7] By examining the science reserve as a contested technical land, I show how the seeming neutrality of scientific knowledge production is mobilized in twentieth-century land grabs. While Galison and others turn to landscapes of extreme depletion or contamination—nuclear sites, mines, etc.—I look at astronomy's so-called clean industry to make evident that "universal science" is tied to specific development agendas and bids for territorial control.[8]

To do this, I look at the history of astronomical development on Maunakea, specifically the 1968 land lease that designated the summit a "science reserve," and the subsequent process of environmental impact assessment conducted for telescope construction and infrastructure building. Environmental Impact Statements (EIS) have produced a specific definition of "environment" that the state can claim is compatible with continued observatory expansion—such a notion of the environment is inimical to Kanaka understandings of land and place. Thinking with the late Kanaka Maoli activist and scholar Haunani-Kay Trask and Dene political theorist Glen Coulthard, I distinguish land from the environment in its meaning for Indigenous self-determination and nationhood. Land, according to Coulthard, is a field of relationships of things to each other; it is relational and it is a form

[4] Jeffrey S. Nesbit, *Space Port: Technical Lands for Departing Earth*, DDes, Harvard University, 2020.

[5] For Peter Galison's work on technical lands, see Peter Galison, Rebecca Uchill, and Caroline Jones, Keynote Panel, Technical Landscapes: Aesthetics and the Environment in the History of Science and Art Conference, Harvard University, April 25, 2017, https://www.youtube.com/watch?v=NnFgnEwN1FU.

[6] The Office of Conservation and Coastal Lands, Hawai'i Department of Land and Natural Resources, General Lease, No. S-4191.

[7] To speak briefly on my positionality as a settler, scholar, and researcher, I see my kuleana supporting kia'i through research and work on the ground. My humble efforts have taken shape in workdays at Manguail's Hamakua Hawaiian Cultural Center and with the Edith Kanakole Foundation, providing supplies to kia'i, still camped at the access road, and digitizing archival material.

[8] And as Sarah Jensen Carr notes, astronomy is often closely connected to destructive militarized practices. NASA and the military have historically worked together in Hawai'i, demonstrating how the Mauna Kea Science Reserve participates in a network of colonial technical lands on the islands. Sarah Jensen Carr, "Alien Landscapes: NASA, Hawai'i, and Interplanetary Occupation," *Avery Review* December 2020, http://averyreview.com/issues/50/alien-landscapes.

9 See Haunani-Kay Trask, *From A Native Daughter: Colonialism and Sovereignty in Hawai'i* (Honolulu, HI: University of Hawai'i Press, 1993); Glen Coulthard, *Red Skin White Masks: Rejecting the Colonial Politics of Recognition* (Minneapolis, MN: University of Minnesota Press, 2014); On environment in architecture during the mid-twentieth century see Larry Busbea, *The Responsive Environment: Design, Aesthetics, and the Human in the 1970s* (Minneapolis, MN: University of Minnesota Press, 2020).

10 Sara Pritchard, *Confluence: The Nature of Technology and the Remaking of the Rhone* (Cambridge, MA: Harvard University Press, 2011), 2.

11 Trask, *From A Native Daughter*, 115.

of reciprocal obligations. The environment is also a set of relationships, an ecological or social system. However, the environment does not have the same political valence as land in Indigenous discourses.

Further, in colonial frameworks, the land is perceived as property and thus can be owned, possessed, and dispossessed in ways that the environment cannot.[9] The division of land and resources into different consulted state jurisdictions such as the Department of Land and Natural Resources (DLNR), Fish and Wildlife Services, and Department of Interior, reinforces separation and offers a definition of "impact" that excludes the voices of many Kanaka communities and ignores Hawaiian science. However, as the literary scholar and settler *aloha 'aina* (love of the land) Candace Fujikane has written, Kanaka Maoli representations of the environment "map the continuities of abundant worlds" and resist the colonial occupation of sacred lands. Looking at a moment where the building of Hawai'i's state bureaucracy met emergent environmental thinking in architecture and urban planning, this essay reveals the limits to the term "environment"— limits both to understanding and control.

Finally, I place this history within a discourse of envirotechnics. Envirotechnics, a term from the historian Sara Pritchard, describes how landscapes become part of technological processes, first by turning nature into a natural resource and then by harnassing those natural resources with machines and infrastructures. There is a political dimension to this, too, as the environment is mobilized in nation-building projects, the land becomes "saturated with power."[10] Drawing on this framework, I ask how we might further science and technology studies (STS) approaches to studying technology and the environment by considering the intersection of environment and technology through a multiplicity of scientific cultures, epistemologies of landscape, and national narratives. What happens when what is at stake is refusing the technical?

Jurisdiction and Possession

In her seminal essay, "Notes from a Native Daughter," Trask writes, "From the earliest days of Western contact, my people told their guests that *no one* owned the land. The land—like the air and the sea—was for all to use and share as their birthright. Our chiefs were *stewards* of the land; they could not own or privately possess the land any more than they could sell it."[11] As Trask describes, the introduction of European paradigms of property ownership was devastating for Hawai'i, particularly because settlers could not recognize communal land stewardship and instead mistook "no one owns the land" to mean "the land is no one's." The right to *possess* the land is critical to expanding industrial development on so-called public lands anywhere. This is true on Maunakea, where a tiered system of lease agreements puts control of the mountain in the jurisdiction of the DLNR, the University of Hawai'i, and the individual corporations that operate the twelve telescopes at the summit.

Missionaries and plantation owners imposed Western property ownership and resource extraction practices on the Hawaiian Islands in the nineteenth century. These practices were considered incommensurable with Kanaka land relations. The result was increasingly brazen forms of dispossession culminating in the 1893 overthrow of the Hawaiian Kingdom and its Queen, Liliuokalani. The United States proceeded to illegally annex Hawai'i as a territory and acquire all land that had been under the jurisdiction of the Hawaiian government and the Queen as "ceded lands." They were now crown and government lands, intended to be used for the "betterment of Native Hawaiians." Maunakea was included in this jurisdiction. The mid-elevation *ohi'a* and *māmane* forests had been protected under an 1876 act by King David Kalākaua.[12] In the 1920s, portions were designated as "Hawaiian Home Lands," a permanent land base for the benefit and use of Kānaka Maoli.[13] Upon statehood in 1959, the Hawai'i DLNR adopted jurisdiction over the crown and government land. In 1968, the DLNR leased the summit to the University of Hawai'i and designated the Maunakea Science Reserve as a "scientific complex, including without limitation thereof, an observatory, and as a science reserve being more specifically a buffer zone to prevent the intrusion of activities inimical to said scientific complex."[14]

The Environmental Impact Statement is one way that land can pass through jurisdictional hands, in this case, authorizing the University of Hawai'i, who leases the conservation district from the DLNR, to sublease to whichever entity is proposing the telescope—be that a national government, a university, or a consortium, as in the case of the TMT. By determining that the environment is not impacted by the construction and operation of telescope facilities, land ostensibly intended for conservation can be developed. This requires definitions of both "environment" and "impact" that frame the terms through a pro-development lens, which obscures and minimizes damages, marshals certain forms of Western expertise, refuses specific kinds of evidence or testimony, codifies arbitrary and imprecise conclusions, and solicits feedback from governmental agencies as opposed to the people who will be affected. Environmental impact statements create a process by which technological instruments are imagined on sacred landscapes. By including new telescopes and the changes they cause within a definition of environment, the EIS enables the creation of technical lands. By presenting Maunakea as a science reserve, the DLNR created the conditions for telescope construction to be deemed acceptable and the land to become technical.

Trask reminds us of the Hawaiian principle of *malama 'aina*, or caring for the land. "The cosmos, like the natural world," she writes, "was a universe of familial relations …. Nature was not objectified but personified, resulting in an extraordinary respect."[15] The state agencies that now administer Maunakea have intentionally framed the mountain as a "scientific" landscape, and characterized opposition to astronomical development as a clash of modern scientific progress vs. "ancient" knowledge and customs.[16] In the debate over impact within this contested territory, though, the environment of Maunakea should be understood through a land-based ethic of care informed by Hawaiian sovereignty and nationhood. Malama 'aina is rooted

[12] Kepa Maly and Onaona Maly, *Mauna Kea: Ka Piko Kaulana O Ka 'Aina: A Collection of Native Traditions, Historical Accounts, and Oral History Interviews for Mauna Kea, the Lands of Ka 'ohe, Humu'ula, and the 'Aina Mauna of the Island of Hawai'i* (Hilo, HI: University of Hawai'i Hilo, 2005), 521.

[13] Hawaiian Homes Commission Act of 1920, https://dhhl.hawaii.gov/wp-content/uploads/2020/02/Hawaiian-Homes-Commission-Act-1921-As-Ammended-Searchable.pdf; Big Island Video News, "Who Owns Maunakea Access Road?" August 14, 2019, https://www.bigislandvideonews.com/2019/08/14/video-who-owns-mauna-kea-access-road/.

[14] The Office of Conservation and Coastal Lands, Hawai'i Department of Land and Natural Resources, General Lease, No. S-4191.

[15] Trask, *From A Native Daughter*, 5.

[16] For example, in a 1976 interview with the *Hawaii Tribune-Herald*, John Jeffries, founder of the Institute of Astronomy, claimed the controversy over plans for new observatories was "mainly due to lack of understanding by those interested in the mountain." Larry Bereman, "Prime Real Estate atop Mauna Kea," *Hawaii Tribune-Herald*, 1976. For more analysis on this see, Iokepa Casumbal-Salazar, "A Fictive Kinship: Making 'Modernity' 'Ancient Hawaiians,' and the Telescopes on Mauna Kea," *Native American and Indigenous Studies* 4, no. 2 (2017): 1–30.

in Hawaiian scientific principles that refuse the separation of progress and traditional knowledge that technical lands create.

Impact and Environment

The first environmental impact statement in the United States was issued in February of 1970, only a few weeks after the signing of the National Environmental Protection Act (NEPA), which mandated an EIS for all construction projects on federal lands, with federal monies, or under federal jurisdiction. It was eight pages long and ostensibly reported on the environmental risks posed by constructing the Trans-Alaska Pipeline and found no impact.[17] During the 1970s, what "environment" meant in these assessments was being actively debated in the courts and iteratively defined in increasingly expansive (though not necessarily more thorough) EISs. The process was a struggle, as pro-development companies, engineering, and planning firms were hired to evaluate the impact and codify the criteria by which construction was evaluated to generate favorable outcomes.[18] By calling in outside experts from public agencies, such as geologists and planners, they could mobilize both the authority and still pro-development bias of state and local government. This is clear in analyzing environmental impact statements for the first two decades of astronomical development on Maunakea.

It was also unclear who should be conducting impact assessments in these early years. At first, engineers and architects took on the role because development companies already employed them. This led to inherent conflicts of interest. Urban and land-use planners began to conduct assessments. However, according to environmental sociologist Robert Burdge, planners did not always have training in environmental and social domains; their expertise was in land-use allocation and design. Planners often ignored environmental information and issues in the design process.[19] However, this goes beyond a lack of training in environmental concerns. In architecture and urban planning, the environment was a category in transition, subject to much theorization. Figures like Buckminster Fuller, Tomás Maldonado, and Ian McHarg, or schools like Berkeley's College of Environmental Design, were actively defining what environment could mean for the design professions, opening the term to encompass landscape architecture, technical systems, and social worlds. While this capaciousness was transformative for the consciousness of architects and urban planners, it also meant that intervening and indeed designing the environment became increasingly professionalized and increasingly understood as a system with many inputs, including the technological, the infrastructural, the social, and the economic. The passage of policy like the NEPA reflected growing distress over the effects of pollution and rapacious consumption of resources, externalities of the postwar economy. Environmental management responded to this distress, but it did so through mechanisms of bureaucracy and jurisdiction, appeasing the American population with technocratic solutions.[20] What this meant in Hawai'i was increased administrative oversight by settler state agencies, bringing the land under state and national control in the years after statehood. Politicians

[17] Rabel J. Burge, "A Brief History and Major Trends in the Field of Impact Assessment," *Impact Assessment* 3, no. 4 (1991): 93–104.

[18] See Burge, "A Brief History."

[19] Burge, "A Brief History," 100.

[20] In his article "Environment c. 1973," Reinhold Martin discusses the Nixon administration's use of environmental policy to manage risk and bring a sense of apolitical unity to the nation through governmental regulation. Maldonado was particularly critical of environmental policy under Nixon; Martin writes, "and so we find him referring sarcastically to Nixon's environmental campaign as evidence of a neutralizing, authoritarian closure imposed on the social system as reflected in its appropriation of ecological protocols, in the form of what he calls the 'fashion of ecology.'" Reinhold Martin, "Environment c. 1973," *Grey Room* 14 (Winter 2004): 82. See also Tomás Maldonado, *Design, Nature, and Revolution: Toward a Critical Ecology* (Minneapolis, MN: University of Minnesota Press, 2019), particularly Larry Busbea's preface; Felicity D. Scott's *Architecture or Techno-Utopia: Politics after Modernism* (Cambridge MA: MIT Press, 2007) also offers a useful history of the use of the term "environment" in architecture. There is much more to be said about architecture's engagement with the environment during this time, but that is beyond the scope of this essay.

often worked in lockstep with architecture and planning firms commissioned for a public project environmental review. In the case of Maunakea, Group 70 International Inc.—the Honolulu design, engineering, and planning firm—was commissioned to conduct many of the EISs. Group 70 worked on a range of government projects in the islands, and from 1970 to 2000, they authored about seventy-five environmental reviews, the majority of which found no impact. The recently established state government used jurisdiction to move land from Kanaka control to the federal government and private sector. Architecture did the work of dispossession by selectively defining environment and impact based on the capitalist ethos of preservation for development. Telescope proponents portrayed the controversy over telescope expansion as a lack of understanding. But, as kiaʻi and practitioner Kealoha Pisciotta was keen to remind reporters: "This is a very simple case about land use."[21]

fig 2

Impact and Development

The first telescope built on Maunakea in 1964 was used to test the seeing conditions at the summit. In 1968, Hawaiʻi Governor John Burns designated the Maunakea Science Reserve, and the DLNR leased the Science Reserve lands to the University of Hawaiʻi to operate a science complex. Since then, fourteen telescopes have been built on the summit.[22] In 1973, an EIS to bring power lines to the summit was finalized—the first for the Mauna Kea Observatories. Already, it set forth a vision of impact assessment within a future-oriented development framework, predicting that electrical power needs would increase substantially as more observatories were added.[23]

The accepted realities implicit in the EIS had already determined what astronomy on Maunakea would be, introducing more telescopes, more support facilities, and more infrastructure. As the document asserted, "the construction, operation, and maintenance of [new] observatories will add greatly to the state's economy."[24] By looking at telescopes as revenue streams, the EIS incorporated economic evaluation into the environmental review and even privileged economic arguments over conservation ones. It also established a cumulative definition of environment where the growth of the science complex itself was seen as a positive impact. Powerlines lay the groundwork for future telescopes. By transforming conservation district land above approximately 1,200 feet into a "science reserve," scientific activity was protected.[25] Infrastructure was used to convert the mountaintop into an instrument. Humidity indexes, infrared light capture, and windspeed readings had represented the mountain through technical media. Zoning had regulated appropriate use. Telescopes, basecamp facilities, roadways, and powerlines made it part of the astronomical apparatus. Subsequent EISs would see the blurring of environmental, social, and economic categories under the mantle of environmental impact and the introduction of specific economic and industrial benefits as measures of positive impact. The 1974 EIS for the "Road to Summit" included sections on social impact and economic impact, revealing a shift in the definition of the environment to include these terms.

fig 3

[21] Dennis Overbye, "Under Hawaii's Starriest Skies, a Fight Over Sacred Ground," *New York Times*, October 3, 2016.

[22] Built and unbuilt telescopes include the Airforce 24-inch telescope and the University of Hawaiʻi's teaching telescope, Hoku Kea in 1968, the University of Hawaiʻi 2.2 Meter Telescope in 1970, the Canada France Hawaii Telescope and the United Kingdom Infrared Telescope in 1973, the Infrared Telescope Facility in 1974, the James Clerk Maxwell Telescope in 1982, Keck I in 1984, the Caltech Submillimeter Observatory in 1986, the Gemini North 8 Meter Telescope in 1999, the Very Long Baseline Array and the Subaru Telescope in 1992, the Keck II in 1996, the Smithsonian Submillimeter Array in 2002. However, this number jumps to twenty-one if you count the antennae used for the Submillimeter Array. The Keck Outrigger telescopes were proposed but blocked in 2006, the PANSTARRS in 2009, and the TMT was proposed in 2010.

[23] Division of Public Works, Department of Accounting and General Services, State of Hawaiʻi, "Environmental Impact Statement for Power to Summit, Hawaiʻi" (November 1973), 4.

[24] Division of Public Works, "Environmental Impact Statement for Power to Summit," 7.

[25] Group 70 International Inc., "Maunakea Science Reserve Master Plan," (Honolulu, HI: University of Hawaiʻi, 2000), http://www.malamamaunakea.org/uploads/management/plans/MasterPlan_MaunaKeaScienceReserve_2000.pdf.

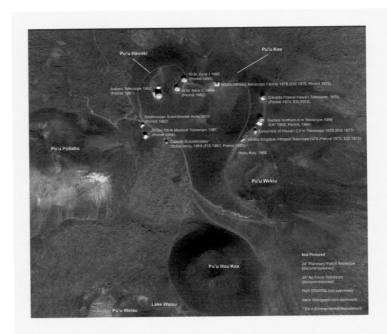

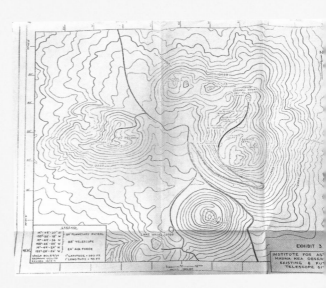

fig 2   Map of Maunakea development. Caitlin
Blanchfield

fig 3   Mauna Kea Observatory, Exist
Future Telescope Sites, 1973. Institute for A

In 1975 the University of Hawai'i hired planning consultants EDAW Inc. to do an after-the-fact EIS for the continued operations of the UH Telescope and the Infrared Telescope Facilities (IRTF) and UK Infrared Telescope (UKIRT) Facilities. This document expanded the economic criteria against which to gauge "environmental" impact; an "environmental impact matrix" included in the EIS established thirty-two environmental categories. Twenty of those categories were "socioeconomic," and twelve were "biophysical." While socioeconomic did include items such as "historical-cultural site" and "unique features," many of these so-called environmental terms described the scientific industry established on the mountain. "Actions" that could have a possible impact were listed along the X-axis of the matrix. These were primarily directed at existing telescope operations and included, for example, "funding," which would positively impact the existing jurisdictional agencies on the mountain (federal, state, county, and the University of Hawai'i). Structure location, traffic, solid waste, and alteration of drainage are delineated as possible actions.

The land became only one category among many, so the fact that it was significantly harmed could be readily discounted and dismissed. Subdivision and quantification were used to obfuscate impact. Meanwhile, the form of the matrix itself gave an impression of scientific authority and neutrality. The EIS broke environment down into discrete categories through different jurisdictions and through the way "impact" was assessed: as archeological, visual, hydrological, geological, cultural, economic, etc. Atomizing the environment into these subcategories made it easier to argue for "no impact," as a positive impact could be claimed in certain areas. In the EIS for the IRTF and UKIRT infrared telescopes, no significant implications for the proposal were found, even though the statement reports that in the "topography and landform" section, that impact would be "high" and would be "negative, long term, and direct."[26] The same EIS also reveals that the construction of the infrared telescopes would also have a "negative, long-term, and direct" impact on the "environmental condition" of the "land use" of the Mauna—specifically for recreation, which at the time included traditional hunting practices. Only by transforming the term "environment" to encompass economic effects, positive impacts on existing infrastructure, and "scientific resources" could the engineers and planners responsible for the environmental impact statements claim that no impact had been made. It was a strategic terminological move that had first been put in motion in 1968, when 13,000 acres of Crown and Government Lands were given to the University of Hawai'i by the state as a *science reserve*, thus erasing a political designation of the territory and replacing it with one that conflated conservation with anticipated scientific development.[27]

fig 4

This logic extended to the cartographic. Maps included in an appendix to a 1974 EIS for the access road to the summit indicate the footprint of future telescopes as though they were already standing. Such projections foreclosed images of other futures for the mountain and created a baseline

[26] EDAW Inc., Environmental Planning Consultants, "Draft Environmental Impact Statement for Existing Operations of the UH Observatory and the Construction and Operations of the New IRTF and UKIRT Observatories," March 1975.

[27] For a clear timeline of events on Maunakea leading to the legal case against the "Thirty Meter Telescope," see Bianca Isaki, Shelley Muneoka, and Kuulei Higashi Kanahele, "Kū Kia'i Mauna: Historical and Ongoing Resistance to Industrial Astronomy Development on Mauna Kea, Hawai'i," The National Academies of Sciences, Engineering, and Medicine Astro2020: Panel on State of the Profession and Societal Impacts White Paper, November 15, 2019.

Figure 15

Actions causing short-term
impacts

Actions causing long-term
impacts

PRESENT OPERATIONS
ENVIRONMENTAL IMPACT MATRIX

LEGEND

N (no impact)

Positive Impacts	Negative Impacts
– minor	○ minor
I moderate	◑ moderate
+ high	● high

Conditions of the Environment

Socioeconomic

JURISDICTIONAL AGENCIES
Federal
State
County
U. H.
UNIQUE FEATURES
HISTORIC/CULTURAL SITES
INFRASTRUCTURE
Power Supplies
Gas and Oil Supplies
Sewerage and Solid Waste
Water Supplies
Roads and Access
LAND USE
Recreation
Housing
Commercial
Industrial
Institutional
SCIENTIFIC RESOURCES
ECONOMY
AMBIENT NOISE
VISUAL QUALITY

Biophysical

TOPOGRAPHY-LANDFORM
GEOLOGY
SOILS
HYDROLOGY
PRECIPITATION
SURFACE WATER
SUBSURFACE WATER
CLIMATE
WILDLIFE
VEGETATION
AMBIENT AIR

EXCAVATING AND GRADING
MISCELLANEOUS CONSTRUCTION ACTIVITIES
TRAFFIC
NOISE PRODUCTION
AIRBORNE EMISSIONS
LIQUID WASTE
SOLID WASTE
ALTERATION OF DRAINAGE
FUNDING

STRUCTURE LOCATION
TRAFFIC
NOISE PRODUCTION
AIRBORNE EMISSIONS
LIQUID WASTE
SOLID WASTE
ALTERATION OF DRAINAGE
FUNDING

IV - 4

fig 4   "Present Operations Environmental
Impact Matrix" from IRTF and UKIRT EIS, 1975.
EDAW Inc.

for subsequent impact statements, in which future observatories would be considered a given. Further, these mappings established a base map or given representation of the site that would be used with slight adaptations in subsequent EISs. Erasure was thus built into the environmental review process. However, maps and drawings of the mountain prior to the seventies would have shown the many shrines surrounding the summit *pu'us*. As Lanakila Manguail told me, "We have the old maps that show all the altars on the lower plateau area. All of a sudden they bring in their maps and all these things are gone ... they're erasing them."[28] *Mauna Kea—Ka Piko Kaulana O Ka 'Aina*, the historical study of the mauna by Kepa and Onaona Maly, for instance, includes many maps of the summit, Humu'ula, and Kalopa *ahupua'a* (land division) that illustrate the names of each *pu'u* (cinder cone), placement of shrines, and traditional trails to the summit.[29] These are accompanied by elevation drawings and distance measurements showing and naming the topography in detail.

By implementing a standard for representation of the summit, one that relied on abstraction, erasure, and projection—projecting future telescopes instead of showing existing structures, place names, and sacred landforms—the maps included in these early Environmental Impact Statements limit the terms by which the land is discussed. They preclude further conversation around how its physical and ontological richness can be protected by simply refusing to show it. Critical cartographers like Mishuana Goeman write about how maps are used as a disciplinary technology to manage dispossession.[30] The cartographic approaches of the EIS mappings show how that management was enacted through select information and geographic narratives. These representations build on a long history of settler depictions of Maunakea as a barren wasteland, even in the face of contrary evidence.

Hi'ilei Hobart has shown how present-day references to Maunakea as "desolate," "lifeless," and "barren" grow out of nineteenth-century tropes of the summit as *terra nullius*, depopulated of Hawaiians, and discovered by white settlers (despite the material signs of Hawaiian use at the summit and the rich oral tradition surrounding the mountain). "Across the course of its development," she argues, "the summit of Maunakea has been systematically recast as a space both otherworldly and anational through its utilization for scientific research."[31] Environment was a tabula rasa in the eyes of the industry seeking to develop it—a representation of a capitalist telos of value extraction. This was, of course, a willful fiction—the *lele* (altars) and *ahus* (shrines) strung across summit cinder cones, not to mention the many *mo'olelo* (stories) of Maunakea climbs, clearly indicated Kānaka use of the land. As landscape historian Vittoria Di Palma notes in her study of wasteland, by the eighteenth century in England the word denoted both inhospitable terrain and land that was not being properly used.[32]

Wasteland traveled as a colonial concept, and it is clear the occupying government saw Maunakea as a wasteland in both senses: inhospitable and improperly used. The later definition opened the mauna up to development

[28] Interview with Lanakila Manguail, April 11, 2021.

[29] Maly and Maly, *Mauna Kea: Ka Piko Kaulana O Ka 'Aina*. Mentioning these maps and diagrams does not discount the colonial history of surveying and its use in expropriating land in Hawai'i, only to say that this information was known to the settler state. For more on astronomy, early surveying in Hawai'i, and settler colonialism, see Jodi Bryd, *The Transit of Venus: Indigenous Critiques of Settler Colonialism* (Minneapolis, MN: University of Minnesota Press, 2011).

[30] Mishuana Goeman, *Mark My Words: Native Women Mapping our Nations* (Minneapolis, MN: University of Minnesota Press, 2013), 20. For more on the epistemology of the map during this period see William Rankin, *After the Map: Cartography, Navigation, and the Transformation of Territory in the Twentieth Century* (Chicago, IL: University of Chicago Press, 2016).

[31] Hi'ilei Julia Hobart, "At Home on the Mauna: Ecological Violence and Fantasies of Terra Nullius on Maunakea's Summit," *Native American and Indigenous Studies* 6, no. 2 (Fall 2019): 42.

[32] Vittoria Di Palma, *Wasteland: A History* (New Haven, CT: Yale University Press), 2014.

[33] Candace Fujikane writes extensively about the "wastelanding" of Maunakea and how it contributes to what she calls the "threshold of impact." See Fujikane, *Mapping Abundance for a Planetary Future* (Durham, NC: Duke University Press, 2019).

in the years following statehood. While environmental impact assessment was ostensibly meant to counter depictions of the Maunakea's upper reaches as a barren wasteland, it was, nevertheless, informed by a wasteland logic that had made the mountain seem empty for development in the first place.[33]

Protest

It is wrong to treat that mountain wilderness so cheaply! Is Mauna Kea just a "junk" mountain to this board? Does the board think that Mauna Kea is valueless wasteland that can be "improved" with technological construction and monstrous observatories? We say no! Big Island people love that mountain .... We protest the EIS treatment of Mauna Kea as worthless land useful only for technological development,

[34] Mae Mull, *The Elepaio* 35, no. 3, September 1974.

[35] Interview with Nelson Ho, Deborah Ward, and Lanny Sinkin, Hilo, HI, April 22, 2021.

wrote Mae Mull in a 1974 issue of *Elapaio*, the newsletter for the Hawai'i chapter of the Sierra Club.[34] Mull was president of the Hawai'i Audubon Society and vehemently opposed the continued "industrial urbanization" of the mountain top for astronomy in newspaper editorials and responses to requests for comment on many of the Mauankea EISs.[35] Her voice was clear and potent in opposition to the efforts of state and county politicians to transform the revered Mauna into an industrial landscape for continued development and extraction. It also encapsulated the spirit of an unlikely coalition of environmental advocates and hunters that first levied public opposition to the expansion of Maunakea in the 1970s. This was an opposition formed through the language of passionate struggle and of environmental management. Increasing infrastructure, telescope density, support facilities, construction, and debris, contributed to what Mull and others termed urbanization. They insisted that no more building of any kind should occur on Maunakea until a comprehensive management plan was written. Her and others' persistence led to the Mauna Kea Plan of 1977 and later the 1985 Mauna Kea Science Reserve Master Plan, which has been used in arguments against further telescope construction that would violate its mandates.[36]

[36] According to Deborah Ward, it is in part because of the master plans that no telescopes have been built in the last twenty-one years on Maunakea.

[37] Bereman, "Prime Real Estate atop Mauna Kea."

[38] Bereman, "Prime Real Estate atop Mauna Kea"; Bruce Benson, "Rush for Master Plan is Tied to Telescope," *Honolulu Advertiser*, August 14, 1976, A-3; Bruce Benson, "Mauna Kea Plan No Peacemaker," *Honolulu Advertiser*, August 6, 1976, A-15.

[39] Webster Nolan, "Board Sets Cooling Period for Ice Age Reserve," *West Hawai'i Today*, June 23, 1977.

[40] Bruce Benson, "Mauna Kea Planners to Try Again," *Honolulu Advertiser* August 14, 1976: A-3

Local papers covered the mounting controversy over the "science city" during the late 1970s.[37] Articles in the *Hawaii Tribune-Herald* and *Honolulu Advertiser* appraised the "prime real estate atop Mauna Kea" and heralded the "rushed" plan "no peacemaker."[38] They also described board meetings and public hearings in hotel conference rooms and district offices where community members could speak out. People like Stephen Kaneai Morse of the Hawaiian Coalition for Native Claims asked for land instead to be set aside "to acknowledge aboriginal land rights" and that access to the mountain be maintained for hunting and other customary use.[39] Hunters like Earl Pacheco called for a moratorium on telescope construction.[40]

By the early 1980s, Hawaiian groups were organizing to express concern in print media about the growing astronomy precinct. A 1980 article in the *Tribune-Herald* written by Faith Bean and Brenda Duquette of the Waimea

Hawaiian Civic Club narrates a 1971 field trip to the summit of Maunakea. A club member shared her family tradition of leaving the piko (umbilical cord) of babies in Lake Waiau, connecting the child to generations past and present, to the island, and indeed to the universe. Maunakea is the piko of the Kānaka, a place of connection and passage across time, space, and state of being. It is a source of energy. In its morphology and agency, the landscape is a piko, so it is there that the piko of the baby is offered, a practice that has persisted even in the face of colonization.[41]

The same 1980 issue of the *Tribune-Herald*—a special feature on Maunakea printed during debates leading up to the 1982 Mauna Kea Management Plan—ran an article by Mike Tulang and Al Inouse of Sportsmen of Hawaiʻi. In it, they outlined the conversations and consensus-building that had led to the 1977 Mauna Kea Plan, what they called "a real honest attempt by the Big Island community to determine what is best for our citizens."[42] Per the plan, the road to the summit would remain unpaved and the mid-level facility at Hale Pohaku—a collection of stone cabins amid the silvery ʻahinahina bushes and māmane trees at 9,000 feet would be protected. Beyond their frustrations with the expansion of the dormitories and work facilities at Hale Pohaku, the authors also conveyed the relationship to land and culture inherent in hunting:

> To most of us [hunting] provides a unique experience, which cannot be measured in [the] amount of food put on the table. The Mauna Kea experience encompasses an appreciation of its natural beauty, an education in its history, an enjoyment in the sport of hunting, and a setting for healthful mental and physical relaxation and recreation. For many of us, the mountain and hunting has been a cultural tradition treasured by families.

If the EIS defined environment through its quantifiability—demonstrated in the impact matrix, in the precise footprints of construction activity, in the reduction of sacredness to the number of ancient shrines—then Tulang and Inouse wrote of Maunakea beyond frameworks of calculability, in a way that joined natural beauty, history, culture through the use of the mountain. Environmental Impact Statements may have undermined an interconnected relationship to the landscape on paper, but those who still used the land preserved it.

As opposed to the Environmental Impact Statement, which subdivides into discrete sociological and ecological categories and classifications, *ʻaina*, or land, is a field of relations that binds physical geography, ancestral memory, plants, animals, and the layers of the earth.[43] In the epigraph to this chapter, Lanakila Manguail speaks of the reciprocal relationship with Maunakea, the elder sibling—Maunakea gatherer of water, abundant with minerals, the flowing, interconnected ʻaina that forges the binds of reciprocity. This understanding of the environment is also evident in hunters' opposition to the development of the mauna. In these newspaper articles, we see

[41] Testimony from kiaʻi, practitioner, and former telescope technician Kealoha Pisciotta at the 2016 Contested Case Hearing against the TMT, describes the piko through the contours of the landscape and ecological cycles: "We see in the physical manifestation as the piko and connecting place between the heavens and the earth, we see how the pikos connect through the water because Mauna Kea is the place that the waters are collected. And we call them kane kawaiʻola, the waters of life of Kane. And they flow down, and they feed the people and the ocean."

[42] Mike Tulang and Al Inouse, "Hunters Express Concern for Mountain," *Hawaii Tribune-Herald*, January 27, 1980, B-8.

[43] For more on ʻaina as a sociological field of relations and how landscape is understood in a Hawaiian world view, see Edith Kanaka'ole Foundation, *Kīhoʻihoʻi Kānāwai: Restoring Kānāwai for Island Stewardship*, http:// nomaunakea.weebly.com/ uploads/1/0/2/2/102246944/ kanahele_kihoihoi_ kanawai_final.pdf.

technical lands refused in favor of self-determination and sovereignty. From the rainforests of Puna just downslope, to the shores of Kahoʻolawe, to ships of the Polynesian Voyaging Society, the Hawaiian sovereignty movement was protecting ʻaina and preserving Hawaiian science. Environmental groups in Hawaiʻi understood the political dimension of land protection. This is at the foundation of the movement to protect Maunakea today.[44]

"Science Reserve" and the Envirotechnical

The DLNR had designated Maunakea a "science reserve" with astronomy in mind—sanctioning telescopes on protected land while still forbidding other construction activities.[45] This move conflated science with technology and, paradoxically, conservation with development, as the telescopes would need to be built for the designated "science" to occur. Historian Sara Pritchard uses the term "envirotechnical systems" to describe the convergence of ecology and technology, revealing the ways that nature and technics shape one another.[46] Drawing on studies in science, technology, and society, Pritchard, along with scholars such as Amita Baviskar, Chandra Mukerji, and James C. Williams, have shown how technologies, and the relationships of power that drive them, become landscape. By thinking of environment and technology categories together, they aim to counter the depoliticization of technologies used in environmental management and instead provide a framework to show how human and nonhuman agents—and their social relations—impact landscapes and history. If Maunakea can be understood on the one hand as an envirotechnical landscape—a site where debates over technological interventions into the land are an extension of political conditions and uneven power relationships, where the word "science" is used as a stand-in for technology in the context of environmental management—on the other it exceeds this category's analytical frame. While STS discourse suggests that the environment is impossible to separate from technology and its social construction, the effort to protect Mauankea shows us that sometimes the task is precisely to separate them. By inscribing Maunakea's summit region as a "science reserve," the state implied that environmental conservation and scientific industry were compatible, even mutually beneficial.

Telescope opponents were resisting a narrative of the mountain as already technological—as the "best site" for astronomical seeing. But kiaʻi have always maintained that they are not "anti-science," as mainstream media and the astronomy community has often depicted the conflict, just that they are against more telescopes on Maunakea. Kānaka have a long history of star knowledge and star navigation. One of the objections to the TMT is that it will block the view planes used by star practitioners to mark the solstice and equinox, the rising of constellations, and alignment with other sacred sites in the islands. Existing telescopes have already obstructed lines of sight and places of alignment, such as to *puʻukohala*, the broad-backed cinder cone on the Kohala coast where King Kamehameha built a *heiau* and launched his campaign to unify the islands. In her testimony to the DLNR, Kealoha Pisciotta framed star practice in terms of Hawaiian science:

[44] On the Hawaiian Sovereignty Movement, see Noelani Goodyear-Kaʻōpua, Ikaika Hussey, and Erin Kahunaʻwaikala, *A Nation Rising: Hawaiian Movements for Land, Life, and Sovereignty* (Durham, NC: Duke University Press, 2014).

[45] See history provided in Isaki, Muneoka, and Kanahele, "Kū Kiaʻi Mauna."

[46] Sara B. Pritchard, *Confluence: The Nature of Technology and the Remaking of the Rhône* (Cambridge, MA: Harvard University Press, 2011).

The religion and spirituality within it is codified, what we know as native knowledge and science. It is thousands of years of observation ... So this knowledge derived from Mauna Kea, this cultural knowledge, traditional knowledge, our traditional resources management models rely on it ... How we make ourselves sustainable in the future will depend on this.[47]

In this way, she makes a case for a landscape that is a place of science and environmental care without the intervention of large-scale technological instruments and infrastructures. Science reserves subdivide land and cordon off summits for the intervention of technology. In doing so, they follow the logic of colonial development, using jurisdiction to put public lands under the domain of leasing entities. They naturalize technological intervention as science, but this land is already scientific in other ways, ways that penetrate and exceed the boundaries of a reserve. This science requires the refusal of the processes that produce technical lands to uphold sovereignty and self-determination at its foundation.

My deepest thanks to Nelson Ho, Lanakila Manguail, Michelangelo McPeek, Tom Peek, Lanny Sinkin, and Deborah Ward for the knowledge they shared with me about Maunakea. Thanks to Kapulei Flores for the use of their beautiful photograph and thanks to Desiree Valadares for comments on an early draft of this chapter.

[47] Kealoha Pisciotta, Testimony and Cross-Examination, Contested Case Hearing for Conservation District Use Application (CDUA) HA-3568, October 14, 2016, https://dlnr.hawaii.gov/mk/files/2016/10/B.01h-Kealoha-Pisciotta-testimony-and-cross-9.26.11.pdf; see also Lauren Muneoka, "Meet the Mauna Kea Hui—Kealoha Pisciotta," KAHEA: The Hawaiian Environmental Alliance, http://kahea.org/blog/mk-vignette-kealoha-pisciotta.

Conjuring the Commons

National Monuments as Technical Lands

Desiree Valadares

During a national conference in January 1967, Dr. Ernest Allen Connally, the first director of the National Park Service's Office of Archaeology and Historic Preservation (OAHP) declared, "About once in each generation, it seems, the United States Congress enacts major legislation to preserve the nation's historical heritage."[1] His assertion positioned the National Historic Preservation Act of 1966 as one in a trilogy of laws that marked a critical juncture in national conservation policy.[2] In promoting this act, Connally recalled the influence of the Antiquities Act of 1906 and the Historic Sites Act of 1935—both intended to curb looting and vandalism of Native American sites in the Southwest at the end of the nineteenth and early twentieth centuries.[3] Connally singled out the Antiquities Act as a cornerstone and a "primary wellspring" for successive federal heritage laws, such as the Archaeological Resources Protection Act of 1979 that established policies to regulate excavation and enforce penalties for those who removed or harmed artifacts.

Connally's January 1967 speech and public statements were authored by his core staff, namely architect Russell Keune, architectural historian William J. Murtagh, and historian Jerry Rogers. They asserted that the Antiquities Act "singlehandedly shaped the national idea of heritage preservation in the early 20th century."[4] Collectively, they posited that the evolution of the American national monument category, spurred by the Antiquities Act, consolidated federal leadership and revealed a gradual awakening of government officials to the importance of a unifying federal preservation framework.[5]

The Antiquities Act is America's oldest law protecting public lands.[6] The act (16 USC 431-433) was signed into law on June 8, 1906, and authorizes the president to designate federal public lands as national monuments without Congressional approval. It is brief, at only four paragraphs long, presidents have broadly interpreted it to set aside parcels of federal land of unlimited size and restrict logging, hunting, grazing, and mining, often under the veil of preservation.

Since 1906, every Democratic and Republican president has wielded the authority of the Antiquities Act to proclaim over 125 national monuments covering nearly 7.7 million acres on land and over 640 million acres of marine sanctuaries. Such unilateral power has created fierce political brawls. Contemporary debates incited by the Trump administration centered on the broad authority accorded to the President under this law to enshrine large swaths of land.[7] President Trump's move to shrink two large national monuments in Utah triggered outrage from environmental and conservation groups and Native tribes.[8] In 2020, Trump shrank the Bears Ears and Grand Staircase-Escalante national monuments in Utah by two million acres with the stroke of a pen. Despite his criticisms of the Antiquities Act, Trump used the same executive powers in 2018 to create Camp Nelson National Monument in Kentucky to commemorate a former supply depot and Union Army hospital that served as a recruiting center for African American troops and a refuge for freed slaves.

[1] Jerry L. Rogers, "The Antiquities Act and Historic Preservation," *The Antiquities Act: A Century of American Archaeology, Historic Preservation, and Nature Conservation,* Dwight Harmon, Francis McManamon, and Dwight Pitcaithley (Tucson, AZ: The University of Arizona Press 2006), 176–77

[2] National Park Service—Pacific West Office Archives, National Park Service History Collection, Ernest A. Connally Collection, RG 53, Box 1- Speeches 1967, https://www.nps.gov/hfc/services/library/connally.cfm.

[3] Carol Hardy Vincent, CRS Report R41330, National Monuments and the Antiquities Act, https://fas.org/sgp/crs/misc/R41330.pdf.

[4] National Park Service—Pacific West Office Archives, National Park Service History Collection, Ernest A. Connally Collection, RG 53, Box 1- Box 7- Speech Engagements 1967–1975, https://www.nps.gov/hfc/services/library/connally.cfm

[5] The Act, in its earliest years, codified established government practice by centralizing power in a group of people through tripartite interagency cooperation that was presumed to be in the best interests of the American public. Today, various state, local, tribal, and private sector policies broaden the scope of legislation on managing cultural resources and historic properties in urban and rural settings. Today, entities such as the National Park Service; the Bureau of Land Management; the US Fish and Wildlife Service in the Department of the Interior; the US Forest Service in the Department of Agriculture; and the National Oceanic and Atmospheric Administration in the Department of Commerce actively consolidate, steward, and co-manage the country's areas of historical, cultural, and natural significance.

6 Dwight Harmon, Francis McManamon, and Dwight Pitcaithley, *The Antiquities Act: A Century of American Archaeology, Historic Preservation and Nature Conservation* (Tucson, AZ: The University of Arizona Press 2006).

7 Section Two of the Antiquities Act (16 USC 431-433) states, "The President of the United States is authorized, in his discretion, to declare by public proclamation historic landmarks, historic and prehistoric structures, and other objects of historic and scientific interest that are situated upon the lands owned or controlled by the Government of the United States to be national monuments." See Lary Dilsaver, *America's National Park System: The Critical Documents* (Library of Congress, 2016), 180–82; and Mark Squillace, *The Monumental Legacy of the Antiquities Act of 1906*, 37, (Athens, GA: Georgia Law Review, 2003): 473, http://scholar.law.colorado.edu/articles/508.

8 For arguments related to its repeal, see John Yoo and Todd Gaziano, "The Presidential Authority to Revoke or Reduce National Monument Designations," *AEI American Enterprise Institute* (March 2017), http://www.aei.org/publication/presidential-authority-to-revoke-or-reduce-national-monument-designations/.

9 While statutes such as the National Historic Preservation Act 1966 effectively decentralized historic preservation (to entities like the Advisory Council on Historic Preservation, the National Trust for Historic Preservation, State Historic Preservation Offices, Tribal Historic Preservation Offices, and local interest groups), the national monuments, designated under the Antiquities Act of 1906, serve as evidence of the story of federal preservation from "inside" the government—the vision of a few people and the discretionary authority of the President to enshrine historic or scientific landmarks, structures, and objects of his choosing.

This chapter offers a close study of the Antiquities Act of 1906 to show how preservation law and presidential directives shape or "conjure the commons." I frame historic preservation and designation processes as political acts that rely on complex technical and bureaucratic procedures that fundamentally alter jurisdiction, land tenure, ownership, stewardship, kinship structures, and land relations. I frame national monuments as technical lands that forge a new legal and spatial imaginary. The Antiquities Act of 1906 can be understood a new, centralized form of land management in the American West and a radical departure from the previous piecemeal public policy on national heritage.[9] I argue that the act's passage enabled a mechanism through which federal officials, interested professionals, and other special interest groups could accelerate preservation goals without popular or congressional consensus.[10] This legislative and spatial history of national monuments is significant to scholars of public land and historic preservation. Yet, scholarly inquiry into the Antiquities Act has been "undervalued, ignored, and discounted" by contemporary observers and historians.[11] The amorphous nature of the act, its quaint title coupled with few statutory limits and shifts in presidential priorities relegate the often-invisible inner workings of this act to specialist circles.[12]

The Formation of the Antiquities Act 1879–1906

National Park Service historian Ronald F. Lee identifies 1879 as a particularly noteworthy year.[13] The year marked the founding of the Bureau of Ethnology in the Smithsonian Institution, the Anthropological Society of Washington, and the Archaeological Institute of America (AIA) in Boston. During the same year, Fredric Ward Putnam's influential book on ancient pueblo sites of Arizona and New Mexico was released.[14] The founding of these professional organizations coincided with numerous sponsored projects and explorations in the American West and Southwest. These events sparked momentum for reform and put pressure on the federal government to institute policies to adequately protect Southwest Native American artifacts and archaeological resources, some of which had already become targets of vandalism and theft, such as Chaco Canyon in New Mexico and Cliff Palace in Colorado. Antiquarians, consisting primarily of a small but influential minority of "privileged and educated easterners," sought a general designation for these sites, making them distinct from the rest of the public domain.[15]

This late-nineteenth-century struggle to protect archaeological sites coincided with the development of broader conservation and preservation efforts throughout the rapidly developing country. During this period, attempts to conserve natural and scenic resources were common practice and championed by individuals and organizations primarily in the eastern United States—many of whom organized around congressional action to set aside forest reserves and nature preserves in the American West.[16] Notable successes among these undertakings included the creation of Yellowstone National Park in 1872, Sequoia, General Grant, and Yosemite National Parks in 1890, the enactment of the Forest Reserve Act in 1891, and the creation of Mount Rainier National Park in 1899.[17] In the American South, efforts to commemorate Civil War battlefields and cemeteries led to the US Congress's 1890 designation of Chickamauga and Chattanooga as national military parks.[18]

The progressive political philosophy of the nineteenth century transformed state and local governments prompted the federal government to take a more active and aggressive role in planning and managing the country's natural resources.[19] National Park Service historians, Richard West Sellars (1997) and Hal Rothman (1989), observed that conservationism gave the nation a way to counter the anxiety created by the disappearance of frontier and wilderness. It instead allowed "for the planning for the future through goals of increased efficiency and equitable distribution."[20] The proposed sites for protection were primarily set in the west in the location of most of the country's public land. Previous acts like the Homestead Act of 1962 and the Mining Act of 1872 were passed to encourage western development and settlement. The Antiquities Act of 1906, however, signaled a major shift. The passage of this 1906 act allowed the federal government to transition from "the unrestricted ethos" of nineteenth-century land management practices to a new pattern for regulating and restructuring land in less-settled regions of the nation. In other words, "the West became a stage upon which the progressive impulse was implemented."[21]

The Antiquities Act thus contributed to developing a new form of land management in the Western United States. It reflected a realignment of the relative power of the executive and legislative branches of the federal government to implement a preservationist ethos on a frontier landscape. Given this impulse, the act implied a federal seizure that instantly proved unpopular among its Western constituency. As Easterners began to mythologize their past, the practical perspective of Westerners put them at odds with the emerging public sentiment. Academics, scientists, and professional organizations were powerful forces who took their efforts to the legislative arena. The same groups that supported historic preservation on the East Coast became critical advocates for preserving the Southwest. From the very beginning, these groups sought legislation that granted powers like those of the General Land Revision Act of 1891. This difference in the perspectives of Easterners, government officials, and settlers in the West generated unrest and resistance.[22]

Monument Wars in the Roosevelt Years

Theodore Roosevelt was not engaged in the legislative drafting of the Antiquities Act between 1900 and 1906, but his philosophy supported those working on the law. In its final form, the act includes three sections: Section 1 prohibits the excavation or removal of ancient items from public land without permission and imposes limits on a host of potentially damaging activities like mining, homesteading, grazing, and logging. The second section of the law authorizes the president to establish, or in the terminology of the

[10] Char Miller, "Landmark Decision: The Antiquities Act, Big Stick Conservation and the Modern State," *Public Lands, Public Debates: A Century of Controversy* (Corvallis, OR: Oregon State University Press, 2012), 66–78.

[11] Hal Rothman, *Preserving Different Pasts: The American National Monuments* (Urbana, IL: University of Illinois Press, 1989), xi.

[12] Harmon, McManamon, and Pitcaithley, *The Antiquities Act*, 1–2.

[13] Roland F. Lee, *The Antiquities Act of 1906* (Washington, DC: National Park Service, Office of History and Historic Architecture, Eastern Service Center), 1970.

[14] Lee, *The Antiquities Act of 1906*, 30.

[15] Rothman, *Preserving Different Pasts*, 12–13.

[16] Francis McManamon, "The Antiquities Act and How Theodore Roosevelt Shaped It," *The George Wright Forum* 31, no. 3 (2014).

[17] McManamon, "The Antiquities Act and How Theodore Roosevelt Shaped It," 330.

[18] Dilsaver, *America's National Park System*, 20.

[19] McManamon, "The Antiquities Act and How Theodore Roosevelt Shaped It."

[20] Rothman, *Preserving Different Pasts*, xiv.

[21] Rothman, *Preserving Different Pasts*, xv.

[22] Lee, *The Antiquities Act of 1906*.

23 *American Antiquities Act of 1906*, 16 USC Sections 431–433.

24 Michael Tomlan, *Historic Preservation: Caring for Our Expanding Legacy* (Springer 2015), 67; Rothman, *Preserving Different Pasts*, 22–23.

25 Roger L. Di Silvestro, *Theodore Roosevelt in the Badlands: A Young Politician's Quest for Recovery in the American West* (Walker and Company, 2011).

26 Roosevelt set aside eighteen natural and cultural landmarks while president. These include Devils Tower, Wyoming (September 24, 1906); El Morro, New Mexico, (December 8, 1906); Montezuma Castle, Arizona (December 8, 1906); Petrified Forest, Arizona (December 8, 1906); Lassen Peak, California (May 6, 1907); Cinder Cone, California (May 6, 1907); Chaco Canyon, New Mexico (March 11, 1907); Gila Cliff Dewllings, New Mexico (November 16, 1907); Tonto Cliff Dwellings, Arizona (December 19, 1907); Muir Woods, California (January 9, 1908); Grand Canyon, Arizona (January 11, 1908); Pinnacles, California (January 16, 1908); Jewel Cave, South Dakota (February 7, 1908); Natural Bridges, Utah (April 16, 1908); Lewis and Clark Cavern, Montana (May 11, 1908); Tumacacori Mission, Arizona (September 15, 1908); Wheeler, Colorado (December 7, 1908) and Mount Olympus, Washington (March 2, 1909). McManamon, "The Antiquities Act and How Theodore Roosevelt Shaped It."

27 "Imperial presidency" is a term used to characterize the modern US presidency, to refer to the use of executive power that exceeds constitutional limits. Arthur Schlesinger, Jr. primarily focuses on the presidencies of Richard Nixon and Ronald Reagan in Arthur Schlesinger, Jr., *The Imperial Presidency* (Boston, MA: First Mariner Books Edition, 2004); for an overview of presidential power see Stephen Graubard, *The Presidents: The Transformation of*

act, "declare by public proclamation" national monuments and reserve them for proper care and management. The plain language of Section 2 of the act states:

> That the President of the United States is hereby authorized, in his discretion, to declare by public proclamation historic landmarks, historic and prehistoric structures, and other objects of historic or scientific interest that are situated upon the lands owned or controlled by the Government of the United States to be national monuments, and may reserve as a part thereof parcels of land, the limits of which in all cases shall be confined to the smallest area compatible with proper care and management of the objects to be protected: Provided, That when such objects are situated upon a tract covered by a bona fide unperfected claim or held in private ownership, the tract, or so much thereof as may be necessary for the proper care and management of the object, may be relinquished to the Government, and the Secretary of the Interior is hereby authorized to accept the relinquishment of such tracts in behalf of the Government of the United States.[23]

Section Three establishes a permitting process, the general requirement for excavations permits, and lists how archaeological sites and objects are to be protected and preserved under the authority of the statues. Although brief, the Antiquities Act provides three necessary criteria for declaration: the national monument must be historic or scientific; it must be situated on lands owned or controlled by the government; and it must be confined to the smallest area compatible for proper management. The act's vaguely defined scope, encompassing "objects of historic or scientific interest," left much room for interpretation, making it "an unparalleled tool" for an expansion-minded chief executive.[24]

Roosevelt's use of the law in the subsequent years of his presidency demonstrates his broad interpretation of the term "American antiquities."[25] During President Roosevelt's three years in office, he cited the Antiquities Act of 1906 to create eighteen national monuments encompassing approximately 1.5 million acres.[26] Of the monuments proclaimed by Roosevelt in the first two years, El Morro, Petrified Forest, Montezuma Castle, and Chaco Canyon were initially selected for protection by the scientific community due to their associations with archaeological resources in the American Southwest, Indigenous history, and imminent threats of unsanctioned excavations and looting. However, Roosevelt's designation of Devil's Tower (1,194 acres) as the first national monument in September 1906 in eastern Wyoming blatantly disregarded the initial Southwest orientation of the act. Devil's Tower, a sacred Native American site made of alkali igneous rock, is in northeastern Wyoming on the banks of the Belle Fourche River and covers 1,347 acres. Roosevelt's use of the act thus set a critical precedent that many successive presidents would employ as chief executives freed from congressional oversight.[27]

Given this unilateral power, Roosevelt's national monuments included a range of sizes and types of resources, including small ancient Southwest archaeological sites recommended for preservation in earlier reports, such as El Morro, New Mexico (160 acres); Montezuma Castle, Arizona (161 acres); Gila Cliff Dwellings, New Mexico (533 acres); Tonto, Arizona (640 acres); Chaco Canyon, New Mexico (10,643 acres); and Tumacácori, Arizona (10 acres). These sites were added to other more unlikely antiquities that encompassed larger areas and featured natural and scenic resources and places of historic and scientific interest.[28] These included significant natural and scenic resources such as the Petrified Forest, Arizona (60,776 acres); Lewis and Clark Cavern, Montana (160 acres); Lassen Peak, California (1,280 acres); Jewel Cave, South Dakota (1,275 acres); Muir Woods, California (295 acres); Wheeler, Colorado (300 acres) Natural Bridges, Utah (120 acres); and Mount Olympus, Washington (639,200 acres); which broadened the definition of antiquities beyond just cultural objects to encompass natural objects and features. Lassen Peak and Cinder Cone were proclaimed by Theodore Roosevelt on May 6, 1907, as "scientific objects" on national forest lands under the Department of Agriculture and other national monuments included four caves: Jewel Cave in South Dakota, Oregon Caves in Oregon, Lehman Caves in Nevada, and Timpanogos Cave in Utah. They would join Carlsbad Caverns, Mammoth Cave, and Wind Cave national parks in the National Park System. In addition to natural features, Roosevelt designated sites of "great historic and scientific interest" such as the Grand Canyon, Arizona (808,120 acres). Francis McManamon argues that despite these antiquities' designations, Roosevelt, by adhering closely to the wording used in the statute, ensured that "any judicial review of his proclamation would give deference to the president's action for its consistency with the law."[29]

Although the eighteen monuments designated by Roosevelt were relatively small areas, controversy ensued. Most notably, Grand Canyon National Monument in Arizona protected over 800,000 acres, and Mount Olympus National Monument in Washington, designated just days before Roosevelt left office in 1909, covered over 600,000 acres.[30] The designation of Grand Canyon National Monument in 1908, in particular, was a bold stroke, given the wording in Section 2 of the act, which stipulated that the limits of monuments "in all cases shall be confined to the smallest area compatible with proper care and management of the objects to be protected."[31] The first challenge to the Antiquities Act concerned the creation of this monument, which was, at the time, by far the largest monument created.[32] The designation drew fierce criticism from the mining industry in the Arizona Territory, and businessman and politician Ralph H. Cameron challenged Roosevelt's use of the act as being beyond the scope of authority granted under Section 2 of the act.[33] He sued the federal government, but the US Supreme Court rejected Cameron's mining claim and upheld Roosevelt's Grand Canyon National Monument proclamation, thus setting the stage for the direct application of the act by subsequent presidents.

the *American Presidency from Theodore Roosevelt to Barack Obama* (London: Penguin Books, 2010), 11; see National Park Service, *The Antiquities Act 1906–2006*, Monuments List, https://www.nps.gov/archeology/sites/antiquities/monumentslist.htm.

[28] McManamon, "The Antiquities Act and How Theodore Roosevelt Shaped It."

[29] McManamon, "The Antiquities Act and How Theodore Roosevelt Shaped It."

[30] Sanjay Ranchod, "The Clinton National Monuments: Protecting Ecosystems with the Antiquities Act," *Harvard Environmental Law Review* 25, (2001): 535–89.

[31] Miller, "Landmark Decision," 66–78.

[32] Brian Turner, "A Grand Precedent: The Supreme Court and the Grand Canyon National Monument," Saving Places, *Preservation Leadership Forum. National Trust for Historic Preservation*, May 2017, http://forum.savingplaces.org/blogs/brian-turner/2017/05/08/a-grand-precedent-the-supreme-court-and-the-grand-canyon-national-monument.

[33] Cameron v. United States 252 US 450 (1920). Congress and President Woodrow Wilson expanded the national monument acreage and created Grand Canyon National Park that year; see Carolyn Shelbourn, "Presidents and Preservation: The US Antiquities Act of 1906," *Art Antiquity and Law* IX, no. 4 (2004): 375.

In the decades following Roosevelt's presidency, the use of the Antiquities Act established a foundation for government policies that recognized an essential public interest in cultural and natural resources and their commemorative, educational, and scientific values. Presidents Taft, Wilson, Harding, Coolidge, and Hoover, who followed Roosevelt, continued to wield this executive order during the first half of the twentieth century, albeit in a less active way than Roosevelt did. They, however, did follow the belief that Roosevelt had pioneered and proclaimed new national monuments in a variety of sizes with a consistent frequency to reflect the variety of important archaeological, historic, natural, scenic, and scientific resources, broadly interpreting the term "antiquities." Following Roosevelt, presidents used the Antiquities Act to expand existing monuments and designate them as national parks or cultural sites. President William Taft was the first president to modify the boundaries of a national monument that Roosevelt had established, thus setting a precedent when he expanded Natural Bridges, Utah, by adding 2,62 acres in 1909 and reduced the original area of Petrified Forest, Arizona, (by nearly 90 percent), Mount Olympus, Washington, in 1912 (by nearly 10 percent), Navajo, Arizona, in 1912 (by nearly 30 percent).[34] Later on, it became standard practice for national monuments to be transferred to state control or disbanded due to management shifts and budgetary changes.[35]

Such land preservation practices became common over time. The national monument category fell into obscurity as the National Park System grew with the founding of the National Park Service in 1916. During the New Deal era, the Antiquities Act and the national monuments became less significant to this federal entity whose primary focus lay in developing existing designations for tourism and economic development rather than creating new monuments.[36] As a result, the agency's focus broadened, and after the end of World War II, how the Park Service perceived the Antiquities Act changed dramatically. New expectations about the role of the agency and a different vision of its future made the Antiquities Act less central to federal preservation than it had been before 1933. The Antiquities Act was used less and less frequently in the early to mid-twentieth century since it offered no provisions for funding new and existing national monuments. Instead, the act was reserved for emergencies and urgent cases whereby the law became a last resort in cases when rapid presidential action was the only way to attract the attention of Congress.[37] The Antiquities Act as a precedent for national conservation policy remained unsurpassed.

Unlikely Antiquities in the Clinton, Bush, and Obama Years

Today, the national monuments under the National Park Service, established under the authority of the Antiquities Act, cover a wide range of objects—coastal areas, marine protected areas, canals, valleys, land bridges, fjords, sites related to the history of science, the Reconstruction period and civil rights struggles, LGBTQ, and women's history. In addition, sacred mounds, burial sites, and World War II sites expand the scope of the national monuments category. This broad interpretation and application of the act

[34] The Presidency Project, William Taft, Proclamation 873, 1186 (UC Santa Barbara), http://www.presidency.ucsb.edu/ws/?pid=76608.

[35] Not all the national monuments proclaimed by presidents over the past century are still national monuments. Eleven have been abolished by acts of Congress. The complete list of transferred, redesignated, abolished or diminished monuments includes: Montezuma Castle, Arizona (1978); Natural Bridges, Utah (1962); Lewis and Clark Cavern, Montana (1937); Tumacacori, Arizona (1990); Wheeler, Colorado (1950); Navajo, Arizona (1912); Oregon Caves, Oregon (2014); Shoshone Cavern, Wyoming (1954); Gran Quivira, New Mexico (1988); Sitka, Alaska (1983); Big Hole Battlefield, Montana (1963); Papago Square, Arizona (1930); Sieur de Monts, Maine (1930); Capulin Mountain, New Mexico (1987); Old Kasaan, Alaska (1955); Verendrye, North Dakota (1956); Katmai, Alaska (1980); Lehman Caves, Nevada (1986); Fossil Cycad, South Dakota (1956); Mound City Group, Ohio (1992); Carlsbad Cave, New Mexico (1930); Craters of the Moon, Idaho (2002); Castle Pickney, South Carolina (1956); Fort Marion, Florida (1948); Wupatki, Arizona (1941); among others; see National Park Service, US Department of the Interior, "The Antiquities Act 1906–2006," *Commemorative Virtual Exhibition,* https://www.nps.gov/archeology/sites/antiquities/MonumentsList.htm.

[36] Donald C. Swain, "The National Park Service and the New Deal, 1933–1940," *Pacific Historical Review* 41, no. 3 (1972): 312–32.

[37] Rothman, *Preserving Different Pasts,* 58–62.

and American antiquities was most evident during the Clinton (1993–2001), Bush (2001–2009), and Obama (2009–2017) administrations. The Clinton administration was responsible for designating Grand Canyon-Parashant National Monument, Arizona (2000), a remote and inaccessible biologically diverse, geologic treasure managed by the National Park Service and the Bureau of Land Management. Fortifications, Castle Williams, and Fort Jay, on Governors Island, New York, were commemorated by President Bill Clinton in 2001 for their defensive role in the War of 1812, the Civil War, and World War II. The same year, Minidoka Internment Camp, Idaho (2001), was designated a national monument to convey the story of the internment of Japanese Americans during World War II.

The Bush administration (2001–2009) used the powers of the Antiquities Act to grant national monument status to an urban site, the African Burial Ground in Lower Manhattan, New York (2006), to commemorate the final resting place of enslaved and free Africans in New York City. Following in the footsteps of his predecessor, President George W. Bush declared the World War II Valor in the Pacific National Monument in Hawaii, Alaska, and California, which includes nine sites in addition to the USS Arizona in Pearl Harbor and the Tule Lake unit in California (2008), to honor the sacrifices and the "high price paid by some Americans on the home front."[38]

President Barack Obama offered protection for important sites associated with racial and ethnic communities and their histories of dissent or struggle for equality and dignity. Designations include the Cesar E. Chavez National Monument, California (2012), which commemorates the farmworker movement and the burial site of Cesar Chavez; the Harriet Tubman Underground Railroad National Historical Park, Maryland (2013), to honor Harriet Tubman's role in freeing enslaved people through a secret network of northward-leading routes and safe houses; the Charles Young Buffalo Soldiers Monument, Ohio (2013), to recognize Colonel Charles Young (1864–1922) and his service in the Ninth US Cavalry, one of the African American troops known as the Buffalo Soldiers that served as the nation's first park rangers. In addition, President Obama designated Pullman National Monument, Illinois (2015), once the largest employer of African Americans as porters, waiters, and maids and America's first planned industrial town; the Belmont-Paul Women's Equality National Monument, Washington, DC (2016), which commemorates Alva Belmont and Alice Paul, leaders of the National Woman's Party, and more broadly honors the struggles of the women's suffrage and equal rights movements. President Obama's designation of Bears Ears National Monument, Utah (2016), though controversial due to its size, honored intertribal history and incorporated a new system of comanagement overseen by Native American tribes, including the Ute Mountain Tribe, the Navajo Nation, the Ute Indian Tribe of the Uintah Ouray, the Hopi Nation and the Zuni Tribe. Obama's other designations include Stonewall, New York (2016), to remember the 1969 Stonewall uprising in the quest for LGBT civil rights; the Birmingham Civil Rights National Monument, Alabama (2017), the Freedom Riders National Monument, Alabama

[38] The Presidency Project, George W. Bush, Proclamation 8327, UC Santa Barbara, http://www.presidency.ucsb.edu/ws/index.php?pid=85048.

39 Monuments Protected Under the Antiquities Act, National Parks Conservation Association (2017), https://www.npca.org/resources/2658-monuments-protected-under-the-antiquities-act.

40 Douglas Brinkley, "Obama the Monument Maker," *New York Times Opinion*, August 26, 2016, https://www.nytimes.com/2016/08/28/opinion/sunday/obama-the-monument-maker.html.

41 In 2014, President Obama expanded the Pacific Remote Islands Marine National Monument by approximately 261.3 million acres. In 2016, President Obama expanded the Papahanaumokuakea Marine National Monument by approximately 283.4 million acres. The two areas contain about 545 million acres of the 549 million proclaimed by the president; see Carol Hardy Vincent, CRS Report R41330, National Monuments and the Antiquities Act, Congressional Research Services, https://fas.org/sgp/crs/misc/R41330.pdf.

42 John Yoo and Todd Gaziano, "The Presidential Authority to Revoke or Reduce National Monument Designations," *AEI American Enterprise Institute* (March 2017), http://www.aei.org/publication/presidential-authority-to-revoke-or-reduce-national-monument-designations/.

43 David Konisky and Neal Woods, "Environmental Policy, Federalism, and the Obama Presidency," *Publius: The Journal of Federalism* 46, no. 3, (July 1, 2016): 366–91; Robert V. Percival, "Presidential Power to Address Climate Change in an Era of Legislative Gridlock," *Virginia Environmental Law Journal* 32, no. 2 (2014): 134–56.

(2017), and the Reconstruction Era National Monument, South Carolina (2017) commemorate African American history and civil rights struggles. Finally, Obama's designation of Honouliuli National Monument, a former prisoner of war and civilian internment camp, in his home state of Hawai'i in 2015, bears associations with other World War II national monuments recognized by the Clinton and Bush administrations.[39]

The Obama administration holds the distinction of enshrining the most acreage of national monuments in the United States than any other president, including Theodore Roosevelt.[40] He designated twenty-three new national monuments in fourteen states and the District of Columbia, ranging in size from 0.12 acres to 1.6 million acres. President Obama also enlarged three monuments, one in California (by 1,665 acres) and two marine monuments (by 261.3 million acres and 283.4 million acres) for a total of 549 million acres under protection.[41] His administration's exploration of areas for national monument designation, including his designation of twenty-three new monuments and enlargement of three others, renewed interest in legislative efforts to restrict the President's authority to proclaim national monuments.[42] Though environmentalists and conservation professionals applauded President Obama's designations, some national monuments were heavily criticized by conservatives, members of Congress, as well as state and local officials.[43] While proclamations in the age of Roosevelt were relatively concise documents describing the objects to be protected and reserving lands from appropriation or use under public land laws, more recent national monument proclamations have set forth more detailed management terms and use restrictions.[44]

As a result, disputes arose concerning monument size, the processes by which the monuments were created, and the management terms included in the proclamations.[45] Critics focused on the perceived lack of consistency between the Antiquities Act and the policies established in other laws, especially the land withdrawal provisions of the Federal Land Policy and Management Act (FLPMA) of 1976, the environmental reviews required by the National Environmental Policy Act (NEPA), and the failure to adhere to public participation and consultation requirements of FLPMA, NEPA, and other laws.[46] Criticism was also expressed by those who oppose restrictions on land uses for extraction (for example, mining, lumbering, grazing) and recreation (for example, off-road vehicle use, fishing, hunting) and ignore the views of local stakeholders. Contentious monument proclamations like Bears Ears National Monument in southeast Utah, designated in 2016, were widely touted as a victory for an intertribal council that now occupies an advisory role. However, critics mounted campaigns to challenge the 109,100 acres of boundary area owned by the State of Utah in addition to the already 1.35 million acres of designated federal land of the area.[47] President Trump's sweeping reassessment of national monuments created since 1996 and greater than 100,000 acres was backed by the Congressional Western Caucus, which called for the president to shrink or rescind controversial monument designations.[48]

National Monuments as Technical Lands

This historical overview highlights how presidential use of the Antiquities Act of 1906 incited opposition, primarily from congressional representatives in the Western United States. They regarded this direct federal intervention in their regional affairs as a violation of state sovereignty. In the late nineteenth century, the act's emergence embodied middle-class, progressive values and contained assumptions that the public would obey its dictates simply because it was the law. Although the monument designation implied federal seizure, the language of the law focused on criminalizing vandalism. In its early years, the term "national monument" was assigned to landscapes deemed valuable by anthropologists, archaeologists, and ethnologists interested in researching a given property. Thus, it discouraged amateur collectors from conducting unpermitted excavations of their own. The monument designation established penalties for looting and unauthorized excavations and enabled the president to impose limits on a host of potentially damaging activities—mining, homesteading, grazing, logging. This ethos, buffered by the Industrial Revolution and advanced by a cohort of like-minded Progressive reformers, drew heavily on European social idealism to shape perspectives on the necessity of a strong central state to formulate a new tool for westward expansion. The evolution in the use of the Antiquities Act, the ease of proclamation, and the law's malleable interpretation of antiquities resulted in its broad application beyond Indigenous Southwest archeological sites. Though the future and the fate of some national monuments remains uncertain, the Antiquities Act remains an audacious piece of legislation. Its history and contemporary usage reveal critical insights into how the creation and management of the commons is a fundamentally technical and bureaucratic process that remains subject to the whims of each presidential administration.

[44] See Proclamation No. 9131, 79 Federal Register 30,431 (May 28, 2014) (Establishment of the Organ Mountains-Desert Peaks National Monument); Proclamation No. 8336, 74 Federal Register 1565 (January 12, 2009) (Establishment of the Pacific Remote Islands Marine National Monument).

[45] *American Antiquities Act of 1906*, 16 USC Sections, 431–33.

[46] Carol Hardy Vincent, CRS Report R41330, National Monuments and the Antiquities Act, https://fas.org/sgp/crs/misc/R41330.pdf; M. Belco and B. Rottinghaus, "The Law: Presidential Proclamation 6920: Using Executive Power to Set a New Direction for the Management of National Monuments," *Presidential Studies Quarterly*, 39 (2009): 605–18.

[47] Matthew J. Sanders, "Are National Monuments the Right Way to Manage Federal Lands?" *Natural Resources & Environment* 31, no. 1, (Summer 2016): 3–7.

[48] National monuments under review by President Trump and Secretary Ryan Zinke included those over 100,000 acres designated in 1966 onward by President Clinton: Grand Staircase-Escalante, Grand Canyon-Parashant, Giant Sequoia, Canyons of the Ancients, Hanford Reach, Ironwood Forest, Vermillion Cliffs, Carrizo Plain, Sonoran Desert, and Upper Missouri River Breaks; President G. W. Bush: Papahanaumokuakea (expanded by 300,000 acres under President Obama), Pacific Remote Islands (expanded by 300,000 acres under Obama); and President Obama: Rio Grande del Norte, Organ Mountains-Desert Peaks, San Gabriel Mountains, Berryessa Snow Mountain, Basin and Range, Mojave Trails, Sand to Snow, Bears Ears and Gold Butte.

Territorial Challenges of Cosmopolitical Design

Roi Salgueiro Barrio

Cosmopolitics and Technical Lands

This chapter discusses territorial-scale projects that devise technical solutions to global climate and ecological crises. These projects design a specific subset of technical lands, named "climate lands," aimed at increasing clean-energy production and improving ecological performance through the technical management of the land. The article considers these climate-lands projects as constitutive elements of a growing type of interventions, collectively leading to a spatial structuring at the world scale, and questions how their conception by design practices can be seen as part of a disciplinary shift towards addressing cosmopolitical questions.

Originally, cosmopolitics was the practice of Cosmopolitanism, the eighteenth-century intellectual movement promoting an idea of world citizenship based on universally shared notions of hospitality, justice, and political rights. Cosmopolitanism thus pursued the incremental construction of a shared and integrated world. However, in its current usage, the notion is mobilized with entirely alternative purposes. The term supports a contra-cosmopolitan project suited for the Anthropocene age of "climate and ecological anxiety."[1] In this context of ecological concern, cosmopolitics renounces cosmopolitanism's universalist drive and faith in scientific neutrality, favoring an inverse privilege of local singularities and world views.

My approach to climate lands builds upon and critically questions this latter meaning of cosmopolitics. The article's first section describes the projects of climate lands and the cosmopolitical criticism of their rationale. The second section presents mainstream cosmopolitical design theory's key characteristics, offering a critique of its limitations in understanding planetary scale phenomena, while the third part analyzes those limitations by contrasting current cosmopolitical approaches to "territory" with previous architectural theorizations of that geographical notion. The concluding section explores how to go beyond the current model of cosmopolitics to reconsider what cosmopolitical design is and its key realms of practice. It focuses on how the recent incorporation of territory into the cosmopolitical vocabulary can contribute to a new form of cosmopolitical practice. My thesis is that cosmopolitical design can build upon the previous architectural theorizations of territory, which situate this notion at the intersection of planetarization and land-technologization processes. Such a conception of territory not only helps us understand climate lands but treats them as integral, albeit problematic, objects of cosmopolitical design.

World Technical Zoning

Climate change and ecological crisis motivate multiple projects to technologize land. Beyond the unrealized impact of geoengineering, diverse design initiatives envisage large-scale territorial interventions to produce renewable energy, which multiply the scale of existing wind or solar farms by hundreds. In so doing, these projects are reconceptualizing geography in relation to predominant forms of technical-land use. Seen together, they

[1] Maja and Reuben Fowkes, "Cosmopolitics," in *Posthuman Glossary*, eds., Rosi Braidotti and Maria Hlavajova (London: Bloomsbury, 2018), 92–94.

start building a sort of world technical zoning, a division of the planet in areas oriented to specific energetic or ecological functions. Even if they may intervene in delimited regions, they produce imaginaries for a global spatial structuring where the technical and the geographic coincide.

A paradigmatic example is 2050—An Energetic Odyssey, an ambitious project exploring the possibility of massive wind harvesting and storage of renewable energies on the entire North Sea. It was designed by H+N+S Landscape Architects together with a consortium that included the Netherlands Ministry of Economic Affairs, Shell (oil company), TenneT (a European electricity transmission operator), the European Climate Foundation, Zeeland Seaports, Rotterdam and Amsterdam port authorities, and some nature conservation NGOs.[2] Aimed at drastically reducing that region's dependency on fossil fuels to comply with the 2015 IPCC Paris agreement, the project requires additional legal and spatial structuring in an already highly regulated maritime resource space to incorporate 25,000 wind turbines (fifteen every week until 2050) upon 57,000 square kilometers of sea.[3] This scalar ambition is echoed by similar energy production projects. AMO's *Roadmap: A Practical Guide to a Prosperous, Low Carbon Europe* is based on previous studies by the Energy Research Centre of the Netherlands and the European Climate Foundation and equally dedicates the North Sea to wind harvesting. The document also conceives North Africa as a provider of solar energy. The recommendation follows the German initiative DESERTEC, promoted by the Club de Rome and the National Energy Research Center Jordan, which considers the entire Sahara as a massive solar farm.[4] In the United States, Princeton University's Net Zero America Report quantifies similarly vast geographic interventions for clean energy production.[5]

Such technical visions of geography constitute an extreme spectrum of possible responses to climate and ecological issues.[6] The other is represented by agroecology and ecosystem-reparation projects, such as E. O. Wilson's Half-Earth Project (which promotes progressively eliminating the human presence and activities from half of Earth's surface), the 30 × 30 initiative of maritime ecological preservation, and ETH Crowther Lab's selection of land areas for the planting of one trillion trees.[7] The contraposition between these two types of projects is ideological rather than methodological. Both rely on upscaling land-zoning procedures to cover increasingly large areas. Despite their conflicting ideological agendas, both design modalities rely upon a similar degree of technicality, requiring data gathering mainly from satellite imagery, data processing, and the digital translation of information to cartographic illustrations. In each project, mapping is systematically the privileged medium of analysis and representation.

In all the previous cases, technicality is procedural before being functional. The procedures these projects use to select, measure, define, and control the conditions of the land are always technologically mediated. In turn, this technological evaluation of the land's conditions determines the specific ecological or energetic function it is assigned, which is then technically enhanced. These projects approach earlier explorations about the

[2] H+N+S Landscape Architects, "2050—An Energetic Odyssey," http://www.hnsland.nl/en/projects/2050-energetic-odyssey.

[3] Cornelis Disco and Eda Kranakis, "Toward a Theory of Cosmopolitan Commons," *Cosmopolitan Commons: Sharing Resources and Risks Across Borders* (Cambridge, MA: MIT Press, 2013), 13–47.

[4] OMA/AMO, *Roadmap 2050: A Practical Guide to a Prosperous, Low Carbon Europe* (The Hague: European Climate Foundation, 2010), 82, https://www.oma.com/publications/roadmap-2050-a-practical-guide-to-a-prosperous-low-carbon-europe.

[5] Eric Larson et al., *Net Zero America Report*, https://netzeroamerica.princeton.edu/the-report. Additionally, the recent government agreement in Germany between social-democrats, ecologists, and liberals includes the mandate to dedicate 2 percent of the national territory to wind farms.

[6] Holly Jean Buck, *After Geoengineering: Climate Tragedy, Repair and Restoration* (London: Verso, 2019), 34–40.

[7] For the Half-Earth project, see https://www.half-earthproject.org/. For the 30 × 30 initiative to protect 30 percent of the ocean's surface, see https://www.oceanunite.org/30-x-30/. For the project of planetary reforestation, see https://www.crowtherlab.com/.

spatial articulation of the world scale, informed by "cosmopolitan" beliefs in common solutions for humanity and a strong reliance on technical-scientific knowledge.[8] Constantinos Doxiadis' 1970s Anthropocosmos model illustrates a paradigmatic example of such an approach to planetary structuring. His model divided the totality of land and sea into twelve differentiated functional zones.[9] Zone 1 required eliminating 50 percent of the human presence on Earth's surface—as E. O. Wilson's Half-Earth suggests. At the same time, the other zones progressively increased the level of human occupation and technological transformation of space. Similarly, Buckminster Fuller and John McHale's coetaneous World Resource Inventory aimed a precise quantification and classification of Earth's energetic and material goods to facilitate a rational and sustainable "world retooling design."[10] Both current climate-lands and large-scale ecological restoration projects seem to replicate these modern, world-planning speculations by sharing a methodological corpus based on large-scale geographic interventions, land zoning, data gathering and processing, and global mapping.

The cosmopolitical criticism of design politics towards planetary problems has insistently questioned this overlap of technical methodologies and mapping—often arguing that it retrofits dominant narratives of Earth altered by all-encompassing, universal humanity that obscure understanding who is responsible and who is affected by the Anthropocene.[11] This criticism states that our experience of planetary challenges relies too strongly upon the accumulation of scientific evidence provided by types of exo-vision such as aerial and satellite imagery showing the global extents of settlements, infrastructures transport flows, and landscape alterations. Representing such conditions from an exterior, extraterrestrial point of view leads to an abstracted conceptualization of planetary conditions that doesn't address the responsibilities behind the climate and ecologic damage to our planet nor its direct effects on the ground.

For cosmopolitical thinkers, the reliance on mapping and similar forms of the exo-vision characteristic of previous attempts at world structuring and contemporary climate-lands projects internalizes this vision's universalizing and neutralizing character, and mobilizes it to support "polytechnical dreams of control" of world space.[12] Ultimately, such an approach only serves to duplicate the social and spatial logics producing so-called Anthropocene. The globalizing understanding of phenomena is necessarily equated to a vast scale of intervention irrespective of local conditions and agents. Cosmopolitical thinkers oppose such a conclusion. Instead, they advocate for an alternative, locally oriented, and locally generated visual and design culture that can reveal the "cosmopolitical present," meaning, in T. J. Demos's terms, the "progressive composition of a common world, acknowledging the presence of those most negatively affected by environmental transformations."[13]

[8] Hashim Sarkis and Roi Salgueiro Barrio with Gabriel Kozlowski, *The World as an Architectural Project* (Cambridge, MA: MIT Press, 2020), 1–20.

[9] Constantinos Doxiadis, "The Ecological Types of Space That We Need," *Environmental Conservation* 2, no. 1 (1975): 3–13.

[10] Buckminster Fuller and John McHale, *World Design Science Decade 1965–1975 Phase I (1963) Document 1: Inventory of World Resources, Human Trends, and Needs* (Carbondale, IL: World Resources Inventory, 1963).

[11] T. J. Demos, "Welcome to the Anthropocene!," *Against the Anthropocene Visual Culture and Environment Today* (Berlin: Sternberg Press, 2017), 7–22; Bruno Latour, *Facing Gaia: Eight Lectures on the New Climatic Regime* (Cambridge: Polity, 2013), 118–20.

[12] Peter Sloterdijk, *Globes Spheres, Volume II* (Pasadena, CA: Semiotext(e), 2014).

[13] Demos, *Against the Anthropocene*, 38

Cosmopolitics

Belgian philosopher Isabelle Stengers settled the basis of contemporary cosmopolitical theory in a series of books questioning the hegemony of Western science, aptly titled *Cosmopolitics*. Later, French sociologist Bruno Latour, design theorist Albena Yaneva, and Brazilian anthropologist Eduardo Viveiros de Castro expanded Stengers's theses, portraying cosmopolitics as a crucial notion when addressing global challenges. This understanding of cosmopolitics negates the validity of the universal ideas of cosmopolitanism, which it portrays as a mere camouflage of hegemonic interests. To avoid such an universalizing trap, cosmopolitics seeks an ontologically plural cosmos constituted by multiple, divergent local actors, each characterized by their world views, lifeworlds, and forms of access to reality. The result of such multiplicity would not be the cosmopolitan universe. Instead, it would be a *pluriverse*, emerging through the intersecting links between these actors' contrasting interests in the absence of an overall ideological framework. In fact, cosmopolitical theory acknowledges and cherishes its own incapacity to methodologically mediate between local debates and global structuring. As Stengers states, "[T]he cosmopolitical proposal is incapable of giving a 'good' definition of the procedures that allow us to achieve the 'good' definition of a 'good' common world."[14]

We are no longer in the cosmopolitan realm of global structuring. Instead, cosmopolitics suggests working at the smallest of scales. Questioning the universalizing ambition of cosmopolitanism, this vision of cosmopolitics implies an inverse privilege of contextual singularities. Under the idea of cosmopolitical design, its translation to architecture has equally claimed the need to primarily intervene on small urban and local scales.[15] There, cosmopolitical designers limit their position to become "embedded in some situations as an ordinary actor," helping to articulate political assemblies around specific ecological controversies.[16] Such ambition requires revealing the different agents involved, including their conflicting interests, as previous steps to finding a possible, provisional, and partial resolution. In so doing, architects and urbanists may contribute to visualizing networks of "quasi-objects." These challenge the understanding of space as a neutral repository of nature and artifacts, and instead favor treating space as a sum of temporary, changing coalitions of human and nonhuman agents, enabled by the objects that structure those collectives.[17]

All the above requires developing a form of "vision from within," a grounded, down-to-earth perspective that can counter the detached exo-vision of the climate-land projects, as well as their external (supposedly neutral) scientific rationality.[18] This operation aims to avoid solutions to climate questions that collapse uneven geographies and ecologies by prioritizing technical fixes.[19] The locality of intervention is also the locality and specificity of knowledge, forms of vision, and means of representation.

Cosmopolitics has brought a much-needed recognition of constitutive political conflicts, power imbalances, and contextual singularities. Yet, its insistence on small-scale local operations and distinct world views has

[14] Isabel Stengers, "The Cosmopolitical Proposal," *Making Things Public: Atmospheres of Democracy*, eds., Bruno Latour and Peter Weibel (Cambridge, MA: MIT Press, 2005), 994–1003.

[15] Donna Houston, Diana MacCallum, Wendy Steele, and Jason Byrne, "Climate Cosmopolitics and the Possibilities for Urban Planning," *Nature and Culture* 11, no. 3 (2016): 259–77.

[16] Albena Yaneva, "What is Cosmopolitical Design?" *What is Cosmopolitical Design? Design, Nature and the Built Environment*, eds. Alejandro Zaera Polo and Albena Yaneva (Farnham: Ashgate, 2015), 7.

[17] Yaneva, "What is Cosmopolitical Design?" 4.

[18] Yaneva, "What is Cosmopolitical Design?" 7.

[19] Houston et al., "Climate Cosmopolitics," 259–77; probably sea-level rise is the realm where it is more evident that solutions to climate change tend to rely on the generalized use of predetermined technical fixes (such as dikes and sea walls) regardless of socioecological singularities. See Kian Goh, *Form and Flow: The Spatial Politics of Urban Resilience and Climate Justice* (Cambridge, MA: MIT Press, 2021).

strong conceptual and practical limitations. Critics of cosmopolitics highlight that the incommensurability of multiple world views is not a solution but one of the key reasons that led the planet to an ecological crisis.[20] Similarly, they argue that the absence of a framework mediating between local and planetary processes impedes assessing the impact of local actions in the constitution of a shared world. In summa, the privilege of small-scale operations, the multiplicity of world views, and the cosmopolitical rejection of shared mediation strategies between local and global risk make cosmopolitics ineffectual.

This criticism has triggered the search, among cosmopolitical thinkers, of spatial categories that can solve this theory's scalar limitations while retaining its interest in singularity. The cosmopolitical revalorization of territory is crucial among those categories to conceptualize a space of proximity linked to a particular community. Bruno Latour suggests replacing the imaginaries of the "local" and the "global" with the imaginary of the "terrestrial" to articulate the politics of what he terms "the new climatic regime." Latour's terrestrial considers that acts of ecological defense are a way to protect the "territories" human groups have historically occupied and shaped, together with the lifestyles those collectives have developed there. Ecology is, thus, not an abstract contribution to an ungraspable, global common good, but the very recuperation of the local singularity.[21] Similarly, for decolonial cosmopolitical thinker Arturo Escobar, the concept of territory refers to situated modes of existence, each involving specific relations between people and Earth.[22]

The recent incorporation of territory to the cosmopolitical vocabulary helps introduce an engagement with geographic materiality, such as Latour's assimilation of territory to the notion of land. It also avoids privileging a single locus of analysis or intervention (such as the city or the landscape) by precisely pointing to the imbrication of different types of geophysical and cultural conditions. Moreover, the category of territory requires the possibility of exerting some form of sovereignty, or political action, upon the land uses. As Escobar has remarked, in territory, communities "engage in a complex interepistemic, and interontological geopolitics aimed at creating alternative territorialities that might result, to the greatest extent possible, in an effective articulation of territory, culture, and identity for the defense of their lifeworlds."[23] As a result, territory can help redirect cosmopolitical discourse to the lands where the most substantial industrial and agricultural production and resources extraction are causing ecological and climatic transformations.

The territorial turn approaches the spaces of actual environmental transformation and enables a more decided scalar response than cosmopolitics' initial focus on small-scale, local operations. But it reiterates some of cosmopolitics' more problematic characteristics: the emphasis on locality, the rejection of meta-frameworks, and the consequent lack of clear procedures to transition between territorial singularities and world. To address these shortcomings, current cosmopolitics needs to be challenged by a

[20] Ihnji Jon, "Scales of Political Action in the Anthropocene: Gaia, Networks, and Cities as Frontiers of Doing Earthly Politics," *Global Society* 34, no. 2 (2020): 163–85.

[21] Bruno Latour, *Down to Earth: Politics in the New Climate Region* (Cambridge: Polity Press, 2018).

[22] Arturo Escobar, *Designs for the Pluriverse: Radical Interdependence, Autonomy, and the Making of Worlds* (Durham, NC: Duke University Press, 2018), 167.

[23] Escobar, *Designs for the Pluriverse*, 176.

theory of territorial production that goes beyond territory's simple characterization as a communal space of proximity. An approximation to such a theory can be seen in a decades-earlier territory claim, which parallels and predates cosmopolitics' territorial concerns. I am referring to an episode within the architectural culture itself whose more explicit manifestations are the theories of territory elaborated by two groups of Italian architects coalescing around the figures of Saverio Muratori and Vittorio Gregotti in the second half of the 1960s. These explorations pertain to a different historical moment than ours and do not directly respond to our current concerns. Hence, they are not a solution to cosmopolitics limitations but an opening to a different understanding of the problems posed by cosmopolitical culture and cosmopolitical design. Such theories contain a more detailed interrogation of the notions of territory and territoriality—one that explicitly approaches processes of land technologization and includes an explicit reflection about the bidirectional mediations and influences between territorial and world processes. The result is an understanding of territory as the key spatial category to affect processes of world structuring.

Territory

24 Stuart Elden, *The Birth of Territory* (Chicago, IL: The University of Chicago Press, 2013), 1–18.

Historically, the term "territory" referred to the area surrounding a city.[24] As such, the initial reflections on territory in the Italian postwar context were mostly responses to urban expansion. Notions as *città-territorio* and *la nuova dimensione* conceived territory as the realm where the functional and dimensional necessities derived from urban growth could be solved. Muratori and Gregotti approach the notion from a different angle. For both, territory is an autonomous spatial category, with its own functional, organizational, and formal problems. Its importance does not derive from city growth but from broader phenomena of massive geographic transformation and global structuring.

The concern with world structuring is explicitly present in the writings of the two architects. Muratori's 1967 treatise, *Civiltà e territorio* (Civilization and Territory), conceives territory as a "new problem," whose relevance derives from the novel evidence of the planetary extent of civilization. For the architect, civilization used to be an expanding phenomenon, affecting only some areas of the earth. It is now a dimensionally fixed system, an "ecumene" covering the entire terrestrial surface. This global condition is for Muratori the result of a system of economic production that converted geographical knowledge into an "active geography" that is not "interested in enjoying reality, but in transforming it." His work proposes creating a new methodology and practice of territory to counter this tendency, which can help inform a new "planning of the world."[25] In turn, Gregotti's "The Form

25 Saverio Muratori, *Civiltà e territorio* (Rome: Centro Studi di Storia Urbanistica, 1967), 52, 45, 291.

of Territory" mobilizes the notion to respond to the emergence of a global, "total environment." The latter results from the vast territorial modifications produced by new technical processes, rapidly accelerating the modification and consumption of physical geography worldwide. For Gregotti, this profit-oriented transformation of land by technical means implies a universalization of the value of nature and delocalization of territory: "The technologization of landscape makes the notion of 'place' less important within our systems of collective values. The idea of place loses its operative value as it becomes dependent on supralocal economies."[26]

Despite the notable differences in their thinking, Muratori and Gregotti problematize territory in a similar manner. Both highlight how territory is imbricated with the articulation of the world scale and how it is now primarily shaped by profit-driven, technically enhanced processes of geographic transformation. In that regard, territory is substantially related to production and land. This theorization is essential for contemporary debates on territory, as it points towards architecture's engagement with a specific understanding of the notion. Recently, geographer Stuart Elden advocated for the need to differentiate the categories of land, terrain, and territory. In this schema, land refers to the ownership of resources, and terrain to military strategy. Territory, in turn, is "a political technology comprising techniques for measuring land and controlling terrain," aimed at constituting bounded spaces where sovereignty can be exerted.[27] The understanding of territory seen in the two Italian architects differs from this political reduction of the notion. It presents territory as a derivative of territoriality, that is, of processes aimed at transforming land and exploiting resources.[28] These are potentially trans-local and lack predefined boundaries. Critically operating within these conditions doesn't require seeing territory as a political technology. It implies, rather, rethinking architecture as a "territorial technology," the purpose of which is to reclaim territory as a material, concrete space that contradicts any attempts to reduce the world to a single condition.

This territorial technology requires creating bidirectional links between territory and planet. Cartographic production plays a crucial role in that process. In the case of Muratori, cartography operates at two contrasting scales. The smaller scale depicts regional territorial formations and their process of generation. These representations attempt to counter the merely productive understanding of territory by highlighting how other dynamics—coming from the spheres of logic, ethics, and aesthetics—have shaped those specific territories. The bigger scale focuses on continental formations, which Muratori names "ecumenes," and shows the global processes that have influenced the territories' composition and the scale that a renewed territorial action would conform. In Gregotti's case, the global scale appears through the visual accumulation of instances of landscape technologization. His procedures of mapping territory require overlaying different readings of the geographical subsoil, the anthropogeographical structures of territorial modification, and transformations produced by planning and economic processes. For both authors, the goal is to create a systematic methodology of reading and analysis that can exceed the particularities of a specific condition.

Contrary to Stengers's rejection of standard procedures, the conceptual effort here resides in elaborating common ways to transition between scales. By working with contrasting scales, these methods combine two forms of vision. A fully grounded, down-to-earth one, approaching the cosmopolitical

[26] Vittorio Gregotti, *Il Territorio dell'architettura* (Milan: Feltrinelli Editore, 2008 [1966]), 72–73, (author's translation).

[27] Elden, *The Birth of Territory*, 322–30.

[28] Claude Raffestin, "Space, Territory, and Territoriality," *Environment and Planning D: Society and Space* 30 (2012): 121–41.

concept of vision from within; plus a detached form of exo-vision, the one characteristic of aerial views and global mapping, which the climate-lands projects use so intensely.

The contrast between Muratori and Gregotti is especially acute in their final objectives. Muratori seeks to create territorial equilibriums, a conservative goal that promotes stability by fixing specific territorial structures. Gregotti, in turn, is fully interested in aligning architectural practices to the ongoing dynamics of territorial change. For him, such an ambition requires recognizing that architecture does not drive the crucial processes of geographic transformation. It is situated alongside them, creating temporary spatial structures. This goal implies ceasing to understand architecture as the construction of concrete objects. In this schema, objects are rethought as "connections, relational knots," instead of "resistant, opaque materials."[29] At the same time, architecture is responsible for assembling the disconnected, heterogeneous materials that populate territory into multiple "quasi-objects" that solidify and allow one to read a set of spatial relations. Quasi-objects are, in this sense, aggregates, compounds of the many elements that can now be taken as architectural "matter"—productive landscapes, infrastructures, buildings; the already existing fabric of territory—which they integrate within a relational structure.

"Quasi-object" is a vital term in cosmopolitical theory since Latour popularized the notion in his 1994 book, *We Have Never Been Modern*. Building upon Michel Serres's previous theories, Latour uses the idea to explain how particular objects structure social relations.[30] Gregotti and his colleagues coined the term previously in the late 1960s and proposed that its operative value comes from being a territorial strategy. For these architects, quasi-objects are orchestrated by linking existing spatial conditions through new architectural interventions. In so doing, quasi-objects impede treating territory as a preexisting, fixed reality. Instead, quasi-objects create "fields" or "ensembles," whose scale and limits are variable, resulting from attending different relations between the elements they bring together. By articulating quasi-objects, designers translate territorial associations into figurative organizations, which are always indissociable from the social collectives that perceive and inhabit them. As a result, quasi-objects produce provisional configurations, reunions of heterogeneous and conflicting social and spatial materials, which neither intend nor allow one to totalize the world into a single image. They instead permit one to understand the environmental processes of organization through specific, partial, formal structures. In this sense, the production of quasi-objects seeks to counter the mere technical instrumentalization of territory. Instead, it ambitions to articulate territory as a cultural, social, and aesthetic space acting as the primary constituent of a world-making, geographic imaginary.

Cosmopolitical Territories

How can this understanding of territory renew cosmopolitical design practices? What could happen to cosmopolitics when it addresses territory?

[29] Michel Serres, *The Parasite* (Baltimore, MD: Johns Hopkins University Press, 1980), 225–26.

[30] Serres, *The Parasite*, 225–26.

First, contrary to the cosmopolitical privilege of small-scale, local operations, the previous theories help us conceive territory as the crucial realm in producing spatial responses to global challenges, be it in the domain of ecological or social transformation, and understand that these responses are the germen of a broader idea of world structuring. In them, territory merges social and geophysical conditions and has the operative dimension to produce scalarly significant changes. They do not treat territory as a predetermined spatial realm but rather as a scale to be uncovered and articulated through design practices. These acts of scalar production through the design of territorial possibilities potentially destabilize existing notions of sovereignty and political articulation. The output of territorial scales responsive to globalization is, in this sense, a fundamental act of cosmopolitical design, both in terms of spatial and political definition.

Second, this vision considers territory a space of technologically mediated processes of spatial and social structuring. It includes conceiving territory relative to specific, primary uses that require a technical transformation of the land, such as vast areas of energy production. This, of course, does not imply disregarding other land uses nor abandoning the critique of mere technical rationality while neglecting social dynamics. Instead, this position recognizes that territory is always the result of technological transformations related to the use of resources and that these processes need to be embedded with a broader social and cultural articulation of territory. The emphasis here is on the necessary coexistence of nature, culture, and technic.

Third, and crucially, territory is a transitional category referring a mediation space. It is not assimilable to the idea of locality. Acting territorially simultaneously requires acknowledging, reading, and enabling local singularities, addressing the globalizing processes that affect them, and operating within the dynamics of deterritorialization and reterritorialization that constantly link territory and world.[31] Recognizing this transitional condition implies elaborating the technologies of vision and interpretation that create bidirectional links between territory and planet, thus forming the meta-frameworks that structure this relation. To do so, it is neither possible to confide in the cosmopolitical doxa of a pure vision from within nor in the cosmopolitical rejection of standard procedures to conceptualize the passing between singularity and world.

Territorial design contributes to the articulation of world-space. This reconsideration of territory challenges the cosmopolitical critique of projects seeking the production of climate lands and suggests instead a potentially positive reading of their ambitions. This positive view recognizes that climate lands are predominantly technical fixes. As such, they are insufficient in addressing the socioeconomic conditions leading to the climate and ecological crisis. Yet, this approach also highlights their constitutive value for a renewed understanding of cosmopolitical design.

Projects of climate lands, as a key, increasingly urgent case of projects that render land technical, require negotiating the conditions of coexistence between technological transformations and the social and environmental

[31] Gilles Deleuze and Félix Guattari, *Anti-Oedipus: Capitalism and Schizophrenia* (New York, NY: Viking Press, 1972).

conditions they may affect. The intense changes these projects can impose on the land act as a methodological proxy for less severe spatial transformations, based on a decided interrogation about the uses of geographical space and how these uses contribute to a broader understanding of world space. These projects' functional component is, in this light, only the trigger for a multilayered spatial project. Technologization always shapes a cosmogeographic a priori.[32] Initially, geographical conditions are crucial for constructing the technogeographic milieu, but then technics reticulate geography within a world structure. This suggests a process of territorial interpretation, uniting understandings of geography and potential structures of world space. Technical lands cannot be thought of only internally.

Projects of climate lands thus may define territorial possibilities of mediation between geography and world. Their spatial proposal creates frameworks for any cosmopolitical structure to come. On one hand, this means that the projects' primary value does not derive from their technical success, but from their capacity to promote global imaginaries about the uses of space. These imaginaries can result from individual initiatives, but they require constructing cosmopolitical agreements through collective discussions. Their implementation is inseparable from the constitution of political frameworks to make them possible.

On the other hand, the projects suggest going beyond existing geopolitical divisions. They question borders *and* the very logic that supports bordering and delimitations.[33] The political demarcation of territory loses relevance vis-à-vis a design process that requires integrating shared ecologies and resources. Rather than the space of sovereignty, the resulting territories are realms where different sovereignties and interests need to be reconciled and put together. Technical lands may be problematic. But their problems urge us to rethink design scales and envisage new, cosmopolitical spatial orders.

[32] Gilbert Simondon, *On the Mode of Existence of Technical Objects* (Minneapolis, MN: University of Minnesota Press, 2017), 191–222; Yuk Hui, "On Cosmotechnics: For a Renewed Relation Between Technology and Nature in the Anthropocene," *Techné: Research in Philosophy and Technology* 21, no. 2–3 (2017): 1–23.

[33] Paulina Ochoa Espejo, *On Borders: Territory, Legitimacy, and the Rights of Place* (Oxford: University of Oxford Press, 2020), 1–26.

Uncommon
*In*terests

Rania Ghosn

In 2008, the oil and gas company Total (now Total Energies) conducted a corporate advertising campaign to articulate its position on the future of energy. This campaign was timed vis-à-vis the UN Intergovernmental Panel on Climate Change recommendations to reduce carbon emissions.[1] Under the motto *Communauté d'Intérêts* (Common Interests), the corporation's media campaign proposed to reconcile the growth objectives of private capital with climate challenges in a slogan that rhetorically articulated, "What if meeting energy demand and combating global warming are inseparable?"[2] In this campaign, Common Interests deployed a visual binary structure with sites of extraction on one side and consumption on the other. For example, one frame featured a prospective image of a polar glacier reflected into the iconic nighttime glimmer of Manhattan's skyline. What is eclipsed from these images is the technological system, including the myriad of tankers, pipes, and terminal ports that connect both geographies. Economists describe these discrepancies with the term "externalities." These externalities are the side effects of the private processes associated with allocating resources. They produce ill effects, notably pollution and the degradation of the commons. To paraphrase the economist William Kapp, who abstracted a general law for capitalism in his 1950 book *The Social Costs of Private Enterprise*, "Capitalism [read here as technological lands] must be regarded as an economy of unpaid costs, 'unpaid' in so far as a substantial portion of the actual costs of production remains unaccounted for in entrepreneurial outlays; instead, they are shifted to, and ultimately borne by, third persons or by the community as a whole."[3] If technological lands do not matter, then energy corporations are not accountable or obligated to pay for the disasters brought about by extractivism.

Technological lands are not inadvertently omitted; they are excised by design. Their "designed" abstraction severs geography into a flattened binary of crude and refined lands, concealing frictions and externalities throughout the system. Indeed, the mandate for "clean" Manhattanism rests on the abstraction of technological lands. Hence, the crisis of Manhattanism (aka the climate crisis) is a crisis of the representation of technical lands. Accordingly, the climate crisis cannot be resolved by introducing more nature into either side of the frame. As Bruno Latour elaborates in the conclusion of *The Politics of Nature*, this is because "nature is not a particular sphere of reality but the result of such a political division."[4] An ecological, counter-Manhattanist approach to the climate crisis addresses the politics of representation that underpin the division line itself and in so doing breaches the closure of "common interests."

The abstraction of technological lands is sustained by a nearly unbroken attitude of wonderment, or "energy myths," extending from the advent of steam power through the spread of fossil fuels. Not dissimilar to John Gast's 1872 "American Progress," technological infrastructures, such as telegraph lines, railroads, and steamships, came to embody visions of progress. Such technical "fixes" reproduce a series of what historian George Basalla calls "energy myths," in which any newly discovered source of energy is "assumed

[1] https://totalenergies.com/media/news/news/campagne-institutionnelle-2008-communaute-dinterets

[2] "Corporate advertising campaign: 'Common interests,'" Total, May 5, 2008, https://www.total.com/en/media/news/news/campagne-institutionnelle-2008-communaute-dinterets.

[3] William Kapp, *The Social Costs of Private Enterprise* (New York, NY: Schocken Books, 1971), 231.

[4] Bruno Latour, *Politics of Nature: How to Bring the Sciences into Democracy* (Cambridge, MA: Harvard University Press, 2004), 231–32.

[5] George Basalla, "Some Persistent Energy Myths," *Energy and Transport: Historical Perspectives on Policy Issues*, eds. George H. Daniels and Mark H. Rose (Beverly Hills, CA: Sage, 1982), 27–28.

[6] Matthew T. Huber, *Lifeblood: Oil, Freedom, and the Forces of Capital* (Minneapolis, MN: University of Minnesota Press, 2013); Hannah Appel, Arthur Mason, and Michael Watts, eds. *Subterranean Estates: Life Worlds of Oil and Gas* (Ithaca, NY: Cornell University Press, 2015); Imre Szeman, *On Petrocultures: Globalization, Culture, and Energy* (Morgantown, WV: West Virginia University Press, 2019).

to be without faults, infinitely abundant, and to have the potential to affect utopian changes in society. These myths persist until a new energy source is deployed to the point that its drawbacks become apparent."[5] The proposed new source of energy, however, is not treated any differently. Rather, recently discarded energy myths are resuscitated and conferred upon the newcomer, replete with familiar images and narratives. These cyclical narratives do not acknowledge, let alone reform, technological lands. Instead, these myths reduce the question of energy transition to a problem of technology, the response to which is to overlook the obsolete and wretched grounds of fossil fuels and displace desire to another energy technology. It is essential to add that myths are not the gap between the technological and spatial, a disjunction that gives rise to misrepresentations that might be corrected with empirical evidence. Myths are geographic projects by design; they remove technical lands from representation and occupy that void with iconographic imagery.

The externalization of costs has been the explicit mandate of the oil industry. No energy myth is greater than the promise of infinite fossil fuels. As the largest single commodity in international trade, both in value and weight, oil has inscribed its infrastructural order as a mode of planetary organization.[6] Over the past 200 years, particularly since World War II, the high-energy content of black gold has tied economic growth to promises of progress and development. Developmentalism praised oil as a mode of energy that could expand economies and advance democracies in producing and consuming nations alike. In social indicators, such as the United Nations Development Indicators, a nation's prosperity was equated with the rate of energy use per capita, contributing to the prodigious expansion of the fossil fuel industry.

The promises of fossil fuels came down with a disastrous twist. The 1970s marked the end of cheap, abundant, and guilt-free petroleum. A surge in global energy demands and the need to manage carbon dioxide have made the imperative for change in energy systems. The question of the transition inherently became a problem of carbon, the response to which was a series of techno-fixes—carbon sequestration, carbon credits, carbon markets—along with low-carbon energy sources from the sun, wind, and tides.

Representation is complicit, possibly foundational in perpetuating such technological myths. The energy myths of zero-carbon alternatives are uncannily familiar, switching off political vigilance on reorganizing the world and its values. AMO/OMA, for example, has explored new energy policies in a series of projects, such as *Roadmap 2050: A Practical Guide to a Prosperous, Low-Carbon Europe*, which proposed a diversified and regional energy network to reduce Europe's carbon-dioxide emissions. A series of renderings visualize how the integrated European network reconfigures the continent's geography away from political boundaries and into energy regions: Tidal States, Isles of Wind, Biomassburg, and Solaria, the latter of which brought together the Mediterranean sunbelt countries. The rendering "Parisian Energy from Sahara Sun" illustrates the promises of Solaria with the Eiffel Tower on one side of the Mediterranean and a camel caravan in a North African field of solar panels on the other. The Solaria symbolizes a promise of a radical transition in energy technology. Its visual structure—the metropolis on the one hand and the extractive hinterland on the other—is an all too familiar organizational trope, reminiscent of Total's Common Interests campaign. It perpetuates the binary organization of the carbon territory and further ignores the scorched, technical lands of oil and gas fields.

Representation is also necessary to dispel myths—to make technological lands visible and to make their externalities matter. In 2005, a time of ecological turmoil, Bruno Latour's *Making Things Public* examined the agency of representation in bringing things (including technologies) to the public's attention.[7] Latour writes:

[7] Bruno Latour and Peter Weibel, eds., *Making Things Public: Atmospheres of Democracy* (Cambridge, MA: MIT Press, 2005).

A matter of concern, is what happens to a matter of fact when you add to it its whole scenography, much like you would do by shifting your attention from the stage to the whole machinery of a theatre ... Instead of simply being there, matters of fact begin to look different, to render a different sound, they start to move in all directions, they overflow their boundaries, they include a complete set of new actors, they reveal the flimsy envelopes in which they are housed.[8]

[8] Bruno Latour, *What Is the Style of Matters of Concern?* (Spinoza lectures, University of Amsterdam, Department of Philosophy, April–May 2005), 39, http://bruno-latour.fr/node/16/.

Matters of concern also accept contingency; they are political *because* they are open to multiple, contradictory interests. Matters of concern demystify a picture-perfect image of progress and a singular politics of improvement and present ongoing contested uncertainties. In this world view, the role of representation shifts from reinforcing consensus on matters of fact to assembling public activism around controversies and other matters of concern.

An "architecture with externalities" counteracts these energy myths by delaminating technical lands and drawing out the scope of externalities *within* the world. Contrary to the nineteenth-century thermodynamic concept of energy, which erased qualitative differences in favor of exchange value, the renewed imagination sees technological externalities as *within* the lands.[9] In this world view, geography is constantly re-formed by the oil network. Timothy Mitchell notes that closely following the oil entrails "tracing the connections that were made between pipelines and pumping stations, refineries and shipping routes, road systems and automobile cultures, dollar flows and economic knowledge, weapons experts and militarism." His analysis suggests a framing of the oil network across the boundaries between the material and the ideal, the political and the cultural, and the natural and the social.[10]

[9] In *New Geographies* 2: Landscapes of Energy, I examined and articulated the emergence of the geographic—then a new, but for the most part latent, paradigm in design—and brought it to bear on the agency of design, energy, and space. The issue invited designers to take on the synthesizing role that geography aspired to play among the physical, economic, sociopolitical, and representational, with the invitation to engage "energy as a spatial project."

[10] Timothy Mitchell, "Carbon Democracy," *Economy and Society* 38, no. 3 (2009): 422.

The representational challenges remain acute because of the narrative and strategic challenges posed by the relative invisibility of the climate crisis and its delayed effects. As Rob Nixon asks in his book *Slow Violence and the Environmentalism of the Poor*, how can we convert the slow-moving disasters that are long in the making into arresting stories, images, and symbols?[11] What is the descriptive machine that makes technological lands visible, political, and speculative? The next challenge for architects, landscape architects, and

[11] Rob Nixon, *Slow Violence and the Environmentalism of the Poor* (Cambridge, MA: Harvard University Press, 2011).

urban designers might be to articulate and deploy a geographic representational machine—more fantastic than the eco-mimetic render—that visualizes externalities and illustrates the relations between form and politics that underpin the organization of all energy systems. A geographic imagination of energy unfolds the technological lands that were squashed into the division-line; it populates them with things deemed to be the mere fallout of progress; it repositions the new assembly at the center of political life.

To frame technological lands as a matter of concern, the research practice Design Earth deploys the architectural drawing and narrative as a method to visualize how technological systems change Earth and speculate ways of living with environmental technologies, such as oil fields and landfills, on a damaged planet.[12] The architectural project becomes the medium to foreground geopolitics that are situated, material, volumetric, populated, heterogeneous, and always grounded. The section drawing brings above- and belowground together in one frame, synthesizing the geological fixity of deep-time hydrocarbon fossilization with the surface order of modern material circulation and accumulation. Furthermore, the axonometric section situates oil reservoirs in a specific site while constructing a topological imagination of the planet. These descriptive geographic drawings unearth relational tensions between the situated and the planetary, the technological and the geographic.

Beyond documentary descriptions, the drawing engages a speculative narrative and sensibility, giving meaning to what otherwise would illustrate the unbearable scale of geopolitical events occurring around the globe, across time. It bestows meaning to facts. The narrative is a thought experiment, envisioning a possible future that opposes a stifling reality imposed by extractive planetary infrastructure. Rachel Carson, whose book *Silent Spring* is credited with launching the global environmental movement, refused to adhere to conventional methods of relaying scientific information. To give shape to the toxicity of pesticides, Carson resorted to using a narrative form. *Silent Spring* opens with "A Fable for Tomorrow," which introduces a "town in the heart of America" that awakes to a birdless, budless spring. "This town does not actually exist," Carson writes, "but it might easily have a thousand counterparts in America or elsewhere in the world," for "a grim specter has crept upon us almost unnoticed, and this imagined tragedy may easily become a stark reality we all shall know."[13] Fabulation becomes a way to reframe reality beyond realism. It plots and gives figurative shape to threats whose repercussions are dispersed across space and time and draws public attention to such long-term, destructive acts.

A speculative drawing is a way to think and look at the carbon present, not as the phantom fulcrum between idealized pasts and salvific futures. The series of drawings recast technological lands with new mythologies that clarify the long-term consequences of the current fossil-fuel usage as the continued energy system on which modern life depends. It is vital to ask how designers speculate on technological lands when we can no longer imagine the world without technology and disaster. The drawings illustrate

[12] See Rania Ghosn and El Hadi Jazairy, *Geostories: Another Architecture for the Environment* (New York, NY: Actar, 2018). On the issue of oil, see Rania Ghosn and El Hadi Jazairy, "A Geographic Stroll around the Horizon," *MONU* 20 (Spring 2014): 12–17; Rania Ghosn and El Hadi Jazairy, "Hassi Messaoud Oil Urbanism," *New Geographies* 6, Grounding Metabolism, eds., Daniel Ibañez and Nikos Katsikis (November 2014): 144–53.

[13] Rachel Carson, *Silent Spring* (Boston, MA: Houghton Mifflin, 1962), 3.

worlds in which "staying with the trouble"—what Donna Haraway says is both "to stir up potent response to devastating events, as well as to settle troubled waters"—is the only ethical option for technological and environmental matters.[14]

[14] Donna Haraway, *Staying with the Trouble: Making Kin in the Chthulucene* (Durham, NC: Duke University Press, 2016), 1.

After Oil

How can speculative narratives reclaim the geographic imagination of energy—the forms, technologies, economies, and logistics of fossil fuels in architectural discourse and political life? Our project, After Oil, visualizes the formal embeddedness of carbon geographies to underline the politics of carbon reform. All energy transitions are no more formally neutral than the forms of carbon urbanism are politically neutral. In the *Geostories* series, After Oil emphasizes the agency of representation in the construction of carbon futures at a moment when the energy-economy-environment triad is at the forefront of design concerns. The project presents three speculative fictions on a future in which the Persian Gulf states and the world will transition away from fossil fuels as forms of energy. The After Oil drawings critically engage the present and future geographies of oil in the Gulf region, charting matters of concern for sites of extraction (Das Island), transit logistics (Strait of Hormuz), and the slow violence of climate change (Bubiyan Island). After Oil renders visible the embeddedness of the oil system in the Gulf region and invites us to imagine the long-range effects of such a crude relationship with Earth.

1. Das Island, Das Crude

Das Island is a critical Emirati offshore oil-and-gas industrial facility. Since the first oil-exploration expeditions in 1953, the island has fueled the urbanization of Dubai and Abu Dhabi, with many of the country's iconic buildings being built with oil wealth. Das Crude makes the value displacement in oil urbanism visible by imagining the island with a subsurface field of depleted oil reservoirs. The United Arab Emirates' architectural landmarks are indexed in relation to oil's geological depths and times of extraction. The volume of excavated soil and stone is assembled in an artificial mountain, a landform monument to the age of oil.

fig 1–3

2. Strait of Hormuz Grand Chessboard

The Strait of Hormuz is a critical oil-transit chokepoint. Twenty percent of the world's oil moves through the two-mile-wide shipping lane in its twenty-one-mile-wide passage. The strait has never actually been shut down, despite the persistent geopolitical anxiety over territorial disputes, particularly the disagreement between the UAE and Iran over the islands of Abu Musa, Greater Tunb, and Lesser Tunb. The Grand Chessboard repurposes the strait as a territorial real estate game, financed by the collective financial oil futures of traditional adversaries across the Gulf. The board game absorbs the three islands among the chess pieces of iconic speculative urban projects.

fig 1 Das Island, Das Crude. Design Earth, 2016

Das Island, Das Crude. Design Earth, 2016

fig 3   Das Island, Das Crude. Design Earth, 2016

Strait of Hormuz Grand Chessboard.
Earth, 2016

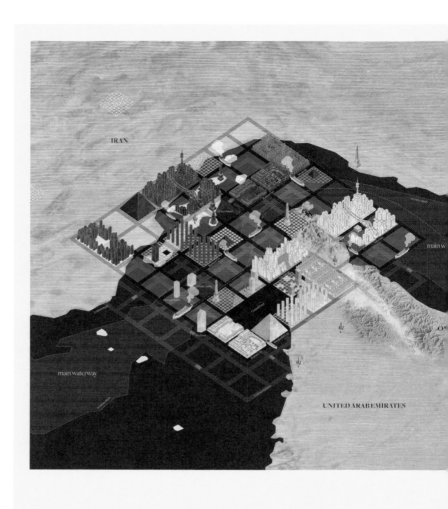

fig 5 Strait of Hormuz Grand Chessboard.
Design Earth, 2016

fig 4 – 6

3. Bubiyan Island, There Once Was an Island

The end of the Persian Gulf War in 1991 was accompanied by one of the largest oil spills, which drastically affected Kuwait's coastal environment. Despite the apocalyptic intensity of this geo-traumatic event, the business-as-usual oil industry, even with the increasing rate of carbon emissions, subjects the world to the slow violence of anthropogenic climate change. Bubiyan Island, flat and low-lying, is vulnerable to sea-level rise. The drawing, *There Once Was an Island*, shows this invisible threat by redrawing the island's shrinking shoreline and its sixteen highest elevations as an archipelago of islands.

fig 7 – 9

After Oil is not a mere switch in energy producers; it is a reformation of the geographic imagination that redeems technological lands from abstraction and rescues all energy technologies from idealism and depoliticization. When energy, economy, and environment are at the forefront of design concerns today, it is important to underscore that all technopolitical projects and representations, including carbon, are simultaneously formal projects (and representations). It is a pivotal design task for energy futures to draw upon carbon's "matters of concern," looking closely at how the techno-carbon system has taken form. Moreover, a geographic imagination highlights the politics and aesthetics of all proposed technological contracts with the planet. It intervenes in representation to render visible the inequality between the promises of technological fixes and the distribution of externalities. If the transition to a low-carbon energy regime is not accompanied by reflection on the geographies on which the current regime rests and by inquiry into its proposed geographies—solar or other—future projects will simply pay lip service to an ecological discourse in urbanism rather than usher in political and economic transformation. The political success of overcoming carbon forms hinges on the reform of the geographic imagination to project a formally and politically situated vision of power in the world's sunbelts and wind corridors.

Earlier versions of this essay were published as "Where Are The Missing Spaces? The Geography of Some Uncommon Interests" in *Perspecta* 45 (2012): 109–116 and "Carbon Re-form" in *Log* 47 (2019): 106–117.

After Oil Project Credits: Rania Ghosn and El Hadi Jazairy, with Jia Weng, Rawan Al-Saffar, Kartiki Sharma, Hsin-Han Lee, Namjoo Kim, and Sihao Xiong.

fig 6   Strait of Hormuz Grand Chessboard.
Design Earth, 2016

Bubiyan Island, There Once Was an
Design Earth, 2016

fig 8 Bubiyan Island, There Once Was an
Island. Design Earth, 2016

Bubiyan Island, There Once Was an
Design Earth, 2016

Vincent Fournier, *SOUSY Svalbard Radar (SSR),*
Svalbard, Norway, 2010. Courtesy Vincent Fournier

Elger Esser, *Morgenland (Morning Land Ser*
Enfeh II, Lebanon, 2005. Courtesy Elger Esser
Silverstein Gallery. © 2022 Artists Rights Society (A
New York / VG Bild-Kunst, Bonn

ent Fournier, *CARMA Observatory*, California, 2006. Courtesy Vincent Fournier

Vincent Fournier, *Noor #2 (Ouarzazate)*, Morocco, 2006. Courtesy Vincent Fournier

Hiroshi Sugimoto, *Black Sea, Ozuluce*, 1991.
© Hiroshi Sugimoto / Courtesy Gallery Koyanagi

Hiroshi Sugimoto, *Sea of Japan, Hokkaido*, 1⬛
© Hiroshi Sugimoto / Courtesy Gallery Koyanagi

Moncouyoux, *Brown Electric Tower Near n Grass Field*, 2015. Courtesy Louis Moncouyoux lash

Paolo Pellegrin, *NASA IceBridge Flight*, Venable 01A, Antarctica, 2017. © Paolo Pellegrin / Courtesy Magnum Photos

Contributors

Caitlin Blanchfield is a PhD candidate in architectural history at Columbia University's Graduate School of Architecture, Planning, and Preservation and visiting assistant professor at the Pratt Institute.

Neil Brenner is an urban theorist, sociologist, geographer, and Lucy Flower Professor of Urban Sociology at the University of Chicago.

Jay Cephas is an architectural and urban historian and assistant professor of history and theory of architecture at Princeton University School of Architecture.

John Dean Davis is an environmental and architectural historian and assistant professor at the Knowlton School of Architecture at Ohio State University.

Billy Fleming is a landscape architect, city planner, founding Wilks Family Director of the Ian L. McHarg Center at the Weitzman School of Design, and cofounder of the Climate + Community Project.

Peter Galison is a historian and philosopher of science and is the Joseph Pellegrino University Professor in history of science and physics at Harvard University.

Swarnabh Ghosh is a critical geographer, architect, and a PhD candidate at Harvard University.

Rania Ghosn is an architect, geographer, associate professor of architecture and urbanism at the Massachusetts Institute of Technology and cofounding partner of Design Earth.

Stephen Graham is an academic, author, and professor of cities and society at the School of Architecture, Planning, and Landscape at Newcastle University.

Florian Hertweck is an architect, professor, and chair of the Master in Architecture at the University of Luxembourg.

Richard L Hindle is a designer, innovator, educator, and associate professor of landscape architecture and environmental planning in the College of Environmental Design at the University of California, Berkeley.

Eric Robsky Huntley is a geographer and designer who is currently a lecturer in urban science and planning in the Department of Urban Studies and Planning at the Massachusetts Institute of Technology and a visiting lecturer in landscape architecture at the Harvard Graduate School of Design.

Nikos Katsikis is an urbanist and assistant professor of urbanism at the Delft University of Technology and affiliated researcher at the Urban Theory Lab in Chicago and Future Cities Laboratory in Zurich.

Marija Marić is an architect, researcher, and postdoctoral research associate of the Master in Architecture at the University of Luxembourg.

Shannon Mattern is an educator, theorist, and professor of anthropology at The New School for Social Research.

A L McCullough is a landscape architect and member of the Climate + Community Project.

Jeffrey S Nesbit is an architect, urbanist, and assistant professor in history and theory of architecture and urbanism at Temple University.

Robert Gerard Pietrusko is an architect, landscape theorist, and associate professor of landscape architecture at the University of Pennsylvania.

Roi Salgueiro Barrio is an architect, urbanist, and founder of the design office RSAU, and a lecturer at Massachusetts Institute of Technology School of Architecture and Planning.

Desiree Valadares is a landscape architect, architectural historian, and assistant professor in the Department of Geography at the University of British Columbia.

Charles Waldheim is an architect, urbanist, and John E. Irving Professor at the Harvard University Graduate School of Design where he directs the Office for Urbanization.

Matthew W Wilson is a cultural and political geographer, researcher, and associate professor of geography at the University of Kentucky and associate at the Center for Geographic Analysis at Harvard University.

Cover: **Siena Scarff**

Editors: **Jeffrey S Nesbit & Charles Waldheim**
Copyediting: **Jake Starmer**
Design: **Siena Scarff Design**
Typesetting: **Stoffers Grafik-Design**
Lithography: **Stoffers Grafik-Design**
Printed in the European Union.

The book was made possible with the support of **Dean Sarah Whiting** at the Harvard University Graduate School of Design, **Dean Robert Gonzalez** at the University of New Mexico School of Architecture + Planning, and **Associate Dean for Research Hazem Rashed-Ali** at the Texas Tech University College of Architecture.

Bibliographic information published by the Deutsche Nationalbibliothek:
The Deutsche Nationalbibliothek lists this publication in the Deutsche Nationalbibliografie; detailed bibliographic data are available on the Internet at http://dnb.d-nb.de.

jovis Verlag GmbH
Lützowstraße 33
10785 Berlin

www.jovis.de

jovis books are available worldwide in select bookstores. Please contact your nearest bookseller or visit www.jovis.de for information concerning your local distribution.

ISBN 978-3-86859-704-2